Social Diagnosis in Casework

LIBRARY OF SOCIAL WORK

GENERAL EDITOR: NOEL TIMMS

Professor of Applied Social Studies,
University of Bradford

Social Diagnosis in Casework

by Eric Sainsbury

Lecturer in Social Administration,
The Department of Sociological Studies,
University of Sheffield

LONDON
ROUTLEDGE & KEGAN PAUL

First published 1970
by Routledge & Kegan Paul Ltd
Broadway House, 68-74 Carter Lane
London, E.C.4
Printed in Great Britain by
Northumberland Press Limited, Gateshead
© Eric Sainsbury 1970
ISBN 0 7100 6829 8 (C)
ISBN 0 7100 6830 1 (P)

General editor's introduction

The Library of Social Work is designed to meet the needs of students following courses of training for social work. In recent years the number and kinds of training have increased in an unprecedented way. But there has been no corresponding increase in the supply of text-books to cover the growing differentiation of subject matter or to respond to the growing spirit of enthusiastic but critical enquiry into the range of subjects relevant to social work. The Library will consist of short texts designed to introduce the student to the main features of each topic of enquiry, to the significant theoretical contributions so far made to its understanding, and to some of the outstanding problems. Each volume will suggest ways in which the student might continue his work by further reading.

The author adopts a wide focus to help students of social work to come to terms with the complex subject of diagnosis in social casework. He accepts the challenge implicit in his recognition of the many different factors that enter any useful discussion of information, diagnosis and goals in social work. 'Thus, the demands of the agency, the variety of theories available to the worker, the variety of human responses to apparently similar difficulties, and the social and professional uncertainties about the nature of welfare, all make for difficulty in generalizing about the relationship of information and diagnosis to goals.' The book begins with a review of some of the main changes in the concept of diagnosis since the classic (partly because unique) work of Mary Richmond earlier this century. The author thereby illustrates, though incidentally, some of the returns we might expect from a reconsideration of the work of such 'historical' figures whose precise contribution to the development of social work is often simply and crudely assumed. The author then raises crucial questions concerning the beneficiaries of diagnosis—social worker, client, agency and 'society'—maintaining a distinction between the professional opinion of the social worker and the client's own parallel and related appraisal of his situation. Chapter 3 is concerned with the steps by which a diagnosis is built up during the whole process of contact between social worker and client, whilst Chapters 4 and 5 consider the skills required in the processes of gathering and structuring information and of formulating plans of help. Throughout the book Eric Sainsbury maintains a useful balance between the general philosophical issues that cannot be avoided (e.g. thinking about diagnosis 'cannot be wholly divorced from a consideration of the wider purposes of social work in our society'), the theoretical issues, and matters of sheer practicality.

A book devoted to Social Diagnosis has an inevitable place in the Library of Social Work for two main reasons: the subject is important, and it has been greatly neglected. 'Diagnosis' or the exercise of some professional judgment on a problem is part of the concept of modern social work. One of the ways in which we can date the beginning of that kind of social work is to ask at what point did 'philanthropists' begin systematically to hesitate before responding, as far as they could, to the applicant's request at its face value; when did they begin to try to understand the individuality of the request. It is, therefore, surprising that, in this country at any rate, diagnosis has not been extensively studied: indeed it seems to be the case that the present book is the first British publication devoted wholly to it. This book is devoted to diagnosis in one particular area of social work, that of social casework, though the diagnostic process obviously occurs in both group work and community work. The present book has obvious connections with other volumes in the Library which deal mainly either with the knowledge social workers use to inform themselves of situations (e.g. Leonard's *Sociology in Social Work*) or with social work methods (e.g. Moffett's *Concepts in Casework Treatment*). Eric Sainsbury helps us to begin to map out our views about social diagnosis at the same time as he provides some of the material which will assist social workers in moving on to the next phase in the development of this subject.

NOEL TIMMS

Contents

Preface

The phrase 'social diagnosis' has a fine, scientific ring to
it. On hearing of the title of this book, a social work colleague commented that, perhaps, we need fewer books on
how to diagnose and more on how to help. In writing
about the first, however, I could not avoid the second.
Suitable subtitles—closer to the content—might, therefore, be *The Thinking in Helping* or *Helping Through
Thinking*.

I wish to record my gratitude to the general editor for
his encouragement and valuable criticisms. I have received
similar help from my wife and my colleagues, Miss Juliet
Berry and Mrs Mary Bromley, who have generously shared
their thoughts with me and borne the brunt of my preoccupation. My thanks are due to Miss S. Fell, Miss B.
Ibbotson, Mrs S. Fuller, Miss B. Petts, Mrs P. Spyve and
Mrs G. Tyack for their help with typing.

E.E.S.

1

What is social diagnosis?

An individual or a family seeks the help of a social case-worker (or is sent to the caseworker) because of an unmet social need or a disturbance in social functioning. These may have an external source; for example, environmental factors beyond the individual's control may lead to shortages of money, of suitable housing or of work. Sometimes the need or disturbance is located wholly within or between individuals: in how they feel about themselves or in their responses to each other. But most frequently the need or disturbance is experienced by the individual or family as both internal and external; as, for example, in the various kinds of loss associated with bereavement, family separation, court appearances, surgery or unemployment. The caseworker seeks to alleviate these difficulties, directly and through support of the client's own efforts, and the elements involved in helping are (a) the skills of sustaining the quality of relationship relevant at different times to the individuals or family in their particular situation, and (b) the rules and procedures of the appropriate social agency or agencies. In short, a problem or need is presented by a client, and assistance of various kinds made available by one or more representatives of social agencies.

There are two elementary dangers which beset this transaction. The worker may so rely on agency procedures, on 'how we always deal with this kind of case', that he loses sight of the individuality and special needs of the client, and erects barriers between the services and those they purport to serve. Alternatively, both worker and client may seek immediate solutions in the goodwill and inspiration of the moment—in the words of a Peanuts cartoon, 'How can we possibly lose when we're so sincere?'—only to find, with mounting frustration, that the 'solutions' do not work. To avoid these dangers some thinking is essential. Social diagnosis is the thinking, and this brief introduction to the subject will attempt to map its content.

The need for diagnosis may best be illustrated by a case situation.

The case of Mrs A.

Mrs A. is a 35-year-old secretary. She makes an appointment with a probation officer at the suggestion of her children's head teacher. She is well-dressed, well-spoken, and calm throughout the interview; she presents her difficulty in an orderly way and without emotional display except (the probation officer notices) that the pitch of her voice rises slightly and her pronunciation becomes more precise when she mentions her children. She left her husband two weeks ago following several months of his moodiness and ill-temper. He accused her frequently of 'being a bad mother' to their sons, aged 9 and 6. She denies this and says that the cause of this accusation is a radical disagreement over her protectiveness towards the children. The husband has often suggested that she is making the boys effeminate by her mothering. She feels this is nonsense but that her husband is obsessed by this danger and is therefore oversensitive to the slightest physical contact between either parent and the children. She left home more in despair than anger. She would not have left the children except that her mother-in-law was staying on a long visit and would willingly care for them; 'and I needed time to think. I can't really think I'm a bad

2

mother, but when you're told something often enough you start wondering, don't you?' Asked about the circumstances of her leaving, she said that she went for a walk one evening when her husband was particularly moody. She visited a former school friend (a woman) after walking aimlessly for a while. When it was time to go home, she 'couldn't face it' and had not returned since, except once to collect some clothes when everyone was out. She supposed that this proved she was a bad mother: she felt miserable without the children, but not sufficiently so to return to her husband. On the whole she likes her mother-in-law, but would feel too ashamed to meet her again. The probation officer brought the subject back to her missing the children, and Mrs A. reiterated how miserable she was without them. At no time did she suggest that *they* might be missing *her*, though she agreed when the probation officer mentioned this possibility. She went on at once to say that she telephones her husband daily to ask after the children, and he allows her to talk to them. She pretends to them that she is away on a holiday and will be back soon; in one way it feels like a holiday as her friend enjoys her company. She has no other family, her parents having been killed in a car accident about six months ago. She was so busy winding up their affairs that she felt she 'hardly had time to miss them', but she misses them now in the present crisis. Her husband never understood how preoccupied she was. 'He thought because I didn't cry I wasn't upset.' At this point in the interview she smiled apologetically, said she was sorry for taking up so much time 'when the advice I want is really very simple'. Neither she nor her husband wants a divorce, but she would like to make some formal arrangement for access to the children. Her husband has said on the telephone that either she should come back home, or should stay away from the children altogether. She does not want a row about this, but wonders what her rights are and whether—if it were discussed with him—her husband might agree to some kind of arrangement. The head teacher suggested that the probation service might advise on this; she had visited the school to tell the teacher about the situation 'as it's only fair to them to know what is happening to their children. As for the rest of it, I shall just have to work it out for myself, won't I?'

Clearly this situation needs a good deal of thought, not least about how much further understanding should be pursued of the motives, feelings and hopes it contains. On the one hand, it could be argued that Mrs A. has decided for herself what help she requires, limiting the probation officer's function to the giving of one piece of advice. On the other hand, as she herself has observed, it has taken her some time to ask her question, and in the process she has implied various other anxieties and needs with which she may, in the probation officer's view, need help, although she has not said that she wants it. Indeed her last comment suggests that she does not want help or at least does not expect it. What follows in this first interview, therefore, will be influenced by the officer's decision about how far it is appropriate to try to understand the situation more fully by leading her into a discussion of key elements in the interview so far: e.g. what she means by 'good motherhood'; her need of the children in relation to their needs of her; the precise circumstances and feelings which led up to her leaving; the impact of her parents' death both at the time and now; what family life, with her parents and with her husband and children, means to her in the context of her expectations of family relationships and of the interaction of roles in family life; and what may be inferred about her expectations and future use of the relationship with the probation officer from those comments which have been recorded in quotation marks. From what is known so far, it could be argued *either* that she would welcome discussion of all or some of these points, *or* that she would regard such a discussion as impertinent or, at best, irrelevant to the specific problem with which she now seeks help.

Thus, we find that the worker's interpretation of his agency's function influences not only the help he gives but also the diagnostic steps he takes and what he regards as relevant to understanding a client's needs. In Mrs A.'s case, the probation officer might argue that his function is concerned with reconciliation in marriage rather than giving legal advice and that, as the client has asked for the latter rather than the former, she should be referred to a solicitor without further exploration of her situation. This argument would depend upon his regarding 'agency function' as the automatic application of standard procedures, and upon his accepting the client's comments at their face value. On the other hand, the officer could argue that 'agency function' is more than a set of administrative procedures against which the needs of a particular client are assessed. He may take the view that the agency has a responsibility to consider the needs of other, unmet, people in this situation in conjunction with those expressed by the immediate client. He may believe, furthermore, that the function of the agency has no separate existence apart from its application to each client, and thus needs re-formulating with each client; if this is so, then in a sense each client contributes to the meaning of 'agency function'. This latter argument implies that the officer would not say to Mrs A., in effect, 'The advice you seek is not my function; I will refer you to a solicitor', but would discuss with her whether there were other ways in which she felt the probation service could help her and her family, in addition to, or irrespective of, the legal aspects of the case.

In short, an integral aspect of diagnosis is recognition of the nature of agency function and the decision whether this concept implies static procedures which limit help, or a dynamic activity, shared with the client, to enhance the help given, even beyond what is initially sought.

The probation officer's diagnostic activity will be influenced also by his personal feelings about the situation and by personal definitions of individual and social well-being. He may feel, for example, that reconciliation *ought* to be pursued irrespective of the present wishes of the client. He may, either explicitly or implicitly, have in mind an end-result of his work based on value judgments about the social duties of wives, husbands and parents. Or he may feel that it is never appropriate to envisage an end-result other than the one defined jointly with the client over several interviews.

These are problems of professional purpose and ethic which lie outside the scope of this book. They are briefly mentioned here in order to suggest that social diagnosis is more than a simple collection and appraisal of facts about clients. Diagnosis demands at its outset some thought about the content and quality of agency function and the philosophical standpoint of each social worker. In practical terms, the probation officer interviewing Mrs A. must determine whether the information he seeks from her should be limited to the problem she states, to the personal problems she implies, or to the social needs (however these are to be defined) of all the people in the situation she has presented.

What conclusions may be drawn from this case about the nature of social diagnosis in casework? First, factual information about Mrs A.'s problem, however neatly and perceptively formulated, will not of itself prescribe how to help her or her family; diagnosis is not simply a balance sheet of information but a process. Second, Mrs A. expects and needs the help to start at once; we cannot require her to sit silently for an hour (or a month) while the worker diagnoses; the process is not one which can be completed before help begins or can be permitted to delay the offer of help. Third, it would clearly be inappropriate to regard Mrs A., for diagnostic purposes, merely as a provider of information; she has already made her own appraisal of her situation and her last comment suggests that she will continue to appraise it; we must assume that, given an opportunity, she can and should contribute to the worker's diagnosis in a far more direct way than is possible, for example, for the patient seeking the help of a physician. This does not imply that the client's diagnosis is of the same quality as the caseworker's, or even in agreement with it, but that the caseworker's diagnosis must include and respect the client's opinion about the source and content of his need, whereas a physician may frequently have to ignore the diagnostic opinions of his patient. Fourth, as the processes of understanding and of helping are concurrent, it is necessary to determine whether the skills involved in these processes are similar or different. Fifth, we should consider how far the worker's intuitions, emotions and value-judgments may appropriately find a place in diagnosis, and whether the worker should seek to be (even if he could) wholly objective and unemotional. Putting this last point another way, is diagnosis a value-free and emotion-free conclusion, built on known facts, or is it a process in which the value-judgments and feelings of both worker and client necessarily play a part? What place, if any, is there for inference and creative imagination on the worker's part? Is there a dynamic quality in social diagnosis which makes it more than a once-for-all assessment of a client's problems and needs? As Perlman (1951, 1968) has suggested, 'The term diagnosis runs a gamut from meaning a static descriptive category of pathology to a fluid appraisal of the meaning and import of a person's behaviour in a given situation, and, likewise, a gamut of emotionalized opinion from contempt of that process to its worship.'

We shall be concerned, therefore, with four main topics in this book.

1. The relationship, both intellectual and temporal, between diagnosis and (a) the investigation of facts, and (b) the giving of help: i.e. diagnosis as an intellectual conclusion determining the whole course of future treatment, or as a continuing process which

7

develops as treatment proceeds.
2. The purpose, content and skills of diagnosis.
3. The extent to which diagnosis is a shared activity between worker and client.
4. The relationship of reason and emotion in diagnosis. Are they compatible or incompatible?

The first of these topics will be considered in this chapter as basic to the discussion of the others.

Changes in meaning

Mary Richmond (1917) offered the following description of social diagnosis:

'In social diagnosis there is the attempt to arrive at as exact a definition as possible of the social situation and personality of a given client ... Investigation (or the gathering of evidence) begins the process; the critical examination and comparison of evidence follow; and last comes its interpretation and the definition of the social difficulty.'

A revised description occurs later in the same book, where the definition of the situation and personality of the client is extended to include other individuals 'upon whom he in any way depends or who depend upon him, and in relation also to the social institutions of his community' (pp. 51, 357). In these descriptions Richmond emphasized the importance of weighing evidence about the history and current situation of the client, and her book draws frequent parallels between this process and the use of evidence in law. For example, she distinguished between verifiable, testimonial and circumstantial evidence, and between facts (i.e. events and expressed thoughts) and the feelings, opinions and inferences of both worker and client. Reliable evidence of sufficient quantity was her first requirement, and only after this had been weighed and assessed was it appropriate to use 'inference', defined as 'the process of reasoning from this fact or facts

8

to another—unknown—fact', which in turn was submitted to further processes of proof or disproof. The difficulties of corroborating both the data and the inferences were recognized, and Richmond usefully summarized the factors affecting their reliability. These difficulties will form the basis of a later chapter. Most of her work, however, consisted of a masterly statement of the sources of evidence (client, relatives, employers and other contacts, social agencies), the principles to be employed in assessing the validity of their contributions, and the proper employment of recording techniques, letters and telephone calls to ensure reliability of information.

In this earlier period of social work practice, when decisions to use or withhold various social resources were central to the activities of many agencies, a stringent examination was essential, both of material needs and of the likelihood of responsibility or irresponsibility in the client's use of help. This examination could most readily be focused upon the client's *history* and *current situation*, evaluated as quickly as possible to meet the urgency of the agency's financial decision. In an investigation of this sort, less emphasis would be placed upon the client's *future* social functioning and his *future* relationship (if any) with the caseworker. Timms (1961) has shown how the activity of investigation was often separated both in manner and time from the process of help by the intervention of a committee decision; the caseworker acted as investigator before the decision, and as helper afterwards if the decision warranted it. Until comparatively recently, a similar distinction was drawn between the activities of probation officers as social enquiry agents and as supervising agents, on the assumption that both client and worker could re-form their relationship upon a wholly different basis following the making of a decision in which neither played a direct part.

For caseworkers today the particular significance of Richmond's work lies in her recognition (albeit more cautious than seems appropriate now) that the processes of investigation, inference and proof in receiving applications for help cannot and should not be wholly divorced from the consideration of future help, nor the relationship between client and worker radically altered in successive stages of the overall transaction between the two. As the objectives of a first interview, Richmond suggested that, besides giving the client himself a fair and patient hearing, the worker should seek clues to other sources of information which might give a deeper insight into his difficulties *and their possible solutions*; and that the worker should *at the same time* establish mutual understanding as a basis of *further intercourse*, beginning *'even at this early stage* the slow process of developing self-help and self-reliance'. (Italics not original.) She recognized also, though only 'in a small minority of interviews, (that) treatment has to begin in an experimental way *before* any evidence can be brought to light upon which a plan of treatment can be solidly based' (pp. 114, 115) and that the worker must, from the start of an interview, begin to draw tentative and conjectural conclusions regarding future needs, even though these conclusions may have to be abandoned later.

Richmond's work, therefore, though generally concerned with the investigation-inference-proof aspect of diagnosis and with treatment as an activity devised by the worker and virtually imposed on the client *after the completion of the diagnosis*, showed signs of some fusion of these two processes, and recognized that diagnosis in casework is not of the same quality as diagnosis in medicine. She appreciated that investigation, if seen as an end in itself, may restrict the purposes to which information should properly be applied, and that excessive concern with whether clients *should* be given help in the *immediate* present may obscure their long-term physical, emotional and moral wellbeing. The implications of this for the case of Mrs A. are evident.

Timms (1962) has pointed out that a fundamental problem in the history of casework was how best to achieve detailed investigation in the initial interview without losing sight of the long-term purposes of help. The particular contribution of the Charity Organization Society from 1869—though set up initially to prevent the abuse of charitable resources—was its concern with the long-term purpose of help as central to its function rather than as a welfare fringe to financial first-aid.

Improvements in basic social provision have lessened the need for charitable gifts from casework agencies, and in casework practice today there is no temporal separation between the investigation of facts and the planning and offering of help. Information is sought, not only to assist the worker to reach decisions about the client's ability to use various kinds of future help, but also to establish an *immediately* helpful situation—at least in so far as enabling the client to express and clarify his needs and their possible solution is in itself a helpful experience. Diagnosis has thus moved its position in the total worker-client transaction from *preceding* help to enhancing the help *currently* available; it is a way of developing in the minds of both client and worker a fuller understanding of the patterns made by the facts investigated, and of the client's feelings about and interpretation of these facts.

The nature and diagnostic use of the client's social history

The 'social history' of a client was at one time regarded as an orderly chronological statement of unchangeable, verifiable and objective facts in his past life. Useful though this may be, caseworkers now recognize that the client's history (in a different sense) exists in his *current* (and therefore changing and changeable) interpretation of past events and in his present feelings about the past. Obviously his history cannot be re-written, but its significance for the client changes in response to his present feelings of success or failure, hope or frustration, anxiety or challenge. For example, the death of Mrs A.'s parents has taken on a new meaning for her in her present isolated (and 'bereaved') situation from her family. It would be possible for the probation officer to help Mrs A. to link the two events in her mind so as to affect the emotional significance of both.

In the same way, present events or future plans are likely to contain elements of feeling which echo similar or related past events and plans. In Eliot's words, 'Time present and time past are both perhaps present in time future, And time future contained in time past.' Recognition of this 'eternal present' of the emotions has had a particular influence upon recent thinking about the relationship of client and worker. Although it is not the purpose of this book to consider this relationship in detail, it is perhaps worth commenting here that, if past emotions inevitably enter this relationship, it is inappropriate for the client's response to the worker to be judged solely upon the purpose of their present meeting. Certainly there can be no place for preconceptions or expectations in the worker of how a client *ought* to behave towards him or his agency. The awe, respect and gratitude expected from clients in the past—forming part of the investigation process, and taken as indicators of the appropriateness of helping—have no significance if they occur today save as facts, to be related to other facts, to be viewed with interest and concern (rather than pleasure and gratification) as aspects and indicators of the client's life history.

From 'investigation' to 'study'

It is apparent also, in post-war books about casework, that the word 'investigation' has been abandoned in favour of words like 'study' or 'observation', suggesting greater passivity in the worker, and a less direct and rigorous form of questioning. This could be an undesirable trend if it implied less attention to detail, or more reliance on sentimental vagueness than on the patient analysis of events and responses with which Richmond's work was concerned.

Two developments in the attitudes and knowledge of caseworkers have led to the disuse of 'investigation' as a basic concept:

First, an increasing emphasis on the need to preserve and enhance the dignity of the client has curbed the discussion of his affairs with those whom Richmond listed as 'other sources of information'. The principle of confidentiality has come to imply a limitation on both the collection and divulgence of information by the worker.

Second, psychodynamic insights have promoted a greater awareness of similarities in the basic emotional needs of people. From this there has developed a greater willingness among caseworkers to exercise their capacity to identify with their clients: to seek the kind of identification which leads to a sharing of the client's emotions, (an ability to feel as he feels) rather than to a sentimental (and essentially self-indulgent) pity for him. The important distinction between sympathy and empathy will be discussed later. This ability to identify with the client, provided there are adequate safeguards of self-awareness and rational objectivity in the caseworker, can promote understanding and reduce the need for direct questioning. It helps to eliminate the risk that the caseworker's questions will appear to the client to be as imperious, impertinent or irrelevant as the word 'investigation' frequently implies.

Diagnosis as an integral part of treatment

We have seen that, in terms of a wide-ranging and comprehensive collection of information, diagnosis is less than investigation. But in its relation to the process of offering help, it goes beyond the scope of investigation. The amount of information sought by the caseworker is limited to what is relevant to the client's present and future needs and to the capacity of worker and agency to provide appropriate help. At the same time diagnosis, unlike investigation, is not based only on *spoken* information and on the *objective* validation of separate facts. It involves an attempt to construct conceptual patterns which interpret and illuminate a client's needs and life experiences—illuminating, that is to say, the complex of thought, feeling, purpose and aspiration which accompanies the client's presentation of his social difficulty and which determines the quantity and quality of help he needs and can use. The understanding which social diagnosis provides goes beyond the comprehension of objective data and their interrelationships. It includes the state of mind of the client: what the facts mean to him at this moment and in this particular situation. It implies the possession of skill and method in obtaining and approaching facts, and an awareness of the purposes for which information and understanding are sought. It requires the worker to acknowledge that to understand a client necessitates some understanding of himself, of himself as the client sees him, and of the emotional impact which each makes upon the other as a result of processes of identification and of the transferring of feelings from earlier relationships.

We may continue with Richmond, therefore, to divide the activities of social casework into three elements: study (investigation and inference), diagnosis and treatment. But they are inter-acting elements in a single process of help, not a series of techniques. It is never appropriate to say there has been insufficient study for any kind of diagnosis to be made, for, as the facts are ascertained (both the objective data of a situation and the meaning the situation has for the client), the worker is seeking a pattern, an inference, an hypothesis, in order that his responses—his prompting, commenting and questioning—are relevant to the client's needs and promote in the client a sense of immediate and helpful purpose in the interview. The study

14

of the situation is never complete, for it is continually supplemented and modified by current events and responses. Similarly, diagnosis starts as a tentative patterning of available information, changing with new information and modifying as the client's needs alter in response to the help already received. At the start of his professional career, the caseworker may be able to achieve this adaption of diagnosis only in a period of re-thinking at the end of an interview; with increasing experience, the process is contained more within the interview itself. Yet however skilled and experienced he becomes, he will still need opportunities for thinking about his diagnosis between interviews. The discipline of writing assessments and summaries to clarify his thoughts, and discussions with colleagues to prevent over-preoccupation with one part of a diagnostic pattern to the detriment of the whole, are additional and essential opportunities to ensure the ongoing relevance of diagnosis to the problems and needs of clients.

Diagnostic labels

With each succeeding interview with the same client, the diagnostic pattern becomes less tentative. Although it may need modifying with each new event and new response, these become less unexpected and more predictable if earlier formulations have been fairly accurate. One may, therefore, reach a stage where some part of the situation can be labelled: with a clinical term like 'schizophrenia', 'reactive depression' or 'psychopathy'; or with a description such as 'rivalry', 'displacement of feeling', or 'work-shy'. But labels can be dangerous. They may look like expertise on the worker's part, but one must always consider for whose benefit they are devised and used. It is doubtful whether they ever benefit the client and it is reasonable to suggest, with Scheff (1966), that they sometimes harm him.

In the present fragmentation of the social services, some

labels are administratively convenient to demonstrate statistically the kinds of problems the agency deals with, and whether the agency is fulfilling public expectations. But the individuality of the client may be overlooked behind the label, and some labels all too easily reduce the worker's concern with individual needs. For example, 'psychopathy' is a label which promotes despair and inactivity rather than help. Labels can imply false similarities between people : are criminals a homogeneous group? Or alcoholics? Or problem families? Do the people labelled in these various ways require the same kinds of treatment? The word 'jealousy', similarly, suggests a stereotype of behaviour and response which may mask very different sources of feeling : a person may be jealous as a reaction to a specific change in his environment, or because of a long-standing personality difficulty, or because of some kind of organic dysfunction. Each of these kinds of jealousy may require a different sort of help; and within each category of help there may be a wide range of precise procedures, from which a selection must be made, relevant to this particular client's jealousy in this particular life-situation and expressed in this particular interview. The way one encourages the client to talk of his feelings should properly relate to the part these feelings play in the life-situation with which he needs help. Simply to label him as 'jealous' and to discuss the nature and source of his jealousy are no part of diagnosis, unless these activities are related to the purpose for which he is in touch with the agency and to the help which the worker can provide.

A further danger in the use of labels is that it encourages a stereotyped response from people surrounding the client, which, in its turn, may reinforce his difficulty. To tell Mrs A.'s friend that Mrs A. is suffering from a depression (which may well be so) will evoke from the friend artificial responses to *one aspect* of Mrs A. in place of the natural response she appears to find helpful. Similarly, to tell Mrs A. herself that she is suffering from a depression (even though she knows this) may reinforce her anxieties about how she will cope with future developments in her family life. She may become more depressed, or alternatively may seize on the diagnostic label as an excuse for future failure.

In formulating a diagnosis, therefore, the worker should ensure that his descriptions do not evoke artificial responses from himself, and do not blinker his perception in such a way that he sees only that behaviour which fits the description. As Scheff has implied, the helping professions sometimes unwittingly adopt attitudes which reward clients for behaving according to a diagnosis, and which make all the more difficult any attempt on the client's part to return to more conventional forms of behaviour. In casework diagnosis the worker defines the needs he can appropriately meet, but recognizes that his definitions do not accurately describe the client's total life-situation. He tries to be aware of the client as a whole person, while remembering that he is not equipped, either by function or competence, to meet all the needs of that whole person.

Towards a definition

Diagnosis is a process of discovering patterns of significance in the information directly obtained or inferred. It is tentatively constructed and refined throughout the whole period of contact with the client. It is a way of thinking about situations so that help is made available now and in the future. Its value can be assessed only by its relevance to (a) the solution of the social problems presented, (b) the client's material and emotional needs (both in the present and, where unfulfilled, in the past), and (c) the capacities of the agency and the worker to help. It is not a static conclusion, for it reflects changes in situations brought about by new events and by the effects of the help already given. To the extent that it is a shared activity with the client, it is dynamic in that it is directly instrumental in changing situations by enhancing the client's perception of them.

2

The purpose and content of diagnosis

Diagnosis for whose benefit?

> 'For the conception of social work must now change. The provision of physical services and resources, and the representation of the individual and the family in the struggle to obtain resources from other departments, and not the practice of individual casework, becomes paramount.' (Professor Peter Townsend, writing about the Seebohm Report.)

Social workers increasingly assume a professional responsibility for evaluating priorities of social need, for enhancing citizen participation in welfare, and for drawing attention to administrative inequity in the services which employ them. It therefore becomes difficult to isolate the processes of casework from other forms of social work and social action. From this standpoint the case situation presented by Mrs A., though intrinsically difficult, seems relatively uncomplicated: the problems she brings are basically concerned with the internal dynamics of her family life, and contain few uneasy issues of social justice, social demand, the allocation of scarce resources (other than the caseworker's time) or the adequacy and relevance of basic social provisions.

In a good deal of casework practice, however, there is an underlying uncertainty of purpose, where concern for the needs of individuals and families is uneasily balanced with a concern for the demands and expectations of society as a whole. This tension can, at best, lead to social reforms;

but it may promote aimlessness in the caseworker and in his relationship with the client. It has been suggested already that diagnosis continues throughout treatment; uncertainty of purpose in treatment will inevitably affect the quality of diagnosis and some attention must therefore be paid to this problem.

It besets the caseworker in three ways:

mixed feelings of responsibility and loyalty towards the client;
anxiety that casework may be an unjustified interference in the client's life;
difficulty in identifying with the agency.

Loyalty to the client

This concerns the practical application of the general principles of confidentiality and acceptance in situations where the caseworker cannot be morally and ethically neutral. Margaret, a severely subnormal girl of 18 under close casework supervision because of promiscuity and inadequate parental control, told her caseworker that she had become 'engaged' to John, aged 19. The caseworker, anxious about Margaret's future well-being and the possible results of marriage, questioned her about John's background and discovered that he was on probation. She telephoned the probation officer, told him of Margaret's mental and emotional state, saying that unless John was a particularly stable man the relationship would probably be a dangerous one. John at this time had been on probation for six months for stealing from his workmates. He was illegitimate, had known a succession of 'fathers' in early childhood, and had been in and out of institutional care for many years. Recently, his mother (with whom he was living) had suffered severe depressions for which periodically she received in-patient treatment. He stayed with her because it was cheap, but there seemed no affection between them. At the start of the probation order the officer met with suspicion and hostility from both mother and son, and for a time doubted whether John was capable of sustaining any kind of relationship; but recently he had kept appointments regularly, had begun to talk about his loneliness and the bitterness he felt about his earlier life. He had told the officer of his engagement; he had spoken affectionately of his girlfriend, but only by her first name, giving no information about her. He said he would bring her to meet the probation officer when he felt ready. The probation officer had not pressed for information or an introduction for fear of losing the very tenuous and diffident relationship that had been established.

The information about Margaret received at this point gives rise to a variety of diagnostically interesting hypotheses about John's needs. For example, although John's manner in interview was often aggressively self-assured, his fiancée may represent his real evaluation of his social acceptability. She may provide him with an unquestioning acceptance unavailable elsewhere. But the utility of this information is affected by the problem of the caseworkers' dual responsibilities to these clients and to society. Is the engagement socially desirable? It is meeting the present emotional needs of the couple, and may be a means whereby John will work through some feelings of earlier deprivation. At the same time, will the relationship continue when this immediate usefulness passes? If it does not, the girl's situation may be worsened. If it does, what kind of family will be founded, and what kind of social problems lie ahead in this and the next generation?

Furthermore, how should the probation officer use the information he has received? It may help his understanding of John's unexpressed needs, but if he does not disclose his knowledge of Margaret's subnormality his relationship may suffer because of the secrecy involved in it. If he admits to this knowledge, John may mistrust the officer's intentions in discussing his affairs 'behind his back', especially if the officer hesitates about disclosing the source of his information and risking John's hostility to his fiancée's caseworker. In this instance caseworkers would probably favour complete honesty with the client. But the decision is not easily made because of the complexity of emotions, and will become even more difficult if one or both workers decide that the engagement is socially undesirable and should be discouraged. Have caseworkers the right, anyway, to assume this kind of responsibility?

Similar problems arise if a client confides information about an antisocial act (for example, committing an offence or defrauding the Supplementary Benefits Commission) where the disclosures may represent the beginning of a trusting relationship in a client who hitherto has been wholly against 'the authorities'.

Divided loyalties of this kind sometimes lie at the root of a caseworker's apparent failure to understand his client; in an unacknowledged avoidance of the dilemma, the worker may expect behaviour and responses from the client which are incompatible with the client's personality, or may assume that the client *ought* to want to behave according to a particular social norm, *ought* to feel and respond in certain ways.

If diagnosis is to contribute to reducing the tension between individual need and social demand, it must involve the worker in three activities: assessing precisely why a particular situation is described as a social problem and how far an agency should accept this as a prescription for action; understanding the client's behaviour and responses sufficiently to regard them as explicable and, therefore, as emotionally if not morally valid; and examining his own emotional expectations in situations and the extent to which these are idiosyncratic.

Casework and interference

The second expression of a social worker's uncertainty of

purpose lies in the anxiety that casework represents interference, sometimes sanctioned by society but not by the
client, sometimes welcomed by a client against the wishes
of others in his family, and sometimes difficult to justify
in relation to the relative urgency of other social problems.
Irvine (1964), writing of one part of this dilemma, suggests
that an essential skill lies in the manner of providing help,
so that the client, though at first perhaps resenting intervention, does not continue to regard it as interference. But
as skills improve, so will the possibility of manipulating
a client into accepting intervention; while at the same time
the public understanding necessary as an effective check
against over-interference may lessen. Diagnosis requires
asking people questions, and it is as necessary for the
worker to assess his reasons for asking as it is for him to
evaluate his skill in doing so.

Agency function

Diagnosis is a means rather than an end; but its content
determines the goal to be achieved with each client. It
cannot therefore be wholly divorced from a consideration of the wider purposes of social work in our society.
For the caseworker, these are partly expressed in the
definition of his agency's function, and any personal
uncertainty about these wider purposes will be reflected
in his mixed feelings about the authority of his agency.
The general lack of specificity in defining agency function
is perhaps useful in making it possible for a variety of
people, whose expressed or undisclosed aims in social work
are not identical, to work together. But vagueness in
definition leads to variations in the exercise of the agency's
powers and in the authoritative or permissive image that
it presents to clients. As clients' responses to the authority
or power of the agency contribute to the diagnostic
assessment of a case situation, the worker needs to recognize his own similar or related feelings, so that his func-

tion as mediator between individual need and social demand is exercised in a manner which avoids collusion with or rejection of either.

So far in this chapter, diagnosis has been seen as one of the processes necessary to help the caseworker to resolve the ambivalences of personal feelings intrinsic to un-resolved moral questions. It is necessary now to consider the other beneficiaries of diagnosis: the client, the community, and the agency in its role as mediator between the two.

Client and agency

Mr and Mrs Brown and their five children come to the Children's Department. Mr Brown hustles his wife and family into the CCO's office and immediately demands that the children be taken into care. They received a notice to quit from their landlord four weeks ago for rent arrears, and at a court hearing this morning were given four weeks to move out. They have been on the local authority housing list for five years, but have been told that they are not yet eligible for rehousing. Mr Brown has not worked regularly for many years, and has been threatened with prosecution on at least two occasions by the Supplementary Benefits Commission. These threats appear to work temporarily in that he finds labouring jobs, but then abandons them fairly quickly because of pains in the back. His manner is truculent and aggressive. He complains that 'people like me never get a fair crack of the whip', that the Labour Exchange has made no effort to find him suitable work, that he did not know his wife had not paid the rent, and that the rent was too high anyway bearing in mind the squalid conditions of the house. He says that he knows his rights: if the CCO cannot get them a house, she can have the children. The CCO comments that she will certainly see what can be done when they have had a chance to explore the situa-

23

tion further. Mr Brown says 'You can suit yourself' and walks out. The children have been silent and passive throughout this interview. Mrs Brown, who has been silently glowering, says laconically, 'That's typical'. She says she does not want to lose the children but has nowhere to take them. She accuses her husband of keeping her short of money so she could not pay the rent; she says he has never done an honest day's work in his life; he never seems short of money himself though she seldom sees much of it; she does not know where he spends his time. She ridicules the suggestion of his having 'a bad back' and thinks that the Labour Exchange and the SBC 'have been too soft with him and I could tell them a thing or two about him'. As Mrs Brown goes on talking, the CCO feels embarrassed that the children should be hearing all this. They continue to be silent, however, as their mother recounts a series of treacheries and violent acts by her husband, and no doubt they have heard and seen all this before. Mrs Brown attributes their present crisis entirely to her husband, and the impression she gives is that the present anxiety is not altogether unwelcome; it can (if she is lucky) relieve her of a husband, raise her own and her children's standard of living, and present them with greater security than they have known hitherto.

Comparing this situation with that of Mrs A. there are important differences apart from those intrinsic to the personalities of the clients. The Browns' case calls into question local housing policy: would it help if rehousing for the whole family were immediately available? It would ease the administrative task of the CCO but would this meet the emotional as well as the physical needs of this family? They might, one supposes, be miserable together in greater comfort. At the same time, at a much earlier period in this family's life, good housing at a reasonable rent might have off-set some of the chronic processes of deterioration. This case raises questions also of the role of the SBC as a provider of resources (to what level?), as an agency with powers of prosecution and as a colleague-service of the Children's Department. One could raise a similar question about the complementary role of the Labour Exchange. One wonders whether this family—in terms of administrative efficiency and human well-being—should have been referred for help at an earlier stage by one of these services or, perhaps, by a teacher or health visitor. Or would this have been an infringement of Mr and Mrs Brown's rights of privacy? Should clients in this situation be helped at all, or is there a risk that, if helped, they will be over-protected against the social consequences of their actions? The CCO is, therefore, confronted with a situation of conflicting personal needs, a long-standing uncertainty of what is socially just in such cases, and a fragmented structure of services which reflects this un-certainty. Her own function in such cases also lacks precise definition on an intermediate level between statu-tory regulations and moral generalizations. The well-being of the children is her first concern, but how is this to be defined, especially when, by their passivity, they give her no direct clues?

The caseworker must rely to a large extent on her own assessment of her function, and assume a professional responsibility for acting independently—for having an inner certainty of purpose while retaining an awareness of the complexity of tensions and conflicts in the case. These personal qualities can be developed by keeping in mind certain key questions which together form the foundation upon which diagnosis is built. They are ques-tions which attempt to ensure that the client's needs and agency resources are adequately matched, and which show regard to the wider social needs and policies of which each agency's work forms one aspect.

A foundation for diagnosis

1 *How should the available services be used?*

These services are publicly provided and in some sense

publicly controlled. What is available rarely fits exactly the needs presented or hinted at by clients, and, therefore, the answer to this first question can seldom be certain. Nevertheless, the caseworker must find an answer of some sort which avoids the risks of colluding with the client against the policy of one or more agencies or against the needs of other citizens (e.g. the client's neighbours), or of identifying with an agency policy or with the pressure from other citizens to the extent that the client's needs are distorted or ignored. Every case in some measure requires a resolution of social conflicts based upon an awareness of the interests, needs and resources of many people (clients, members of the general public, agency employees, etc.). Sometimes a caseworker, after considerable thought, may permit (even encourage) a demonstration of conflict between these interests where he feels that the price of resolving the conflict is too high—if, for example, it invades the integrity and rights of individuals. But initially he strives to decide how the services available can be tailored to meet the needs of the client without betraying his responsibility to wider public expectations of how those services should be used.

2 *In the light of existing social resources (e.g. services for income maintenance, health, education, etc., the availability of local neighbourly support) can this client manage his affairs to his own satisfaction and without harm to others in his environment?*

This question lies at the core of professionalism in casework. If the answer to it is yes, then time spent on casework *may* not be justifiable however much the client may wish to retain a relationship with the caseworker. The more adequate local resources become, the greater will be the caseworker's responsibility to assess whether his professional skills are really needed and justified, so that manpower may be more sparingly used and basic services and resources more efficiently employed.

26

3 *Of the kinds of help requested by the client (both materially and emotionally) which are or should be available?*

This question draws attention to two aspects of diagnosis which benefit the client by protecting him from unnecessary intervention and overdependence. In the heat of the moment, the client may hint at problems which on reflection he will wish he had not disclosed; a caseworker who zealously pursues every hint of a problem may reinforce a client's feelings that he has divulged too much. Distinctions must be drawn between what is momentarily wanted by a client and what he needs, and between the needs which, with encouragement but minimum intervention, he can satisfy for himself, and those which require a longer period of external intervention. Of those requiring intervention it is then necessary to ask whether the appropriate quality of help is actually available. In the case of John and Margaret it could be argued that John's feelings of loneliness, beside needing alleviation through the support and concern of the probation officer, might also be helpfully traced back in discussion to earlier feelings about illegitimacy, separations from home, and reception into local authority care. But if the officer lacks the time or skill for making these discussions feel helpful to his client, it is best that the problems hinted at, though recognized as existing, should not be pursued.

4 *What are the requirements of self-discipline and self-awareness in the caseworker to ensure the efficiency of the agency?*

The efficiency of an agency requires that the caseworker's concern for his clients should be matched by the capacity to avoid prejudice (against particular clients, colleagues, or other agencies), and by a willingness to evaluate and employ a greater variety of approaches and techniques than might be intuitively and spontaneously used. As an example of the first of these : Mr Brown does not appear as a likeable person; Mrs A. does. Caseworkers cannot be expected to experience no feelings of liking or dislike for particular clients, and it is no part of the professionalism of social work to encourage caseworkers to expend emotional energy on trying to deny the experience of these feelings. In any event, work based on a denial or rejection of feelings is arid. But an intellectually self-disciplined attempt to formulate needs can prevent an emotional display which, either by excessive warmth or rejection, imposes unrealistic demands and reactions on clients; and it can help the worker to offset the kind of over-involvement which generates depression when meeting a depressed client, vacillation when meeting a drifting family, and anxiety or cynicism when confronting those whose lives seem to be built upon recurrent crises.

Objectivity of this kind (to which the word detachment is frequently but unfortunately applied) may also, though indirectly, help the client to achieve a similar standpoint of thoughtful observation of his own situation. But the 'thoughtful observer' position is primarily a safeguard against the debilitating involvement of the worker's own feelings to the detriment of the agency's work, and it makes possible the capacity to evaluate and employ a wider range of methods of helping than the worker would intuitively use.

Diagnosis as a professional opinion

One of the least comfortable experiences in verbatim or process recording is acknowledging the limited range of one's intuitive responses to others. A worker, by these means, may find that he has a tendency always to be per-missive and never directive, always to avoid or to welcome hostility, to be alert to certain facts in situations while ignoring others; so that diagnosis is unwittingly inaccurate
28

both in describing people and in indicating the kind of help they need. An awareness of these limitations has given rise at various times to an argument which questions the worker's right to make a diagnosis. The argument, briefly, is that the activity of diagnosis, because of its inevitable defects, does intellectual (possibly even moral) violence to the personality of the client who, though never fully understood, is treated as if he were and as if the outcome of the caseworker's activities and policies can be accurately predicted. This view would deny the right of the worker to include a predictive element in diagnosis, and suggests that help should be based only on an ongoing attempt to communicate in such a way that both worker and client become more aware of each other as *whole* human beings. From this process the client would, it is argued, become more aware of himself and of the way he relates to those near to him, and thus more able to express himself and to meet his own needs within an increasingly realistic understanding of his environment.

Several arguments have been levelled against this view. Such an approach is so client-centred as to remove the caseworker's responsibilities to evaluate public provisions, to assess priorities of work in his agency, and to advise on changes in policy. Caseloads would need reducing to an unrealistically low level. Many clients would be unable to benefit from this approach. Applied to some of the simpler but essential tasks of the caseworker, it would be like employing Escoffier to boil an egg. It assumes without proof that social problems or social disorders are symptoms of unknown and perhaps unknowable underlying needs, whereas, possibly, the 'symptom' *is* the disorder. It seems to confer on caseworkers a right to unlimited intimacy with the client's emotions.

One cannot in a short space do justice to any of these arguments, some of which imply radical philosophical disagreements about the nature of man and the place of the helping professions. Those emphasizing treatment through whole-person-to-whole-person communication lay stress on the primacy of the individual, and tend to view social structures *either* as only collections of individuals *or* as 'games' or conspiracies against which the individual needs to assert his integrity and mental health. The opposing view, while not minimizing individual rights, would define mental health as indicative only of a comfortable conformity to prescribed roles, and thus would require the worker first to evaluate which social roles are required of the client and then to help him achieve a comfortable acceptance of these requirements. Whatever the arguments against the whole-personality approach, it provides a reminder of the essential complexity of human personality; while the alternative approaches, based on role definition and on prescriptions for role adjustment, provide an antidote to any facile assumption that intention and relationship matter more than the precise quality of actions, or that any human being can be wholly free from the influences of social expectations, roles and habits.

A further question is posed, however, by the recognition of the inadequacy of the caseworker's perceptions in diagnosis. This concerns setting the limits of enquiry— whether round the problem as presented (the possible inadequacy of this was evident in the case of Mrs A.) or more widely round the whole person or the whole family. This question will be discussed later, but it is appropriate now to consider one way in which it is frequently expressed: 'How far is it right to probe?' Clients vary in how much they are capable of defending themselves against probing or against the emotional consequences of being probed. Margaret probably cannot defend herself very effectively, though her subnormality may preserve her from some of the anxieties of being questioned; Mr Brown defends himself by hostility; Mrs A. by her intelligence, though this is offset by the 'hints' which seem both to resist and to invite further questioning. (How far her hints are deliberate should exercise the probation officer's diagnostic thinking both now and in later interviews. Is she asking for help in an indirect way? Is she expressing feelings before she has thought about them? If so, would she cease to express them if they had been thought out?) The question of probing is related to the nature of the help required and available. Mrs A.'s problem may be capable of solution only by reviewing past events and feelings; the Brown family need help with an immediate crisis, and the solution for them may lie less in reviewing the past than in meeting the present need in a way which will enhance their capacity to cope for themselves with future crises. The investigation of feelings relevant to Mrs A. may well be irrelevant (at least at this stage) with Mrs Brown, not only because of differences in personality and needs, but also because the help they require lies for each at different points in time. To ask a general question about the right to probe is invalidated by its implication that clients form a homogeneous group and that all casework help is of a single kind. The limits of diagnostic enquiry must be related to the circumstances of each case, and the decision where to draw limits based partly on the response of the client to the worker's attempts at communication (see Chapter 4), partly on the task set by the client and the agency's function in relation to that task, and partly on the recognition that different helping processes may, for their effectiveness and their theoretical integrity, require the worker to possess certain information from the client or from others in his environment.

At the same time, the worker's concern and respect for his client should ensure that as far as possible he discusses with the client what he has in mind to do and the reasons for his questioning. Emphasis on diagnosis as a professional opinion should not obscure the aim in casework 'to engage this client with his problem, and his will to do something about it, in a working relationship with this agency, its

31

intentions and special means of helpfulness'. (Perlman, 1956.)

Aetiological, clinical or dynamic?

It has been suggested in this chapter that diagnosis is a means of enhancing the caseworker's capacity to relate together the needs of clients, social demands, agency function and service efficiency. In situations where social purposes are ill-defined, the activity of diagnosis—forming an opinion and prescribing action—is central to the claim of professionalism. This activity may require (as in the situation of Mrs A. and of John) some knowledge of the client's life history in order to understand aetiologically how his present situation arose and why he invests certain feelings in particular aspects of it. At the same time, within the relationship between client and worker, the client's responses may themselves indicate the quality of some earlier relationships: Mr Brown's attitudes to the CCO tell us something about his attitudes to women and his earlier transactions with workers in other agencies, so that the deliberate exploration of *some* earlier relationships becomes less necessary, except to verify what is inferred. His responses are made to his preconceptions of the worker's attitude and function rather than to the worker as she is, and the worker may thus be able to deduce what her role should be in their future meetings. There is a similarity here with the clinical relationship of patient and therapist.

It has been suggested, however, that casework diagnosis is not concerned with the attachment of clinical labels; neither can it lead to the imposition of treatment regimes as if social problems were diseases with cures. As we have seen, casework diagnosis involves some sharing of opinions with the client about the facts of his situation, the location and sources of his problems, and his own capacities to satisfy his needs. It includes his views about the emotional

32

implications and priorities of his situation, and the patterns which apparently unrelated facts form within his mind. A casework diagnosis is always tentative, capable of development and modification, and provocative of new ideas in the minds of (at least) two people, and for this reason is described as a dynamic activity.

The sharing of diagnosis between worker and client is, however, only partial, and it is necessary to distinguish between the worker's professional opinion and the client's parallel and related appraisal of his situation. The caseworker's opinion is derived from:

some scientific understanding of the likely relationships between certain events or experiences in the client's life, and between his social background, developmental history and present behaviour and needs;

some awareness of the predominant stresses in the client's life and their sources: e.g. in the environment, in his feelings of guilt, in perceptual distortions, in ungovernable impulses;

some awareness of the values implicit in social policy; knowledge of the availability and use of social resources, and of the agency's policies and priorities in meeting needs;

some assessment of the client's motivation in seeking help; i.e. an appraisal of past responses to help from other sources, and an attempt to compare the values implicit in the client's request with those of the worker and the agency. For example: Does the client wish to change his situation? Has he the capacity to do so, and in what ways? Is it appropriate to assist him in these ways? The worker cannot be neutral to the outcome of events in the client's life and it cannot be assumed that the definitions of 'well being' as sought by worker and by client are identical or of equal emotional or moral validity.

Diagnosis as a professional opinion, therefore, involves several different intellectual processes: the *analysis and*

33

interpretation of facts; the *evaluation* of several value-systems; and the *comparison* of the validity and feasibility of various solutions.

As the outcome of these processes should be the formation of *operational predictions*, it may be helpful, as guide lines in diagnosis, to set out certain questions which to some extent could be asked about the three case situations already described. The answers to these questions would suggest operational predictions for the focus and nature of future work:

1. In view of the problems presented, the emotional significance which the clients attach to them, and the feelings and expectations they have about the worker as a possible source of help, which are the most helpful starting points for further discussion?

2. Which of the problems presented may most appropriately be discussed and helped by this agency? What would be the implications for the client(s) of the introduction of other agencies or professional helpers?

3. What significance has the starting problem for various members of the families concerned? What will happen to all the people in these situations if no help is given with the problems presented? What are the likely effects on each of them of various kinds of help or intervention?

4. What solutions would be acceptable and possible to the clients and the families in their social situations and within the limits of their personalities and resources? What would be the effects of these solutions on others in the environment (neighbours, other professional workers, the agency's other clients)? To what extent will environmental factors contribute to success or failure in the efforts of the worker?

5. If each problem is wholly or in part an emotional one (not the direct outcome of the lack of material resources) why does it persist? Are there any senses in which some solutions would feel worse to the client than

34

the retention of the problems? For example, if Mr Brown were given an immediately suitable job and a good house at a low rent, would he, in the long run be (and feel) helped, or would he come to resent the sudden loss of objects to blame in the environment? And would his family's situation deteriorate as a result? Similarly, does the client need to retain certain kinds of problem behaviour in order to remain acceptable to other significant people in his environment?

6. What kind of personality would the clients ideally need the worker to possess in order to help them in their personal emotional development? The assumption implicit in this question is that all people in their earlier years pass through phases of development which require modified responses from others. Development may become halted and may, therefore, need a compensating and appropriate relationship to be established with reference to the phase reached. Here again there may be a conflict of wanting and needing: Mr Brown hints at his dissatisfaction with the failure of the social services to gratify his demands for dependency (giving him a house, finding him the right job) while at the same time his aggressive manner and abrupt departure reduce the likelihood of these demands being met. Conflicts of needs will be discussed at greater length in a later chapter.

7. To what extent do the social difficulties experienced by the clients reflect problems in role-definition or in role-confusion? If a worker is to assist a client in establishing or maintaining particular social roles, the client's present role-performance needs assessing: i.e. the extent to which a specific role meets the clients 'felt' needs, the needs of others in his environment, and the demands and expectations of society in general. (See Ruddock (1969) for more detailed discussion of roles and relationships.)

Answers to these questions can sometimes be inferred from comments made by the client. Sometimes the client himself raises questions of these kinds as, through discussion, he seeks his own solutions to his problems. The manner in which he perceives his experiences (as forming a pattern or as fragmented events) and the quality of his comprehension (whether in intellectual or wholly emotional terms) will determine how far he takes the initiative in exploring his problems in ways similar to the questions suggested here. But the principal purpose of these questions is to enhance the worker's awareness of the client and his adaptability and responsiveness to the client's needs; however modified, they are unlikely to form a framework of discussion with the client, at least during earlier interviews. Sometimes, in the later stages of a relationship, such discussion becomes possible, but until then much of the caseworker's opinion is the product of informed but unverified conjecture.

Thus a diagnosis is not a blueprint for action but an exercise, in part a private one, in assessing what is known (the facts of the situation and the explanatory theories which might be employed in understanding these facts), in creating receptiveness and understanding, and in developing a lively sensitivity to the possible outcomes of different courses of action.

Diagnosis as shared understanding

We should not regret this lack of blueprints. Any partnership between worker and client, and any hope of enhancing the client's capacities to resolve his own difficulties, depend on the worker's acceptance of the essential uncertainty of his diagnosis, and his need therefore to listen to and to learn from his client. Experts in medicine and law are valued; self-professed experts in social living are not. If, in Mrs A.'s situation, the probation officer said, 'What you should do is ...' or 'I'll see your husband and work something out', Mrs A. would infer, possibly with resentment, that the probation officer feels her problem is simple and that she is foolish not to have solved it; or that his superior wisdom renders further communication impossible; or that her feelings, opinions and assessments are irrelevant; or that her situation runs 'true to type' and is not individual to herself.

The help available to a client, particularly in the first interview lies, therefore, neither in the production of immediate solutions nor in the worker's total absorption in asking the questions and receiving the facts which will form part of his professional diagnosis. It is, for example, neither courteous nor useful to interrupt the client's opening remarks (or to precede them) by insisting on the immediate completion of the agency's forms, however useful these may appear to be for diagnostic purposes. Neither, at a more sophisticated level of performance, is it helpful to absorb the client's comments and withhold any tentative observations indicating that one is beginning to understand and to clarify ways in which one might help. Both worker and client will be withholding some part (possibly a large part) of their thoughts from each other; both independently will be understood the situation a little more clearly, formulating more precisely the needs to be met and how each thinks they may be met most effectively. Both, in a sense, are engaged in diagnosis: the worker starting his, the client reformulating his. The client derives help from the recognition that they are engaged in a similar process, and that their ability to share ideas will increase in later meetings. In this way the sensitivity of both worker and client is heightened without the accompanying risk of undermining the client's morale. Both worker and client are likely with each meeting to find new significance in facts and events (as, for example, when the client says, 'I've never thought of it in that way before' or 'I've just remembered that ...'). If sensitively listened to and prompted, the client recounting past events gains a new understanding of their significance and, possibly, a new awareness of what he or another person is really like.

Yet as we have seen in the Brown case, the client's

37

expectations of the relationship may be very different from the relationship the worker would choose to make. The client may consider that the worker lacks experience and understanding (specific or general) of his personal and cultural background, of 'what it feels like to be me', and he may (perhaps projecting his hostility) assume that the worker will not be willing to learn from him. This is not always expressed in overtly hostile terms. It is more frequently found in silence, 'flat' responses, sullenness, or cynicism. Sometimes it appears in excessive self-justification, in endless reiterations as if the client were battering the caseworker into understanding or submission. In some cases, therefore, a prerequisite of sharing in diagnosis is the worker's willingness to recognize (and introduce discussion about) the stages and feelings the client went through before their meeting, and the mixed feelings he has about coming to the agency and receiving help. For some people, seeking help runs counter to a personal standard of self sufficiency; a visit to an agency represents a surrender of self-esteem, an admission to a stranger of personal inadequacy, a further proof that the problem they are bringing is insoluble and hopeless. Some may fear that the existence of a problem in one area of life will be interpreted as symptomatic of *general* inadequacy; a client who bursts into tears after presenting a problem may be relieving tension *or* may be surrendering to the debilitating effects of seeking help. For many clients, visiting an agency for the first time adds a fear of the unknown and considerable personal inconvenience to the problems which motivate their coming.

More subtle hindrances to shared understanding lie in the unrecognized value the client may place, for example, on individuality, on the nature of human beings in general, and on action. Some conduct their lives on a basis of sharing, while others value their independence; some tend to believe the best about other people, others the worst; some value activity, others passivity.

38

Similarly the agency may have restricted functions, administratively defined, which, however concerned the worker feels for the client, prevent the provision of effective help, especially for problems which lack adequate definition. If no existing social service can provide for the felt needs of a particular client, effective sharing in any part of the helping process is limited. A caseworker should therefore be alert to the importance of evaluating existing social provisions, ready to identify the possibilities of new forms of service, and ready to acknowledge inadequacies in the ideologies of existing services. New and experimental forms of help (for example, the appointment of detached workers or the establishing of informal agencies in local communities) can be effective only if the exploration of new techniques is matched by an exploration of alternative ideologies in helping. (See Timms, 1968.)

Summary

Diagnosis necessitates an identification (albeit critical) with the employing social agency. The problems with which caseworkers are concerned are *social* problems, and are—for the most part—recognized as such by the clients themselves as well as by the community. Clients become aware of their need for help through experience of difficulties in social roles and socially required tasks; as Perlman (1953) has pointed out, they rarely approach the caseworker saying, 'I need help in myself, in how I feel about myself,' but rather, 'I need help *in relation to* my marriage, my job,' etc. Thus, diagnosis is not a process of defining and prescribing for all maladjustments but only those affecting the client's capacity to maintain his social roles and social responsibilities. It is not fruitful to examine the dynamics of the client's personality in isolation from the dynamics of his social environment and of wider social pressures and expectations.

Diagnosis is a psycho-social process, and, as Marshall has said (1965), 'the question is on which half of that compound adjective you put the emphasis. In the matter of welfare ... the emphasis should be bang in the middle, on the hyphen. At that point of perfect balance the social worker can exercise an expertise which is not that of the psychiatrist, a systematized procedure which is not that of the bureaucrat, and a personal influence which is not that of the moral censor.'

Diagnosis starts with the attempt to answer questions: What is the problem? How is the client coping with it and reacting to it? What is he trying to say about his problem and the quality of the help he needs?

From questions such as these, the caseworker begins to form opinions and hypotheses about the patterns made by the facts and their implications for help, the sort of relationship the client needs to experience, the social ends and priorities to be served, and the social values to be expressed in the relationship. At the same time he seeks to engage the client in sharing ideas and feelings about the problem and its solution, to enhance the client's capacities in locating, defining and attributing priority to that part of the complex of needs at which help should begin. The facts of the situation need ordering according to their significance for the client, and need to be understood by the worker not only objectively but affectively. Past and present facts in a client's life are, by recall and discussion, subject to affective redefinition.

Reference has been made to value elements in diagnosis. The caseworker is concerned not only to discover the best form of intervention in the client's life, but whether it is appropriate to intervene at all and the possible outcome of his not doing so. He must consider and compare in each situation what society and the client would regard as 'change for the better'. He must consider various social expectations of how the client ought to behave alongside what the client can realistically be expected to achieve in the light of his life history, his personal resources and his immediate environment.

40

3

The relationship of diagnosis to facts and theories

The purpose of this chapter is to look at the steps by which a diagnosis is built up during the whole period of contact between worker and client. Hitherto emphasis has been placed mainly upon the caseworker's thinking in advance of and during a first interview, and upon the needs of the individual client. In this and the next chapter, the longer-term process of diagnosis will be considered and some attention given to diagnosis in situations of marital and family conflict.

Two elementary but essential points must be re-iterated :

Treatment begins at the first meeting of worker and client and runs concurrently with diagnosis; diagnosis is modified in the light of the results of help, and the help given is refined in the light of greater diagnostic under-standing. Thus, as Davison (1965) and Perlman (1956) have suggested, the first task is to determine where and how to start helping; the criteria they suggest are :

1. the aspect of need which most immediately concerns the client;
2. where several needs hold equal importance for the client, those which appear to be most representative or typical of the whole range;
3. those which seem most manageable and capable of fairly quick solution, so that the client experiences as soon as possible that help is available through dis-

cussion, and that more complex and intractable difficulties may also be resolved in time.

Secondly, as new facts emerge, new events take place, new emotional significance is attributed by the client to past events, and new qualities of relationship are experienced, so the process of diagnosis in respect of these facts and events will be resumed. Some hypotheses will be at the stage of testing while, possibly in another area of the client's life experiences, new patterns of behaviour or hints of feelings are emerging which have not yet been sufficiently understood to make possible an hypothesis. In attempting to systematize the process of diagnosis, therefore, it must be remembered that different parts of the process may be going on at the same time with reference to different aspects of the client's life and needs.

The process of diagnosis

1. The principle source of information is the client. The worker starts with problems as they are perceived by the client and introduces discussion which the client sees as relevant. Facts are sought about the duration and extent of the difficulty, the way it came about, how the client feels about it, the source and circumstances of his referral to the agency.

2. From this information the worker begins to construct descriptive pictures of how certain facts and feelings interact to form the case situation. He will start to gain some awareness of which factors have an individual significance for the client and which represent commonly shared experiences in the client's family or social group—whether, and to what extent, in his family and local associations he is 'the odd man out' in some aspect of behaviour and feeling or in some professed or implied value. Some impression will be gained whether the problem is contained within a small area of the client's experiences or is promoting parallel difficulties in several areas. The worker

will also be trying to estimate whether the quality of the client's feelings seems appropriate or inappropriate (for example, excessive, misplaced, insufficient) to the problem as presented.

3. According to the range and extent of the difficulties described or inferred, the worker will then decide which related areas of the client's life and experiences need more systematic exploration. These may include, for example, the composition of the family, his expectations of the agency's function, his education or employment record, his health, his income and the management of the household budget. Some aspects of present and past family relationships may seem to have a direct bearing on the problem as the client experiences it : for example, changes in allegiances within the family; bereavements and separations in earlier years; the way in which the family is reacting to the client's problem and is likely to react (or has already reacted) to the caseworker's intervention. Insufficient attention is sometimes paid to what happens in the family immediately after some aspect of family life has been discussed with one member, or after the caseworker has ended a home visit. For example, a middle-aged woman in chronic marital tension which, for the most part, was displayed by silence and moodiness, was encouraged in one interview to talk about happier times with her husband before the birth of the children. The interview ended on this note of cheerful nostalgia. On her return home, she immediately and vociferously found fault with all the members of the family in turn, and precipitated a major (and, for them, unexpected) row, thus increasing the unhappiness of her children and promoting a general hostility to the caseworker.

It is important to ensure that the client sees these explorations as relevant, and some of the necessary skills are examined in the next chapter.

It may be appropriate also to discuss with the client in this phase of diagnosis the need for information from other sources, or the involvement of other agencies in providing help, taking care not to prejudge whether the intervention of other agencies will help or perhaps confuse him. Sometimes further referrals should be delayed until the client 'knows where he stands' with the worker: that is to say, until he has gained confidence in the worker's intentions towards him and has established some role for himself in the agency. Richmond (1917) suggested that, in approaching other sources of information and help, especially in the early stages of a case, it is wise to concentrate on those who can increase the worker's understanding rather than those from whom co-operative work is sought. In the interests of not bewildering the client by excessive intervention and of helping him to establish a sense of partnership with the agency, this remains a useful guide, even though it seems to delay the provision of some kinds of help and may (in problems of great complexity) make the worker feel inadequate and isolated. It is useful also at this stage, as Richmond suggested, to group external sources of information as main or subsidiary. If, for example, in the case of John, it became relevant to future discussions with him about his earlier life at home, school and work, to seek verification from external sources, it would be best first to approach the Children's Department, in whose care he has been on several occasions, than to pursue random enquiries of employers and headteachers, or perhaps even of his mother, who may well feel that a discussion of her son's earlier life is irrelevant. Similarly, external sources may be grouped according to their possession of direct knowledge or their reliance on hear-say.

4. The next phase is to structure these data. The data comprise thoughts, feelings, events and responses which, to a greater or less degree, form in the client's mind a coherent pattern of part of his life. For the worker, some of the facts, feelings and responses may seem (at least for a time) anomalous. Similarly, for a client who has suffered traumatic hardships or a succession of bewildering experi-

44

ences, the pattern may seem to have broken down; some events, and his responses to them, seem unexpected and inexplicable. Thus the structuring of information can sometimes usefully be shared with the client as part of the process of helping. But shared activity of this kind should be based on tentative prompting by the worker, not on the imposition of the worker's own structures upon the client's perception. The following interview with Mrs Charles illustrates this process:

Mrs Charles (aged 20) visited the caseworker at the suggestion of a solicitor whom she had approached because of her husband's persistent cruelty. The husband (aged 23) has worked on the railway since leaving school. They have a son of six months and have been married for 17 months. The solicitor telephoned to make the appointment, saying that it seemed 'a hopeless case' as the husband's behaviour recently had been very violent: he had thumped and kicked his wife on several occasions without any apparent provocation from her. The couple were buying their own house, but Mrs Charles and the baby had now returned to her parents, and more recently the husband had returned to his.

On arrival at the agency Mrs Charles was well-dressed; she was smiling and looked light-hearted. She said it was kind of the worker to see her, but she really saw little point in coming as she would never return to her husband. The caseworker commented that she must have been having a worrying time recently, though she did her best to seem cheerful, and perhaps she would like to tell him about it. She nodded, paused rather uncertainly, and produced a handkerchief as if about to cry, but did not do so. She then began to talk about her courtship and marriage in the historical order of events, and with a surprising degree of detachment. It had been a whirlwind courtship lasting only a few months; her husband had been considerate, seemed hard-working and attentive to her. After only two weeks of marriage, however, he became sullen and aggressive

45

in finding fault with her housekeeping. When she went into hospital for her confinement, her husband took her cousin out on two occasions (so she had been told by a friend); 'I don't know if he did anything wrong with her; he said he didn't, but I wouldn't put anything past him.' More violent behaviour started on her return home. He began to drink heavily, frequently got drunk, and came home at all hours. She had been taught by her parents to keep 'respectable' hours. 'My father never liked him and said he wouldn't be any good.' Her parents had agreed to the marriage, however, because of her insistence and because her mother thought it would be all right.

The caseworker commented that it probably worried her that her father never liked her husband. This sometimes happens between people who are rather alike in some way. Did she feel they were a bit alike? Mrs Charles paused, and said that they both drank too much; this had caused trouble between her parents for many years. She had not wanted her marriage to go the same way. At the same time, she did not blame her father; her mother was 'a terrible nagger' and this used to make him worse. Her husband had not got the same excuse; she herself had never nagged him. The caseworker said 'Not in words', paused, and suggested that sometimes people feel they are being nagged in other ways—by the way people look at them, or even in the way other people show their affection to them. Perhaps her husband was a bit like that, and sometimes felt he was being nagged even though she did her best not to nag him. Mrs Charles looked surprised and a little anxious: 'I'm worried because he doesn't seem interested in me; that's what makes me think he's got someone else. I don't throw myself at him, and perhaps I've been too cold with him. . . . He's so possessive sometimes, as if he's jealous.' The caseworker asked if this had become even worse since she came out of hospital. Mrs Charles began to be tearful at this point, spoke of how he ignored the baby and hit him when he cried. 'It all seems hopeless; I wanted my marriage to be so different' [from what?] 'I don't really want to leave him, but we can't go on as we are.'

This case illustrates the linking of two aspects and periods of Mrs Charles's life in an attempt to help both client and worker to find explanation and coherence in her feelings and responses in marriage. The link is, till verified by the client, a guess on the worker's part based on a theory that earlier relationships, without recognition, influence the choice of marriage partner and later relationships within marriage. It was, for the worker, a leap from known facts to unknown facts capable of verification by the client; at the same time the client's attention was drawn to emotional links not readily available to her but which can be used to increase her understanding of some aspects of her present difficulties.

In ways such as this the structuring of information may take on a creative aspect, and some writers, for example, Hamilton, (1951), Lehrman (1954) have emphasized this aspect of diagnosis. Richmond wrote of inference as an essential part of the process by which synthesis and creative interpretation contribute to understanding. This creative thinking must not be confused with defensive intellectualizing or with phantasy; it is not a *retreat* into theory or into unreality, but rather an attempt to get nearer to what it feels like to be another person.

Clearly this can be dangerous. A caseworker may embrace a theory of human behaviour which, by encouraging one interpretation of the facts, blinkers him to the possibilities of alternative interpretations, so that he unwittingly discards inconveniently anomalous facts. Safeguards are, therefore, important. Diagnostic probability rests on the degree of certainty in the facts themselves, on the objectivity with which they are perceived, and on the degree of verification possible both of the facts and of general theories of explanation. In any case situation the data can be structured in a variety of ways to provide a

47

variety of patterns; any action or response in the client may be rooted in several interdependent factors. In the process of arranging the data, therefore (whether in private reflection or in discussion with the client), distinctions must be drawn between what is known and verified, what is reasonably inferred, and what is guess-work.

It is necessary also to ensure that the diagnostic patterns constructed from the data contain at least an acknowledgement of the complex interactions which make up human personality: physical constitution and health, cognitive capacity, experiences, values and norms and their sources, external demands and expectations in the present and the past, and the feelings and responses about the interactions of these various aspects. The marital difficulties of a man who suffers with a duodenal ulcer cannot be understood without reference to the pain he experiences, his possible anxiety about his illness, the restrictions of various life activities because of illness, his wife's behaviour and attitude in relation to these aspects of his life, his norms of marital interaction and of manliness, etc. An assault on the police may be a source of guilt or a means of social acceptance. Among social groups, one member may be regarded as a 'legitimate' victim or a 'natural' ally. Poverty will be experienced by one family when they cannot buy bread, by another when they have to sell one of their cars.

5. Hypotheses are then developed about the relative probability of the various structures and about the likely effects of intervention of different kinds upon all the people involved in the case situation. Hypotheses suggest what might usefully be discussed in future interviews, both as part of the helping process and as part of the verification of information. Hypothetical explanation may be sought, for example, for (a) the fact that the client reiterates certain pieces of information, or is resistant to discussing what appears to be a central aspect of his difficulty; (b) whether he introduces new information as an invitation to further discussion or as a defence against what is already

48

being discussed; (c) how far his feelings about certain people are transferred from earlier relationships, or are displaced from others in the same environment, or are projections of feelings about some aspect of himself; (d) whether aspects of his behaviour are responses to uncontrollable inner pressures, to role uncertainty or confusion, to critical ambivalences of feelings, or to overwhelming pressures from his environment; (e) how far any or all of these may play some part in his present behaviour.

At the same time, the strengths or resources in the client and in others (including the caseworker) need assessing according to their relevance in overcoming the client's difficulties.

6. As new information is added, so the structures and hypotheses are revised; the help given so far is evaluated as part of the client's changing environment, so that future help may be made more relevant.

The relationship of the person, the problem and the environment

Hamilton (1951) and all later writers have emphasized the danger of attempting to separate these three variables in any part of the casework process, and this has particular relevance to the structuring of data in diagnosis. Casework is concerned with problems arising from the interaction of people and their environments. Even when the social difficulties appear to be entirely environmental, they are capable of definition and of help as social problems only in so far as they are experienced by *people* and, moreover, are experienced in particular ways. The environment of a person—for helping purposes—is what he *perceives* to be 'out there' rather than what actually is. Some writers extend the concept of 'environment' to include inner factors such as illness, ideals and intelligence in that these are not controllable by the client or are experienced as, in a sense, external to the 'real-me' core of his personality.

49

The structuring of data involves, therefore, not only the collecting of details under discrete headings but also the attempt to find categories which reflect the interaction of person and environment from which social problems and social needs are derived. Hollis selects three such categories which, when related together, make possible hypotheses about the nature of the help required:

1. the continuing presence and reinforcement of infantile needs which promote inappropriate demands and responses in the client's relationships with others;
2. the current pressures from the environment (conceived, as noted above, in both internal and external terms);
3. distortions in the client's perception (of other people in the environment or of social demands) which give rise to loss of adaptability in social behaviour, together with distortions (arising from an over-punitive or over-permissive conscience) in the client's perception of his own responsibilities.

Difficulties in the first and third categories may add to the problems in the second; see, for example, the case of Michael in Chapter 4.

Questions for further consideration

This outline of the intellectual process of diagnosis suggests issues which require further discussion. The success of the process relies considerably on skill in eliciting facts through interviews, and in Chapter 4 there is some discussion about the manner of asking questions, of listening and prompting, and of building upon the client's responses. We must consider what is meant by the 'strengths in the client'. We must also review the difficulties of seeking understanding by combining intellect, feelings and imagination. This difficulty is sometimes suggested by the use of descriptions which are essentially paradoxical: 'dis-

interested sympathy', 'the maximum of detachment combined with the maximum of involvement'. A paradox is not
necessarily a nonsense; it may represent, in Dr Johnson's
words, 'a truth standing on its head to attract attention'.
These and related topics are discussed in Chapter 5 where
we shall consider the planning of help as an attempt to
balance the worker's need for objectivity with the client's
need for someone who is willing, if necessary, to become
emotionally involved and morally committed in helping
him.

Evaluating the process of diagnosis as an intellectual activity

The only access to facts is through individual perception;
and descriptions of facts (and the capacity to reflect upon
them) are confined within the language available. In
Leonard's words (1966) 'Facts are ... sense data perceived
in terms of a scheme of concepts'. Words are an imperfect
medium for describing emotions and needs. Some clients,
confronted by complicated mixed feelings about their
relationships with others, especially in marriage and family
life, are 'at a loss for words' and present their difficulties
incoherently or indirectly. Sometimes the words required
may be embarrassing to the client, or he may be uncertain
whether he ought to use them to the caseworker. This is
often so in problems involving sexual difficulties, where
the most commonly used words and phrases have aggressive and pejorative overtones, and where the client, therefore, sometimes presents alternative problems (for example,
complaints about mismanagement of income). Sometimes
the client hopes that the caseworker will infer the central
problem and present it in his own words. Sometimes the
secondary problem is used as a test of the reliability and
sensitivity of the caseworker before more intimate problems are presented. The secondary problem may itself be
serious, but if regarded as the central or only concern of
the client the structure which the worker applies to the

information he receives will be distorted, and his hypotheses will lack relevance. The formation of hypotheses is therefore always secondary to the attempt to understand what the client is trying to say, and to a willingness to assume the initiative in discussing the client's hints, even when these represent embarrassing topics.

Sometimes the nature of the problem can be inferred from the kind of agency the client approaches. A man of 22 came to a marriage guidance counsellor; his opening comment was 'I wish you'd have a talk with my wife. She doesn't get me up for work in the morning.' He then sat in flushed and embarrassed silence. Receiving the answer that this had gone on for six months (since the start of the marriage), the caseworker assumed *either* a broad dissatisfaction with marriage (a regret, perhaps, for lost freedom and lost home life) *or*, bearing in mind the man's age and the nature of the agency, a problem of sexual disturbance. He asked, therefore, whether the man had come because of some sexual difficulty or because, perhaps, he was wondering whether he was abnormal in some way. This was a fairly reasonable guess. Even apparently sophisticated clients may need equally direct help.

The caseworker's approach, especially in view of the limitations of language, is therefore often empirical. If asked to produce diagnostic justification for what he does, he might present a mixture of speculation, intuition and personal values as well as some verified objective data. Diagnosis rarely satisfies demands for scientific stringency. It need not be condemned for this, for the caseworker is more concerned with the meaning of the situation for the client than with scientific objectivity. But intuition and speculation, however plausible, often fail to provide a valid interpretation of the client's meaning, and therefore require testing against a continuing and rigorous observation and an awareness of alternative theories and explanations of human behaviour.

The multiple causation of all important human actions

must also be recognized. No married man would be able *completely* to answer the question 'How and why did you choose your wife?' because of the complexity of conscious and unconscious motives and ambivalences present in this relationship. No single theory as yet encompasses all these complexities. In meeting people's problems, therefore, one may need to move from one theory to another, from one set of concepts to another, evaluating how far these alternative theories are compatible or incompatible, and alive to the possibility that a desire for certainty, for a final and undeniable truth about a situation, may indicate less a wish to help the client than the worker's own need for intellectual and emotional security. The pursuit of 'truth' can lead to rigidity in relationship and to a disregard of what the client is trying to say.

One possible safeguard lies in ensuring that any discussion of past events and feelings is related forward to *present* experiences and needs. (We have already considered examples of workers who succeeded and failed in doing this, and the effects in treatment.) Hollis (1968) suggests that, central to the caseworker's responsibility both to the agency and to the client, is the analysis of the effectiveness of a client's present performance in his necessary roles. She defines role as a 'learned patterned action', and observes that, though the psycho-social history of the client may indicate which factors have prevented the identifications necessary to this learning, and may draw the worker's attention to the residual effects of earlier role confusion, the history is not an end in itself. Most interviews are properly concerned with describing, 'ventilating' and reflecting upon here-and-now problems rather than with the study of personality dynamics and early causation. Similarly Gottlieb and Stanley (1967) suggest that casework is concerned with improvement in the client's present social functioning (i.e. with his expressed and overt needs and symptoms) rather than with his personality development.

At the same time a change in one aspect of the client's present social functioning may lead to other changes and to a development in personality. Effective work in the present may mitigate some of the damage in earlier development, just as some understanding of earlier development may help the worker to establish a relationship which *feels* helpful to the client in the present and which matches the quality of support he currently needs. Reiner and Kaufman (1960), for example, relate the various stages of emotional development to the client's capacity to tolerate and use permissive, unstructured, directive or authoritative relationships. Each stage in life presents goals of maturation and achievement, and it is therefore possible to assess which stresses experienced by the client are (or were) intrinsic to a stage in development and which represent an individual variation in the capacity to integrate new experiences and new learning, or in the quality of role-expectations and role-reinforcers in his environment.

In assessing current life patterns or earlier stages of development, it is wise to remember that, whereas events in one's personal life often form a coherent pattern when viewed historically, each event *in its own time* may appear to possess a quite different relationship with the past or with the future. In retrospect, one sees patterns in a marriage, but the significance of each stage or act in the marriage was not *at the time* perceived in this way. There is little feeling of prediction in human life and relationships; though life may seem deterministic in retrospect, it seems much less so in prospect (save possibly in compulsive or neurotic conditions). This suggests that the client's memory of his past life (and the worker's of his interviews) is a selective process which constantly re-interprets the significance of past events, so that even the unexpected is *subsequently* perceived as part of a pattern. What seems significant now (both for worker and client) may derive its significance from the memory of past events. Its significance may later diminish or increase when viewed retrospectively.

It is necessary, therefore, to review data-structures and hypotheses from time to time, and to involve the client periodically in a discussion of progress, so that the case-worker has the opportunity of re-starting the intellectual process of diagnosis in the light of changes in the significance ascribed to earlier events.

The diagnostic importance of the family in understanding the needs of the individual client

It has already been suggested that, depending upon the need presented by the client, it may be relevant to seek information about some aspects of family relationships. It is sometimes asserted that all casework is family case-work. This is a clumsy assertion, for it implies a degree of intervention out of keeping with some problems referred for help. But it contains two important truths: the neces-sity for awareness of the needs and responses of others relative to the client, and the recognition in diagnosis of the pervasive influence of past and present family relation-ships on individual behaviour and attitudes beyond the family circle. The family is the primary social institution in moulding the individual's emotional and social life; it helps or hinders subsequent adjustments to a variety of social relationships by enabling or preventing development through the various phases of socialization, and by per-mitting or denying the influence of external values; it pro-vides or inhibits experiments in role-taking and the incorporation of the expectations of others from which develops the individual's fundamental attitude to himself. The family mediates between social forces and the indi-vidual member, and permits or denies compensations for failure in his socially ascribed roles. In the family, the individual may privately act out many needs denied to him elsewhere—to dominate, to be aggressive, to be dependent, to love, to 'show off'.

55

Caseworkers are concerned diagnostically with the family life of the client because of the insights it provides into individual development and the emergence of social problems, and because the family can be promoted as a powerful resource of help to the individual. The intimacies of family life are never more than partially known, but any information obtained may be structured under four general headings relevant to the worker's understanding of the individual client's needs:

1. The values expressed by the activities of the family: the extent to which the client's individual needs are satisfied or denied in accordance with these values.
2. The mechanisms by which the needs of the individual are reconciled with those of other family members; for example, who makes the decisions which affect him, who shares which satisfactions and loyalties with him, who allots his responsibilities within the family, how are his difficulties resolved or denied by the family?
3. The emotional climate surrounding the client; how this has changed over the years; the relationships between generations; how much of the client's life is lived inside and outside the family; where he expresses and satisfies particular needs.
4. The relationship, so far as this can be ascertained, between the inner psychological life of the individual client and the manner of his interaction with other members.

As information accumulates under these headings, so it becomes possible to assess whether and in what ways the family, or certain members, may be helped to assist in resolving the client's difficulties.

Diagnosis in marital problems: the conflicting needs of two clients with a shared problem

Reference in the last paragraph to the *inner* life of the

individual in the family draws attention to the tensions which may exist between emotional needs and the opportunities for their expression and fulfilment, and between ideal and reality. The tension may be overtly recognized by partners in a marriage. '[At first] she corresponded to my myths and I corresponded to hers.... After a year or so I began to know her. Then I found we were totally unsuited to each other.' (Quoted by Dicks, 1967.) At other times the tension is *consciously* denied, but experienced as a general unease or dissatisfaction : as with a couple whose conversation was full of endearments but who, in the presence of the interviewer, curtailed each other's sentences so that neither could ever complete a remark. In marriage—unless a scapegoat can be found (possibly among the children, the in-laws or the neighbours)—the conflict of ideal and reality is focused intensely in a single relationship, the foundation of which is rarely, if ever, capable of clear and rational definition. One partner may lose sight of the reality of the other beneath a weight of projections.

The inner ideals which each partner brings to the marriage may be verbally indefinable save as vague general feelings ('a rosy glow' of falling in love) or may be projected, e.g. as photographic pin-ups. They may be based not on what can be achieved within present reality but on 'what might have been', on the nostalgia of unfulfilled attempts at earlier emotional satisfaction. Several writers have drawn attention to the emotional stresses which may arise in the attempt, within the relationship of husband and wife, to satisfy both the unmet (and possibly forgotten or suppressed) needs of the past and the conscious needs of the present. It has been suggested, for example, that some sexual impotence within marriage may be explained in this way. It may be supposed, then, that all external situations (the behaviour of the marriage partner, the birth and behaviour of children, the relationship with the caseworker) will be subject to partial interpretation and

57

evaluation in the light of this inner reality of ideal and expectation. Many who seek casework help with marital problems probably would not need to do so, but for the unease engendered by this internal tension between the satisfaction of conscious needs within present reality and the pressure of residual earlier needs still seeking unrealistic and impossible gratification. This tension is often apparent in the incoherent and disordered presentation of the marital difficulty. The case of Mrs Charles illustrates these conflicting needs: she sought, and still seeks, to make a marriage different from that of her parents, yet finds herself impelled (perhaps needing) to repeat their mistakes.

It will be useful to continue the case of Mr and Mrs Charles at this point, as providing additional examples of the issues raised so far and as a preface to further discussion.

Mr Charles responded to an invitation to visit the caseworker, and launched immediately into a series of complaints about his wife. He justified his anger with her first on the basis of her incompetence in managing the housekeeping and in not getting his meals to time. The caseworker tentatively commented that he seemed to be suggesting that his wife was not matching up to the standards he was used to before he was married; but Mr Charles irritably exclaimed, 'My parents don't come into this at all', and began a further tirade about his wife's jealous accusations about his drinking and his unfaithfulness, saying that he only went out drinking on Sundays, and that he is indeed faithful to her '... not like the other men at work—they're always on about the other women their wives don't know about'. After several minutes of complaint and self-justification from Mr Charles, the caseworker asked if the trouble was all his wife's fault. Mr Charles grudgingly said that he supposed it was fifty-fifty, and described himself as short-tempered '... though she drives me to it'. (Cf. Mrs Charles's earlier comments about nagging.) The caseworker asked if there were any things they did *not* argue about; Mr Charles talked of his son in affectionate terms; he was obviously proud of being a father though agreeing that life with his wife had got worse since the baby's birth. There followed a tense discussion about the lack of love-making in the marriage, Mr Charles's certainty that his wife did not want him, and her unjustified accusations of infidelity. He angrily blurted out, 'Why, I only had sex twice with her before we got married.' He spoke about the kind of talk that goes on between the unmarried men at work, how he hoped he was better than they are, and, finally about his hopes that he and his wife 'could start again'. His work interests him, and his ambitions were discussed at some length, concluding with his wish that his wife could accept the awkwardness of his working hours and his interest in the job; 'I warned her before we got married that she was marrying the railway as well as me.'

In the following interview with Mrs Charles, her anxieties about not managing the housekeeping money played a large part. There were further complaints about her husband's persistent drinking (every night), and the amount of time he spent at the weekend with his parents compared with his never taking her out. 'When I ask him to, he answers me back. You don't want to trust him, he's not the angel he looks.' Her fear of the caseworker's taking sides against her was discussed and the interview concluded with her saying that the baby had come too soon, and that she sometimes got as fed up with it as her husband did; she had hit the baby sometimes herself. She felt that she and her husband ought to be able to get together again, but not yet; she needed time to think it out.

Later Mr Charles returned unexpectedly, saying that he had been thinking about things; he said he thought they had both been stubborn, and that he particularly had said a lot of things to his wife that he should not have said. The caseworker commented that Mrs Charles also was 'thinking about things', and wondering, for example, how she could manage the housekeeping a little better. Mr Charles looked surprised about this, and commented that his wife had never discussed 'things' with *him* in that way. The caseworker agreed that it was sometimes difficult for two people to talk honestly together about what they really felt about themselves and each other. After further discussion, Mr Charles suggested that the caseworker might arrange to see them both together. The caseworker suggested that Mr Charles visit his wife to ask her opinion about this. He was very hesitant, but then said, 'Perhaps I'll ask her out for an evening—not really to talk—just to enjoy ourselves.' Two days later, Mrs Charles arrived to say that they were together again.

(Clearly the case is not finished at this point; the couple have entered a 'honeymoon' phase, which is encouraging for them and for the caseworker, but there is no reason to hope that the internal complexities of feeling are so quickly resolved, and many more problems have been raised by both clients than have been adequately explored. The caseworker has helped, and probably knows or infers enough to go on helping. But there remain factual discrepancies, e.g. about the husband's drinking, about which both clients have apparently told the truth as they see and experience it. How important is it, diagnostically, to pursue an objective truth about such matters?)

It is not possible in this book to review comprehensibly the various sources and kinds of marital disharmony. It is evident however that, in addition to information about the present behaviour of the partners, the caseworker sometimes needs to establish an historical perspective of how present needs and earlier unfulfilled needs are interacting both within the individual partners and between them.

The quality of disharmony may change according to the age of the marriage. In the early stages, the couple may fail to establish the necessary minimum of physical or emotional relationship, the past remaining influential for one or both partners to such a degree that the marriage is not recognized or accepted as a major change in roles, responsibilities and opportunities. Failure of this kind may indicate a residual dependence upon parents or, possibly, a lack of self-acceptance as a capable adult. Or failure may draw attention to a difficulty, rooted in earlier experiences, in giving or accepting intense affection. A wife's need for dependence may have been one of her main attractions in courtship, but may later be resented by her husband when marriage provides her with an unlimited opportunity for expressing this need. Similarly a dependent husband may jealously resent the birth of a first child, and in turn meet a resentful response from his wife. The case of Mr and Mrs Charles permits speculation on some of these points.

At a later stage, a hitherto happy marriage may founder because of different maturational speeds in the partners. One or both may develop hitherto undetected facets of personality, or may no longer be meeting the changing needs of the other. What started as a complementary relationship may cease to be one.

Later still, the very intensity of the partnership may promote a return to the kinds of earlier emotional responses that one or other partner had with a parent. A woman of 55, with two adult children, began to address her husband, and to refer to him, as 'Daddy'; she used the word affectionately, but it evidently irritated him. Nevertheless it fairly accurately described the relationship that had recently developed. The husband complained of her increasing over-dependence upon him, telephoning him at work, and seeking to keep him at home every evening. At the same time—in his more affectionate moods towards her— he willingly held her hand when they went out together. In later periods, also, with the departure of the children from the home, new roles and new redirections of emotional and social life are required of the parents, which may again intensify inner conflicts between acceptance of the present and nostalgia for the past.

Some writers have suggested that at the root of many of these difficulties lies a failure of self-esteem in one or both partners. He or she, anxious and possibly guilty about the presence of mixed emotions towards the other, experiences a sense of personal confusion and unworthiness. He may take into himself the added burden of the least loveable parts of the partner for whom he cannot or dare not admit feelings of dislike. Lacking self-acceptance and self-assurance, he may make insatiable compensatory demands for affection, or may, almost deliberately, promote quarrels and seek rejection. A wife, subject to such feelings, may increasingly mismanage the household while increasingly demanding forgiveness; she may complain that her husband is overdemanding ('he uses me') or under-demanding ('he doesn't love me').

An extreme problem of this kind was presented by Mrs Jones, in her late twenties, who came to discuss her marital situation following her husband's complaint of her recent frequent associations with other men, which with professions of guilt she had voluntarily admitted to him. She was an attractive woman. The marriage relationship hitherto had been satisfactory, and some indication of its strength lay in her confiding in her husband about her behaviour, which she described as compulsive and virtually uncontrollable during the last four months. During this period she had denied her husband sexual intercourse though assuring him (and both accepted this) that she loved him. Hearing of her promiscuity, the husband had been resentful, angry and ashamed; the wife responded with increasing expressions of guilt and the suggestion that it might be best for him if she left him, though she did not wish to do so. Both seemed to find their situation inexplicable. The caseworker in the first interview concentrated upon the apparently sudden onset of this behaviour and upon the woman's experiences in the months preceding her promiscuity. An unusual and traumatic history of ill-health was

62

presented: a seriously deformed baby had died at birth, and a second pregnancy terminated because of a deformity of the foetus; on medical advice she had been sterilized, and had undergone two supplementary operations. On several occasions in the first interview she referred to her body as 'bad', and the caseworker inferred and suggested that possibly she saw herself as wholly bad. Mrs Jones agreed, talked at length of her unworthiness of her husband's affection, and of her own recent behaviour as 'wicked'. She wanted intercourse with her husband but would not permit it because 'it would not be right for him'. She spoke as if her body would damage him in some way. She had not said this to him ('because it sounds so silly') and his resentment made her feel worse. They had not spoken much for some weeks until she confided in him about her promiscuity.

The presence of a physical causative factor in her behaviour cannot be ruled out; neither can the possibility of an unconscious need to hurt her husband. It seems apparent, however, that a dramatic loss of self-esteem played a part in this situation. It was evident also in later discussions that this loss, combined with her bereavement problems, her ambivalence about a relationship which had produced abnormal births and which had indirectly removed from her the possibility of maternity ... in short, the whole complexity and confusion of feelings within her made her incapable of recognizing the impact of the situation on her husband in spite of her affection for him. What she had interpreted simply as his resentment contained strong elements of uncertainty about his capacities as a husband and of grief for the lost children.

This case together with that of Mr and Mrs Charles illustrates marriages at two stages of development, in which inner ambivalences and tensions of need are apparently present. In both, the problems of interaction are accompanied by feelings of inadequacy and guilt, and in the Charles's situation the presence and influence of the

63

parents can be detected. Both cases merit fuller discussion, but the following notes suggest how the information available in each might be structured so as to promote the forming of hypotheses of need and of help. Although these notes are specifically related to marital relationships they may, with modification, suggest a framework for discussing the relationship problems of parents and children. The examples given with each note are not comprehensive, but serve as starting points for further thought.

1. The discrepancies in the impressions of each partner as to the nature of the present difficulty and the precipitating factors.

   Example: Mrs Charles points to her husband's brutality and possible unfaithfulness and drunkenness, and wonders whether she unwittingly made a bad choice of husband. Mr Charles admits to the brutality but denies his wife's other suggestions which, he infers, are her way of covering up her own mismanagement and bad temper. Mr and Mrs Jones are agreed as to the overt problem, but lack awareness of each other's emotional responses to it.

2. The relationship may satisfy certain needs, if not all. The behaviour of each partner in the relationship may represent an undisclosed attempt to satisfy needs which do not accord with the expectations of the other.

   Example: Mrs Charles is perhaps trying to prove to her parents that she can make a better marriage than theirs, and resents that her husband has retained a closer bond with his parents than she with hers. Both partners are seeking dependence on each other but neither is prepared at first to admit this; resentment increases, in different ways, as the unacknowledged need is not met. Mrs Jones seeks protection from her husband while hurting him and denying her worthiness of it.

3. Inferences concerning the development of these needs through earlier life; the resultant attitudes towards the people most important in the life of each; the capacity for affection; the quality of sexuality.

   Example: compare the attitudes of Mr and Mrs Charles to the caseworker and in their loyalties to their parents. The hints of variation between their family norms and the acceptance/rejection of these norms. Differences in what the child means to them, and the ways in which the child is used as a focus of disturbance. For Mrs Jones her sexuality is at present a means of harm rather than a means of displaying affection; her promiscuity is not for gratification but for punishing her corrupted body.

4. The anxieties and fears which prevent the enjoyment of satisfying relationships.

   Example: Mr and Mrs Charles's inability to talk about and verify their feelings about each other. Mrs Jones's anxiety about her physical 'badness'; her sense of unworthiness. Mr Jones's resultant loss of certainty in his own capacities as a husband.

5. Factors which may suggest the intensity of help required.

   Examples: (a) the duration, severity and extent of the disturbance; (b) the presence of infantile reactions (e.g. Mr Charles's violent episodes); (c) the presence of strengths (e.g. Mr Charles's relationships, reliability and loyalty outside the home; Mrs Charles's surprising degree of objectivity and flexibility in early discussions; her husband's initiative in approaching her after his last interview, in spite of the possibility of rebuff; Mr Jones's seeking help rather than breaking his marriage); (d) the presence or absence of discrepancies in social values and religious beliefs; (e) the presence or absence of relatively smooth periods in the earlier relationship.

6. Areas of particular anxiety which the client has

difficulty in putting into words, and where he may need support.

Example: Mrs Charles's admission that she, too, beats her child; the Jones's problems of bereavement.

7. The extent to which one partner colludes with the behaviour of the other, and re-inforces it, in spite of expressed disapproval.

Example: Mrs Charles's complaint of her husband's behaving as if she were nagging him, and her subsequent recognition that, in a sense, she was doing so. Was she punishing him in place of her father? Did she need to promote his unsatisfactory responses in order to convince herself that she is really the innocent and aggrieved party in the marriage? How far did Mr Jones connive at the discontinuation of the sexual relationship?

Diagnosis in work with the whole family

Some caseworkers now base their work largely on whole-family interviews, in which the family is treated as a unity rather than as the sum of the interactions between individuals. This is not a denial of the individuality of members, but a recognition that the expression of individuality may be better understood in the context of a wider unity, of which the basic process is the achievement of a satisfactory pattern of 'separateness' and 'connectedness'. If some or all of the help is provided through whole-family interviews, the worker will be collecting *at first hand* information about the quality of interactions, similar to that of the group-worker. It may therefore, be necessary for the caseworker to develop a diagnostic framework for the family group parallel to the framework devised to meet the needs of individual members: he may need two frameworks to match the variations in the methods and skills of helping in the individual interview and the group interview. The second falls outside the scope of this book, but it may be appropriate briefly to outline the content of this supplementary framework:

the patterns by which decisions are reached concerning issues affecting all the members;

the patterns of shared activities;

the contributions individuals make to the character of the family: i.e. to the way in which a neighbour would describe *it* rather than *them*; and the response of individual members to this corporate character by their behaviour both inside and outside the family; the interactions which appear to contribute to the successes and difficulties of different members;

the extent to which members share or differ in their views about themselves, each other and the whole group;

the quality of the group's reactions to critical events; whether one person becomes the source of strength for the whole group; whether the family tends to unite or to disintegrate in crisis.

As has been suggested by Bell (see Handel 1968), it is difficult, especially when the extended family is geographically closely knit, to draw clear limits between family influences and wider neighbourhood influences. A chronically disturbed nuclear family is likely to involve the extended family in its internal conflicts so that the disturbance becomes so pervasive as to appear as a natural characteristic of life; the members lose sight of alternative norms of behaviour and of alternative solutions to their difficulties. The family may become a closed system, on the defensive against the wider community, and maintaining patterns of interaction, however unsatisfactory, for fear that any alternative will be worse. In other families, rejection may be directed towards a scapegoat, chosen because he embodies the essence of a disagreement between other members, or a tension between the family and neighbourhood which cannot be admitted or expressed. For example, parents who are divided on methods of discipline may scapegoat the child whose behaviour is most unpredictable or who most associates with others in the neighbourhood. The scapegoat may be chosen because of a facet of personality resembling a disliked part of another person (a parent, a marriage partner) who cannot be rejected. Once the selection is made, the scapegoating is rationalized; by his reactions to the rejection, the scapegoat 'proves' that the family was 'right' to reject him.

In studies of family life, such as those of Elizabeth Bott (1957), these processes are described in families who neither seek nor need casework help, who regard their behaviour patterns as normal, and who are accepted by others in this way. By 'isolating' a family or a marriage for casework help, an agency may imply abnormality which is unrecognized by the family itself or by the family's neighbours whose patterns of behaviour are similar. It is appropriate, therefore, to consider briefly the notions of norms and normality in relation to diagnosis.

Norms and normal

These words may be used in three senses: as representing a statistical average; as describing behaviour which in a particular group (or family) is deemed to be morally right or customary; and as reflecting an ideal of behaviour possessed by an individual or a small group. The second of these uses is the most common in everyday speech. It tends towards the making of generalizations, so that behaviour which is accepted by a group is assumed to have a moral validity for a much wider group. As Bott (1968) has shown, however, even where there appear to be areas of agreement in the norms of various groups, these areas lack precise definition; in terms of social behaviour there is probably far less consensus on norms than is commonly supposed.

The acquisition of norms, and of the moral component associated with the word, involves continuing processes of projection and introjection. Parents provide the primary models (to emulate or to improve upon) in the establishment of norms for marriage and family life; to their influence is added that of friends and neighbours who serve either as reinforcers of existing norms or, by contrast, as negative indicators of what the norm should be. Sometimes, a family will reinforce their norms by making friends with those holding similar ones. In general, therefore, norms about family life are internalized from the experience of the behaviour of others; if the various potential models differ in their norms, the individual or family will tend to select those most nearly similar to their own, and will thus ascribe a wider validity to the norm.

As norms are built up throughout the life of the individuals, so some will be nearer to consciousness than others. Some recently acquired may be in conflict with earlier norms; these conflicts may then be internalized and, as described earlier, give rise to ambivalent feelings about personal behaviour, the behaviour of a partner in marriage or of a child.

In full consciousness, however, will be retained a single standard of what is normal, and this will usually be seen as a majority standard. Goffman (1961) has demonstrated that within institutions behaviour which would be regarded as abnormal outside the institution is judged normal because it represents majority behaviour. The collective norm of the institution, maintained (sometimes unwittingly) by the majority, assumes an autonomous reality which is experienced as a moral obligation by its members. This phenomenon occurs in social institutions of all kinds; though more apparent in the collective life of a closed institution, it is an influence in the lives of members of families, small groups, clubs, schools, social agencies, professions.

In short what is normal or abnormal will vary in different situations, and these words when used in diagnosis have little value unless the reference group is defined or reference made to the traits, abilities, values and behaviour expected in a particular culture or sub-culture for a particular age group at a particular time. Furthermore it should be recognized that behaviour which is, by these references, clearly disturbed may not always be pathological; some disturbed behaviour (particularly perhaps in adolescence) may be a necessary forerunner of learning and change.

Regrettably these words are sometimes used without qualification of any kind; they become in themselves social facts while what they purport to describe may not exist as an objectively significant condition in the case situation. Laing (1967) has suggested that social prescriptions are sometimes introduced not to deal with the conditions which require help but as responses to these unqualified descriptions used as if they were diagnostically valid. Help may then become divorced from the need or problem as experienced by the client. (Similar difficulties may be inferred in the use of administrative and legal terms like 'truancy' or 'delinquency' in diagnostic assessments.)

Problems in marriage and family life not infrequently focus upon a complaint of abnormal behaviour in one member; the behaviour described may also be judged abnormal by the caseworker on the basis of his own norms. Even so, it is necessary to question how far the word indicates a need in the person using it or in the person described by it, and to examine whether the latter would or would not apply this description to himself.

We need, therefore, to be hesitant in speaking of 'normal' or even 'healthy' families. But caseworkers are concerned with 'change for the better'. As Caplan (1961) has suggested, the worker's concern is not simply to meet the need as presented but to meet it in such a way that the individual's or family's resources are strengthened for coping with future crises. This may involve helping a client *not* to put a brave face on a situation (even if to do so represents normal behaviour for himself and his group), if there is risk of a delayed reaction at a later time, or a risk that he is avoiding the problem by denying its importance or by redefining it unrealistically. Treatment may, therefore, be at odds with norms in pursuing change for the better.

The caseworker is concerned with the interpretation of normative and prescriptive values which are seldom seriously debated: the value of 'individual maturity', of 'happy family life', of individual 'integrity', of loyalty and responsibility in bonds of mutual affection. Although we should hesitate to describe a family as abnormal or unhealthy, we must nevertheless have a notion of families who need help and families who do not. The important distinction is that 'abnormal' often implies a standard which families are morally obliged to achieve, irrespective of their capacities to do so, whereas, 'in need of help' implies that, even by its own standards and within its own capacities, the family is failing to fulfil all its functions: for example, it allows for the individuality of some members but not of others (the parents, perhaps, unwillingly sacrificing themselves to their children); it emphasizes unity at the expense of individual differences (problems arise when the adolescent children want to go on holiday with their friends); it is unable to recognize that sharing and complementariness are possible only between individuals who could potentially be in conflict, and that some conflict may be essential, however threatening it may appear to the stability of relationships (like the young wife who runs home to her mother at the first irritable remark from her husband).

Casework is concerned with reconciliation rather than with the maintenance of external and idealized standards, with the acceptance of difference rather than with the search for conformity. It seeks in family relationships to replace prejudice (which the word 'normal' frequently implies) by awareness of the self as a real person and of others as equally real, not as environmental extensions of the self.

4

Observation within a relationship

We have noted the sense in which all casework is family casework: the feelings and attitudes invested in a problem by an individual, a married couple or a family group cannot be understood without regard to the past and present influences of the family, in one or more generations, as the primary force in socialization and in personality development. We have also seen the inadequacy of attempting in the diagnosis of a case-situation to separate the individual from the environment.

The caseworker, therefore, needs to decide in each situation whether to arrange whole-family interviews, separate individual interviews with each member, or interviews with a selection of the members individually or together; whether to interview only the person who expresses or experiences difficulty, or to spend some time with others who may not themselves show a need for help but who may be contributing to the problem or, potentially, its alleviation. The process by which decisions of this kind are reached has been described. Information is collected and structured about the problems presented, the reasons for their existence and presentation, the conflicts of satisfactions and allegiances. Hypotheses are made concerning the interactions of needs, the accessibility to help, the priorities in forming relationships with particular clients, and the probable effectiveness of such relationships. The caseworker decides whether or not to make a home-visit, whether a married couple should be seen together or apart, or whether a father should be invited to accompany his son to the agency for a joint interview. Sometimes a joint interview or a home visit seem unwarrantably risky; for example, when there appears to be an irreversible trend in the breakdown of a relationship; or when the motivation of one person is dominantly (even malignantly) destructive; or when there is a major personality difficulty in one member (paranoia, psychopathy, serious perversion). Sometimes one member has an important personal secret which cannot risk disclosure. Sometimes the worker infers that one member has such rigid defences that a serious personal or group breakdown may occur if he is virtually compelled into discussion with other members of his family.

In each situation the caseworker retains wide discretion, while aware that what he sees and infers may unwittingly be selective and distorted, and what he chooses to do affected by his individual attitudes. Reference has been made to the need for objectivity, self-discipline and self awareness, combined with emotional involvement, and this need is the central concern of this chapter and the next. In this, we shall be considering some of the interviewing skills required in gathering and structuring information; in the next, the interviewing skills required in formulating plans of help.

These skills cannot be taught mechanistically; they are not 'useful tips' or 'know-how'. They are individually acquired by caseworkers through practice, and through the lively interaction of theoretical knowledge of various kinds with the attitudes of the individual worker towards other people and their needs. Often they are exercised as if they were wholly intuitive; but they should be capable of evaluation so that they can be consciously and deliberately employed in situations where, for various reasons, the worker's intuitions would lead him towards inappropriate assessments and responses.

The caseworker's attitude and manner in discussion

All people use relationships as means of achieving, maintaining or validating a sense of personal identity. The caseworker's particular contribution to the client's sense of identity lies in expanding his understanding of the personal and social resources available to him, and in strengthening his ability to use these resources to satisfy both his own needs and the expectations of others concerning his behaviour. The problem the client brings is the starting point of a relationship; it is there to be solved. But it also makes available a means whereby the client can establish or develop his sense of identity. A client may say, 'I feel a lot better for coming', not only because of the partial solution of his problem but also because of a heightened feeling of well-being. A 'good' relationship in casework is one which both client and agency perceive as purposeful and relevant at both levels; for example, in each case discussed in the last chapter, the worker's concern is with the future of the marriage as a social contract, with the social implications of the behaviour of individuals towards each other, but also with helping the individuals to feel better in themselves.

The caseworker is, therefore, the medium of social expectations and demands, the conciliator between the expressed needs of individuals in social relationships, and the support available to the individual's attempts to resolve inner tensions (of conflicting needs, ambivalent emotions, confused roles or frustrated ideals) which reduce his feeling of well-being, his sense of identity and of personal integration. In helping an adolescent in serious conflict with his parents, or engaged in delinquent acts, the caseworker is concerned not only with the social and individual consequences of behaviour but also with helping the client to accept and cope with the fact that he cannot—however much he wishes—separate himself from what he perceives as the outside world. The world as he sees it is incorporated

74

within him, and, however much he may rationally or irrationally reject the values of others, some aspects of those values are effectively operating within him and giving rise to conflicting standards, attitudes and beliefs in respect of particular situations. When the adolescent says of an action, 'I knew it was wrong; I don't know why I did it', he is not necessarily denying responsibility, nor inviting a rational debate; he may be simply expressing the kinds of inner tensions to which reference has been made. It is often, therefore, less helpful in diagnosis to ask people *why* they acted in certain ways than to enable them to recall the conflicting feelings present at the time of particular actions. Finding the words necessary to describe these feelings may in itself provide the client with the means whereby the conflict can be contained and future actions controlled.

The caseworker's manner, therefore, should enable the client to express what kinds of help he requires, and to accept the help he needs. The skills involved are those which (a) assist the client to retain and express his sense of personal identity and encourage the development of his capacity for interdependent relationships with others, (b) permit him to talk honestly about the anxieties and tensions he feels, and to find the words necessary both to control these and, at the same time, to define their resolution, and (c) assist the client to establish or maintain his social roles.

The first two areas of help primarily concern the client's feelings rather than his intellect; the last requires a more calmly intellectual appraisal. As most situations are perceived emotionally before cognitively, the caseworker's manner in discussing the facts of the situation needs to modify appropriately, depending on the intensity of feelings present, and the relative inhibition or display of those feelings. The early stages of diagnosis, therefore, are concerned with eliciting the client's feelings about the problem and his determination about problem-solving by obtaining information in a manner which is not intolerant or impatient of incoherence in the presentation of facts. Comforting though it may be to the caseworker to complete his 'front sheet' as soon as possible, or to make notes of information that he does not wish to forget, these activities may interrupt or disturb the client's presentation of his problem *in the manner in which he experiences it*, so that distortion enters the diagnosis from the start of the case. The taking of notes may be left until the end of the interview or to that part of it when the client has completed the presentation of his problem and is able to recognize the usefulness of the worker's note-taking as a way of ensuring the relevance of future help and as an opportunity for him to review the content and purpose of the interview so far.

The worker may sometimes need to exert some control, however, on the client's flow of information, comment and feelings in this early phase. Some clients respond to an accepting and permissive manner by disclosing more information than they would wish. Sometimes also, an uncontrolled flow of complaint or anxiety increases rather than reduces depression. A client may be unable at this stage to move beyond the reiteration of self-justification or self-blame, of circumstantial rather than real grievances, or of projections or introjections of guilt. The caseworker's concern, therefore, is not simply to collect as much information as possible, depending upon the client's willingness to talk, but rather to assist him to experience a feeling of purpose in the interview. This may involve overcoming feelings of reserve about meeting a stranger whose function and purpose are initially unknown, setting aside some of the 'public' attitudes he has hitherto displayed about his problem, and overcoming inappropriate loyalties towards others in his environment. In order to help Mrs Charles, for example, it was necessary to get behind her cheerful façade and, later, that she should be able to talk of her parents' difficulties unhampered by inappropriate expressions of loyalty to them.

As the relationship develops, the client is helped to move from the general to the specific in expressing his feelings and needs, to elucidate them in such a way that both he and the worker are able, as part of the sharing of diagnosis, to detect relationships and patterns in the emotions attaching to *apparently* dissimilar people, experiences and events. By encouraging the client's expression of difficulties in these ways, the worker's later activity as mediator or conciliator between people, or between client and social demand, is made possible.

Skills in diagnosis are closely related to skills in communication. The client is helped through as nearly as possible an honest and equal exchange of ideas and feelings. Reference has already been made to the difficulties attendant on the use of words in this process: some people cannot easily use words; some use words defensively. Sometimes, therefore, the caseworker needs to listen to the sense which lies behind the literal sense of the words used. Sometimes he needs to employ non-verbal means of communicating—for example, stretching out a hand to a frightened child, preserving a calm manner in a tense situation. All purposeful communication tends, whether verbal or non-verbal, towards one of two goals: change through rational comment and evaluation, and change through the emotional impact of personalities and the transmission of ideas through the use of feelings. Some techniques of communication serve both goals at once: a lecturer may employ more of his personality than his intellect in communicating with his students. The caseworker uses both forms of communication, but should be clear in every situation which of them he is employing, and the extent to which the use of one form or another will promote the client's participation in identifying and solving his problems. All change effected through casework is based on the interdependence of client and worker in assessing needs; the caseworker's manner of communi-

77

cating may increase or reduce the client's capacity to share in this activity and, by extension, in activities with others. Every communication influences a little the client's sense of his own reality and the nature of his social situation, and modifies for better or worse the defensiveness he needs to adopt inside the agency and elsewhere.

Starting and finishing where the client is

Many writers have stressed the importance of 'starting where the client is'—of understanding the complexity of feelings and influences which accompany the client's presentation of his difficulty. An earlier case-illustration suggests the importance also of concluding interviews (during which ideals, aspirations or past events have been discussed) with some recognition of the environment to which the client will return. In diagnosis, a further meaning can be added to the idea of starting and finishing 'where the client is'. An interview starts at the first meeting between client and worker; this may precede by seconds or hours the formality of sitting down and initiating a systematic discussion. For example, the caseworker may meet the client on the stairs, and some comments are likely to be made informally by both before the door of the interviewing room is closed. A probation officer on court duty may have only a few minutes with a new probationer in which to arrange an interview on the following day; but these few minutes are the first interview. In both instances, the client's feelings about his situation may be more readily accessible (because the meeting is informal or contrasts with the experiences immediately preceding it) than they will be when the interview-situation has been formalized or when the client has had the opportunity of rehearsing what he intends to say. This is not intended as an invitation to 'catch the client out', but rather to suggest that, as diagnosis is concerned with understanding,

78

any clues the client makes available should be respected and acknowledged.

Similarly an interview may not finish with the completion of its formal part. A client is about to open the door and then says (e.g.) 'By the way, I thought I ought to mention ...' Some things are more easily said when an 'escape route' is available or when the client feels more in control of the situation. Final comments such as this may not be as trivial as their manner suggests; the worker may decide to invite the client to resume the interview; often it is possible and appropriate for useful interviews to take place on doorsteps.

Finally, a brief note about lies: deliberate lying by a client in producing information may be irritating but the caseworker's diagnostic concern should be less with the irritation than with seeking or inferring an explanation why the client found it necessary or useful to lie. Sometimes it is unclear whether misinformation is deliberate or not, as in the matter of Mr Charles's drinking habits where, in any case, the search for an objective truth seemed irrelevant to the needs of the clients at that time. A client's capacity for honesty is, of course, worth knowing about: in diagnosis it may be regarded as an important strength. But not all lying represents moral weakness: interests of varying moral and emotional validity may be served by the client's lying; he may be 'lying' to himself as well as to the caseworker, and for powerful emotional reasons. Care is therefore necessary in any diagnostic attempt to test out the client's honesty. For example, when information is already known, the caseworker should not pose questions to the client to test out the honesty of his response without seriously considering whether, by asking the question, he is encouraging the client to lie or is more interested in trapping the client than in understanding him better. People who are caught out in a lie rarely contribute more honestly afterwards.

Asking questions

The responsibilities of the caseworker towards the client and towards agency administration (and the tension that may exist between these responsibilities) influence the questions asked and the manner of asking. Questions form part of the diagnostic process relevant to both administrative and personal needs; so do answers, and their relevance and honesty in these two related purposes depend in part on the form of the questions. When related to emotions, aspirations and viewpoints, questions should as far as possible be 'open-ended'; that is to say, they should not infer that the answer is expected in a particular form, or that a particular answer is the 'right' one, and should avoid engaging the client in a pattern of monosyllabic answers which, besides becoming a habit, denies him the experience of partnership.

Partnership is promoted further if questions about his history are directly related to present experiences in social functioning. For example, 'What jobs have you had since leaving school?' might be better asked as, 'How long have you been in your present job? ... How does it compare with your earlier ones?' and from this (working backwards rather than forwards in time) to a full work history.

Members of some social groups, more accustomed than others to answering questions, verbally or on forms, may have greater skill in accommodating their responses to defined categories and in avoiding irrelevance. An answer which apparently changes the subject of the question may reflect a lack of skill in framing responses rather than, necessarily, a wish to change the subject. Similarly it should be recognized that questions are of various qualities: they may be about actual events, hypothetical events of varying degrees of probability, personal attitudes or values, or may be entirely open (e.g. 'How are things?'). Not all people are used to being asked questions of these kinds, and cannot therefore be expected to answer all kinds with equal facility. It may be necessary to rephrase questions to increase the client's opportunity of expressing his views.

Sometimes several questions need to be asked in succession. They may be arranged to form sequences of two kinds: the sequence of rational development (often apparent in survey questionnaires and record sheets) and the sequence of emotional relationships in which the logic is less immediately apparent. If the answer to a question in a rational sequence is accompanied by a high level or unexpected quality of feeling, it may be appropriate to change the kind of sequence at this point. For example, a young woman recounting her work history in chronological order says, 'Then I went to work at X's, but that wasn't much good' (she giggles) 'so I went to Y's, and was there for a year, and then ...' If the problem for which help is sought bears (or might possibly bear) any relationship to her attitudes to workmates or employers—if, for example, she finds it difficult to make friends of her own age or to relate satisfactorily to people in authority—it might be appropriate to return to her work experiences at X's in greater detail and to pursue the relatedness of her feelings in that situation to other different but parallel situations, rather than to maintain the earlier chronological sequence of job-changes.

Listening and prompting

People attribute different cognitive and emotional meanings to the same words, and reference has been made already to the importance of prompting the client to be more specific in describing his attitudes, feelings or views about events, partly so that he may find the words necessary to increase his own understanding of his needs and partly to ensure that the caseworker himself achieves a more precise understanding of what is being said. One of the greatest difficulties experienced by caseworkers confronted with distressed clients, or those fumbling painfully to find words, is to avoid the glib use of reassuring phrases such as 'I understand' or 'I see what you mean', in situations where it is apparent to both that understanding has not been achieved. Listening to oneself is harder than listening to the client, but of equal importance if the client's responses are to be adequately evaluated as part of the diagnosis. At the same time, clients sometimes make comments which are evidently full of feeling and which require a supportive response from the worker, yet where the sense is too uncertain for the worker to be sure what to say. Such comments may be detected by their apparent irrelevance to the discussion up to that point, by their reiteration within the same interview or over a series of interviews, or (as in the preceding section) by the unexpected intensity or absence of feeling which accompanies the rational sense of the words being used.

Example 1: a boy in early adolescence, whose conversation often appeared to be random and casual, said, 'There's a boy in my class in geography who always draws his maps upside down', and then laughed for several seconds before going on to talk of something else. This comment and merriment were repeated in the next two interviews. Casual conversational replies seemed inappropriate after the third occasion. In the following interview, therefore, the caseworker asked how the boy was getting on who drew his maps upside down. The boy laughed and said he was just the same. The caseworker commented, 'Well, we none of us know where we are sometimes.' The boy nodded seriously and asked the caseworker to help him draw a map with his house on it. This became a routine for several interviews at the boy's request, the caseworker drawing a rough map, and the boy inserting his house and drawing pictures of the members of his family, talking as he did so of the difficulties at home and about how he was not as good as the other children; in his drawings he was always separated from the rest of the family.

Example 2 : Mrs Charles's complaint about her husband is 'interrupted' by the comment, 'My father never liked him'. There is no indication at this point whether she is introducing her father as a 'good' man who would support her complaints, or as someone equally 'bad' as her husband. In this instance, the caseworker explored the second possibility.

Example 3 : Mrs Smith, visited regularly by a caseworker for help in budgeting to pay a number of debts, developed a weekly routine of sitting next to the caseworker for general and easy conversation about the family; she would then volunteer to fetch the weekly payment, and having paid the worker neither resumed her seat nor continued any conversation. She always professed to be keeping clear of further debt, to be managing well, and to welcome the caseworker's visits. This 'switching off' in each interview was disconcerting, and was thought to indicate either an underlying hostility towards the worker or anxiety or guilt about further debts. Trying to cover both possibilities the worker commented at this stage of the following interview how difficult it must be to manage financially in view of the weekly payment, and that she would not be surprised if Mrs Smith found it impossible to avoid running up the occasional additional debt. Mrs Smith sat down : she wanted to talk about a further debt that she had not liked to mention before.

Several similar examples, involving projection, displacement or denial of feelings, might be cited : the probationer who says that his former probation officer 'wasn't much good' may be implying the same of his present one; the woman who repeatedly says that she ought to go to her doctor but never finds time to do so may be implying something about the doctor as a person, or about her wish not to visit the caseworker as a similarly unwelcome person, or about her fear of illness.

In all such instances, the caseworker's assessment will

83

depend on the skill with which he detects the sense behind the words, and by his prompting and comments allows or encourages the client to bring this hidden sense into open discussion. One such 'prompt' may be silence, provided the worker is fairly certain, through previous knowledge of the client, that the client can use silence constructively and not be unduly bewildered by it. At other times, the worker may comment that he is finding difficulty in understanding; implying, however, that this difficulty is not the result of the client's failure but represents a more general problem, experienced by many people, of putting feelings into words. Sometimes, however, the expression of feelings or their further exploration may be too threatening for the client to tolerate; certain kinds of depression increase rather than reduce through discussion, irrespective of the skills of the interviewer. In such instances it is appropriate and sufficient to recognize the client's difficulty (to acknowledge it with him) and to help him move on to another topic. The worker's understanding may need to be sacrificed in the emotional interests of the client, and sought later through discussion of other topics at various emotional distances from the area of distress. Somewhat similarly, the disturbed paranoiac phantasies of a client may be reinforced by exploration; however much the client invites and welcomes this, it can be argued that a diagnostic interest in the content of phantasies should not be pursued in such a way as to weaken the client's grasp of reality.

The complexity of this kind of situation is apparent in the problems of clients with virtually uncontrollable and socially unacceptable impulses, who only by the constant exercise of self-discipline can prevent or delay the gratification of these impulses : for example, the drug addict attempting to avoid places where drugs were available to him in the past, or the aggressive man attempting to avoid fights. On the one hand it can be argued that, for some clients, prompting by the caseworker to talk of these impulses (and of their gratification) delays the need for satisfaction or makes satisfaction available in idea rather than in behaviour. On the other hand, such prompting may appear to condone the expression of the impulse, and thus weaken the client's resistance to it, or to increase the strength of the impulse by focusing attention upon it.

This is a dilemma for both diagnosis and treatment. For many clients the prompting of discussion about feelings and needs aids casework in both its diagnostic and treatment aspects. For some, however, diagnostic and treatment interests appear to be at variance; for these, diagnosis involves careful examination of what the client wants to talk about in one aspect of his personality, and what he *needs* to talk about in another aspect in order to reinforce socially acceptable behaviour. In psychoanalytic terms, some areas of discussion will tend to support ego, superego or id; the problem for the worker is which of these aspects to support in opposition to or in allegiance with other aspects. In some instances the choice rests largely on conjecture and inference, where the pursuit of diagnostic certainty involves a risk in the client's subsequent behaviour. Inference may be based on knowledge of the client's past actions, and he may be prompted to recall the circumstances of past behaviour, but the linking of earlier behaviour patterns to present impulses will be tentatively undertaken and possibly omitted entirely.

Transference elements in relationship

The transference of emotional responses from earlier relationships to the worker, to another member of the family, or to another person in the environment is a phenomenon related to those already discussed. Close relationships in the present may promote an association of feelings from earlier intense relationships. If not recognized for what they are, the worker will be surprised by the strength of hostility or affection displayed towards him, or by the client's talking to him as if one or both were considerably older or younger than their ages. In such cases the worker's response may be relevant to the phantasy element in the transference but inappropriate to the client's conscious expectations or to the agency's responsibilities for effecting changes in his situation. This will be the case, for example, if irrational hostility begets hostile responses. In transference situations, therefore, the worker needs to think out whom he represents or symbolizes in the client's perceptions, and to determine whether the transference should be accepted as an essential preparation for the client's future social adequacy, or should if possible be halted and reversed. The manner and timing of doing so will depend on an assessment of the client's capacity to tolerate discussion of the phantasy element in the relationship, and the availability of supportive relationships in the environment.

Involving the client in locating and identifying problems and in finding patterns

It has been seen that the relationship of client and worker sometimes contains ambivalent, transferred, displaced and projected feelings, indicating the presence of needs which the client is unable to express in other ways. The worker may comment and prompt the client in such ways as to draw his attention to characteristic patterns in his responses to people, and to the ways in which his present needs and problems are in some sense reiterating unresolved difficulties in the past. The worker can assist the client to stand back from his own life for a brief period and to observe what is going on within it. But the client who does this will—like an observer—find his experiences intelligible only if they are seen as patterns and sequences and if he can recollect the feelings which attach, or have attached in the past, to relevant parts of the pattern or sequence.

86

The client cannot assume or discard his emotions, roles and behaviour patterns at will: they are retained from one situation to another as internalized modes of action and response. One can never make a wholly fresh start in one's life. A simple illustration of this is the experience of Mrs Lambert who, with her family, was about to be re-housed. She had been energetic in securing the new tenancy, and the family was enthusiastic to move. Yet, in the last two weeks before moving, Mrs Lambert became increasingly and (in her own view) inexplicably tired. She did not arrange for the removal of her furniture in spite of urging by her caseworker, and all preparations came to a halt. The worker asked her about her previous experiences of changing houses, and made tea while Mrs Lambert recounted the disasters of the last move; she had felt responsible for all that went wrong, and had had no help. The worker listened, commented about these past difficulties and about how she must be dreading the next move. Mrs Lambert spoke at length of her need for 'a magic wand' but later began to assess the differences between the new situation and the old. (If she had not done so, the caseworker would have need to prompt this.) Subsequently, with no direct action by the caseworker, but with support, Mrs Lambert completed the arrangements for the move and carried it through successfully.

In this case the client's response to the crisis was governed by earlier crises with which she had not come to terms. It was likely that, even with continued urging to action, she would have 'coped' with the new crisis by avoiding it, because its emotional demand was beyond her present resources, and was undermining her recent resourcefulness. Casework was based not on a feeling of disappointment but on the opportunity provided by the situation for demonstrating how similar crises can be met or prevented in the future. The manner of help *at this moment* assisted Mrs Lambert to identify more closely with the helpful intentions of the agency, yet was preparing her to be less reliant upon the agency in *future* difficult situations, and possibly assisting her a little to understand better her characteristic responses to crises. It was clearly preferable to help her in this way than for the worker (in sympathy, frustration or anxiety) to make all the arrangements, and indirectly contribute to Mrs Lambert's present lack of resource.

Involving the client in diagnosis of his needs and of his capacities in solving them requires also that he should be helped to understand the extent and limitations of the purposes, resources and skills available in the agency. This cannot be achieved by giving the client a statement about the agency's work. Clients learn about the agency's function by contributing to and experiencing its exercise, and are unlikely to be receptive of the worker's views if these contrast with their own expectations or experiences. But there are situations when the client's co-operation can properly be sought only on the basis of some understanding of this function (for example, when a child care officer makes home enquiries in preparation for a report to a court), and of some recognition of the worker's limitations in skill or powers of assistance. Limitations of any kind should be conveyed less as a regrettable defect in the worker or agency than as a reality factor which need not prevent useful shared activities. After all, it is unrealistic to expect a client to play a responsible part in the agency's work if the agency's worker presents an impression either of general inadequacy or of super-human competence.

Michael, aged 26, was brought to the agency by his mother (a good-natured but fussy and over-protective woman) because of his increasing withdrawal from all social life outside the home. Though of high intelligence, he had remained an assistant in a small back-street shop since leaving school; his employer was a family friend with whom he felt at home. Most evenings he stayed at home, painting or making rugs. He had no friends, but would occasionally go out to watch a local crowd of youths playing football though they never spoke to him or he to them. Michael's mother spoke of his father as a colourless man whom Michael despised; they seldom spoke to each other. Michael's present behaviour began three years ago. Up to then, though never very sociable, he had led a reasonably full life; he had had a regular girlfriend, went dancing with her, and ran a motor bike. Michael was interviewed alone on several occasions. He described, with difficulty and requiring a good deal of support, how a change took place in his life following the extraction (because of an abscess) of most of his bottom teeth. After the extraction, about which he felt badly because of its effects on his appearance, he met his girlfriend in the usual way. When she laughed at the change in his appearance, he went home, attempted to gas himself, and was taken to hospital. As an in-patient he was treated for 'depression' by E.C.T. He was ashamed and still distressed by his suicide attempt (perspiring freely as he spoke of it) and by having been 'a mental patient'. In later discussions, he mentioned his fear of going to the barber, saying that, as his hair was being cut, he felt as if his body were shrinking in size. He wished his mother would not fuss so much about him, but at the same time he was grateful to her for doing so much on his behalf.

Several events and ideas are presented here for diagnosis. Whatever the nature and source of his feelings at the time of the teeth extraction, it is evident that he has not come to terms with them. The loss of his teeth, his feelings about having his hair cut, his going out to look at other youths playing football all combine to suggest possible hypotheses of physical or male-role inadequacy, latent homosexuality, even (perhaps) castration anxiety. His ambivalent feelings for his well-intentioned but essentially dominating mother, and his rejection of an inadequate father, give additional weight to the possible hypothesis of homosexuality while suggesting also that he wishes to escape from being homosexual. On the other hand, this evidence, together with the shame he felt about his hospitalization and his attempt at suicide, can be employed in other hypotheses of widespread anxiety and guilt inhibiting the making of relationships. The steady girlfriend and possibly the motor bike suggest that at an earlier time he achieved a satisfactory male role, and might, therefore, do so again, given the opportunity of new relationships with people who could, without fuss, accept the knowledge of his earlier behaviour. One could pursue other structures of this information and other hypotheses as to his present needs and their basis.

Clearly some of these hypotheses suggest treatment within the competence of a caseworker, and others not. If latent homosexuality is indeed a factor the caseworker can do little about it except help Michael to accept himself as he is. About castration anxiety, the caseworker can do nothing: and interesting though Michael's feelings are about having his hair cut, little purpose would be served by pursuing them. New identifications and relationships may, however, be within the caseworker's capacity to provide in some way or another, and these could lead in turn to a reawakening of Michael's ability to pursue his own relationships, and possibly to find different and more challenging employment. The caseworker may also help the parents to make a more effective contribution to Michael's situation. Furthermore, the caseworker can help Michael—it may be necessary on more than one occasion —to talk about the experiences of three years ago, helping him to make sense of them, and, by accepting them without blame, helping him to come to terms with them and to be less influenced by his memories and regrets. Such discussions could be diagnostically useful to the caseworker in his future work, as well as helpful to Michael. It may be possible, through them, to decide with Michael whether psychiatric help is necessary and whether what at present looks like a difficulty in sexual adjustment is a basic problem or a symptom of more general social inadequacy. But help of these various kinds can be made available in a relevant and orderly way only if Michael is willing to discuss his difficulties in spite of the embarrassment and anxiety attaching to them, if he is helped to see in what ways the caseworker can and cannot help, and if he understands at least some of the reasons behind the caseworker's prompting (which may need to be persistent) of the memory of earlier experiences.

Diagnosis in such a situation requires an expression of function, skill and intent by the worker, and assistance to the client in recognizing the value of his own intentions and aspirations, and in identifying those aspects of the process of change where his contribution will be more effective than the worker's.

This idea can be extended to diagnosis in marital or family situations where several members ostensibly share the same problem. Within the family, one client will have views not only about his own needs but about the needs of other members. Various views may be in disagreement and none may accord with the worker's. But a client's view of the needs of others merits serious consideration in diagnosis if, possibly at a later stage, his help will be enlisted in meeting these other needs. Ackerman (1954) has suggested that help in marital difficulties involves a search for the possibilities of 'complementarity' between people as well as a process of meeting the needs of individuals in their own right; work which aims exclusively at producing a major psychological adjustment in one partner may adversely affect the possibility of reconciliation within the partnership, in that any hope of complementarity is destroyed. Engaging clients—at some point—in examining the patterns of compensation used by others to maintain complementarity may lead in time to an examination of the ways in which each can be assisted to help the other: for example by demonstrating increased tolerance or support for an immature emotional need, for irrational projections of feelings, for compensations against anxiety, for distorted perceptions. This phase of helping—the process of conciliation—may be a late one, but becomes possible only if, from the start of the relationship and in the whole process of diagnosis, the client feels that his impressions and views about the needs (as well as the behaviour) of others are respected. This suggests that special care should be taken in inviting to the agency the second marriage partner in a marital problem, or other family members in problems primarily focusing on one (e.g. delinquency). The aim in the invitation is not merely to seek confirmation or denial of information already received ('to hear their side of the story'), but to demonstrate that the worker recognizes the interaction of needs between people, and that others beside the 'first' client have views to contribute to the understanding and treatment of a shared problem situation. Casework diagnosis requires a capacity, through relationship with a client, to see a situation through his eyes and through the eyes of others, so that he and they in turn see each other with equal acceptance.

5
Formulating plans of help

Some processes in diagnosis are themselves aspects of helping; some ends are both expressed and achieved in the means employed. This chapter will summarize and extend earlier ideas with particular reference to the goals of diagnosis.

Self-direction and setting goals

We have seen that, in the last half-century, the client has become the central, primary and most important source of information about himself and his needs. In establishing the goals of helping, greater reliance is now placed than formerly on the client's selection of important factors and problems in his life. The worker observes and notes the client's defences, gestures and feelings when discussing parts of his life history and his current needs, not in order to devise a programme of help to be imposed on the client, but to ensure that by his own manner and focus in interview he is more able to involve the client in recognizing where to start in solving the problem and determining goals for the future. 'Treatment in casework should be based on goals that are consciously and mutually agreed upon by the client and the worker' (Gottlieb and Stanley 1967). 'Goals are finally implemented only when they are shared by both client and worker' (Hollis 1968). The practical advantages of identifying goals in this way are that the worker enlists the client's personality as a progressive force in treatment, and is given more realistic opportunities for reviewing progress and for testing hypotheses than would be available if his goals were formulated in professional isolation.

The case of Mr and Mrs Brown has shown, however, that goal-setting as a shared task may not for various reasons be easy to achieve.

Firstly, problems may become perceptually and cognitively isolated in such a way as to distort the life situation of the client. For example, the client is referred for help because of debt, or because her husband has contracted a disease. All people categorize particular events or problems, but they seldom *experience* these in the isolated form suggested by the category. Caseworker and client may appropriately focus their efforts on resolving a discrete difficulty, but it is necessary to recognize that this focus is neither so exclusive nor, perhaps, so central in the client's life as it may seem to be to the worker and to the agency. There is a danger of over-emphasis.

Secondly, the client's view of his needs may be different from the worker's. The client may not look beyond a particular material need (like a new house, or clothes for a baby) while the worker may infer more general problems of family interaction. Sometimes aid given at the material level may be as much as the client is prepared to receive, and assistance with a simpler task may effect changes in unexpressed needs or responses without further intervention. It sometimes happens, however, that solving only the problem as presented encourages greater future dependency, or promotes resentment when the client subsequently realizes the inadequacy of the help given. If the worker, therefore, considers that the client's goals are unrealistic, he has a responsibility to help him to review these and to seek more satisfying or more attainable ones. At the same time, he should not, exhilarated by the client's agreement upon the task to be attempted, allow this task to become an exclusive concern which prevents awareness of other issues with which the client

94

may later need help.

Thirdly, the pursuit of mutually agreed goals may be more time-consuming than the worker envisages or the agency can tolerate. The worker may consider that, to help one member of a family, several others should be consulted for their agreement and co-operation and prepared for possible changes in the behaviour of the principal client. But the need to speed up a process of help in the agency's interests of economy may require the caseworker to reduce this intensity of work.

Fourthly, the client's goals may be, and may remain, incompatible with the caseworker's wider responsibilities in social welfare. Not all goals are equally valid, and the client seldom expects the worker's assent to all goals. A totally permissive worker may create unnecessary insecurity in the client, just as he will certainly be condemned by those who make and implement social policies.

An implicit goal in all casework is the maintenance or development of the client's responsibility for others. Wootton (1959) has written of the setting of goals, 'The plain fact is that social work is only undertaken with the object of changing people's behaviour in a particular direction and, no matter how conscientiously criticism of the client may be withheld, norms are inevitably implicit in the caseworker's goals.' The problem then is to decide which goals, if any, should be allowed to become immutable ideals. The trouble with 'ideal' goals is that any disappointment in achievement may harden the caseworker's attitude to his client and lead to an increasing manipulation of responses; so that improved social behaviour is accompanied by reduced rationality in the client's exercise of his responsibilities.

Some general conclusions about goals

Casework in some agencies is related to changing standards

of problem-definition, social expedience and administrative efficiency. In some others, work is related to a more or less rigid external standard of duties and responsibilities. Within these agencies the caseworker establishes functional goals, while recognizing that sometimes these may exceed or fall short of the goal-aspirations of his client.

A caseworker, seeking to share the formulation of treatment plans and goals with his clients, must in each situation respect the autonomy of his client (lest his interpretation of mutuality becomes one of 'getting him to see things my way') but also avoid professing his respect for this autonomy as an excuse for abandoning his own responsibility and for colluding with the client's goal when it is unreasonable or impractical. The agency requires the worker to take the ultimate responsibility for clarifying and establishing goals; responsibility—when required to do so—for defining need, the reasons (though not, perhaps, the causes) for the need, the changes which are requested, appropriate and possible, and their means of achievement.

Compromise may be necessary in the employment of resources and between goals of near-equal validity. The caseworker hopes that his client will experience a feeling of personal fulfilment while finding adjustment to environmental demands, but a necessary adjustment may deny some of this feeling. Some probationers, for example, at least initially, experience the demands and goals of the probation order as irksome and restrictive. And, as already observed, the maintenance of complementarity in marriage may be possible only if one partner is *not* wholly released from infantile or neurotic needs and responses. Such compromise (like the wider social uncertainty about the nature and aims of welfare) may partially frustrate the worker's efforts to achieve a sense of partnership in setting goals.

In formulating a diagnosis, therefore, information from

and about a client needs to be limited by reference to the goals that lie within the agency's capacity to achieve. A worker may be aware that his own professional development and the interests of research require diagnostic information not directly related to the plans for helping a particular client, but in this case, the client's co-operation must be sought afresh in producing information which he knows is unrelated to his needs or to the plans of help.

It has been suggested earlier that diagnostic limits are sometimes set by the theories of behaviour explanation and treatment embraced by the caseworker. A psycho-analytic approach in diagnosis comprises an intensive knowledge of the 'why?' of past and present responses: all responses become grist to the diagnostic mill. A diagnosis based on learning theory would probably require more limited information related to the mechanisms of future change. With the application of 'crisis' concepts to casework practice, and with the growing use of role theory, problems arise about the relevance to treatment goals of much of the data presented by the client or sought by the worker. 'Crisis' work for example, relies on active and intensive intervention for limited periods of time to ensure the prevention of ego damage and a more satisfactory resolution of future crises; it is less concerned with providing opportunities for the client's calm recollection of past emotions, though the case of Mrs Lambert shows an attempt to combine these approaches. Similarly, work based on here-and-now interactions in family life, on communication patterns and role playing, may appear (in one sense) in opposition to the exploration of individual emotions in depth. Thus, the diagnostic purpose of discussion and the relevance of what is discussed may be seen differently by different workers or by a client and worker together; all might agree on general long-term goals, but there may be explicit or implicit disagreement on the short-term steps by which these are to be achieved:

97

i.e. what should be discussed or done in the next interview.

Thus, the demands of the agency, the variety of theories available to the worker, the variety of human responses to apparently similar difficulties, and the social and professional uncertainties about the nature of welfare, all make for difficulty in generalizing about the relationship of information and diagnosis to goals. The worker's discrimination in collecting information will be based on moral attitudes, different sources and kinds of 'relevance', particular theories of helping, and the extent to which various goals can be identified as compatible and feasible within the limits of personality and social environment. The client offers some information as part of the shared experience of trying to formulate agreed goals; some information is sought to establish the client's eligibility for help of particular kinds in relation to the social responsibilities of the agency; some is sought by the worker to assist his own understanding of the factors which have contributed to the client's difficulties; some is gratuitously given by the client simply because he wants to talk. Goals will initially be selected on the basis of the more conspicuous or emphatic factors presented, but in the awareness that, in any social situation, there is more than one possible goal and more than one way of achieving an agreed goal. Thus, diagnosis may sometimes involve a review of the past life of the client and at other times a horizontal examination of roles, reference groups, values, family structure, and of the agency as a social system which contains the client and about which the client has views and feelings. The goal may be concerned with change in individual, family or environment. To achieve it may require an assessment of the capacity and availability of various sources of complementary help, including some (for example neighbours, local leaders) whose helpfulness to a client rests upon their *not* regarding him as a client. There is no single right way of helping people, no single right plan of help; and no single way of measuring success in achieving goals. Success in some cases may lie not in achieving advance but in preventing forseeable disasters. In others, it may lie in achievements which initially lay well beyond the aspirations of the client. We cannot generalize about the nature of success in casework or about how to establish long-term goals for all clients. We can, however, strive to find accurate ways of examining the results of what we do. Skill in diagnosis and in the review of diagnostic formulations is an essential component in this aspect of professional development.

The capacities of the client in problem-solving

These may be assessed by evaluating what the client has achieved (recently and in the past) in resolving his difficulties unaided, and his 'ego strengths': namely,

1. his competence in various social roles. A client bewildered by his failure to cope with a difficulty in performing one role may be encouraged and helped by discussion of his success in others;
2. the feasibility of the solutions he suggests;
3. the extent to which he sees, or can be helped to see, his present difficulty as explicable, can appreciate 'cause and effect' in situations, and can tolerate accepting some responsibility for the situation as it is and for changing it. Two aspects of this particular strength in Mr Charles were his preparedness to see his marital difficulty as a joint responsibility with his wife, and his willingness, at the risk of rebuff, to get in touch with her again;
4. the extent to which the client can be both patient in awaiting change and optimistic about the possibility of change. This capacity can sometimes be enhanced by recalling memories of happier times, provided that these will not be used negatively to make the present situation seem worse. Similarly, to help the

99

client think constructively of the future (whether unpleasant—as in waiting for an operation, or desirable—as in coming out of hospital) may help him to integrate his present experiences within a sense of purpose, so that his behaviour is neither vacillating nor whimsical, because of depression or of his defences against being depressed;

5. the extent to which he is appropriately sensitive to the needs of others, neither manipulating them in relationships, nor assuming that he has no rights in relation to theirs; the extent to which any of his relationships successfully avoid over-dependence or over-independence.

6. his adaptability to new ideas and his willingness to attempt to find new modes of behaviour.

The assessment of these strengths cannot be based simply upon what the client says about his successes in life; it is necessary to observe and discuss how he actually behaves and feels. Helping the client in discussion to find appropriate words to describe his feelings and needs may enhance his resources in that they provide him with a mechanism both of self-control and of control of his environment. (As suggested earlier, putting a desire into words may be a necessary step in learning to control it by means of symbolic gratification.) This occurs, however, only if the words used are precise and specific in meaning and describe reality rather than perpetuate phantasy. For example, a girl may justify her promiscuity by calling it 'love'—i.e. play Humpty Dumpty with the word to make it fit, and thus justify rather than control, the desire. Diagnosis of the client's personal resources contains a regard therefore for the client's need for help in finding words and for the quality of his current use of words.

The caseworker's recognition of his own capacities

The caseworker's awareness of his own capacities and

limitations is also essential if diagnosis is to promote the formulation of realistic goals (see the earlier case of Michael). This awareness requires an appraisal of skills and suggests the need for supervision to avoid distortion in diagnosis and in selecting goals. It requires also identifying one's characteristic approach and manner in casework, which may influence the relationship made, irrespective of the client's needs. Productive work is possible only if a worker is able and willing sometimes to think about himself; effective concern for others is not achieved by assuming indifference about oneself; nor is it achieved by the kinds of over-activity which prevent evaluation of what one has done and the personal motives and needs expressed in the doing.

Observation of the behaviour of another person will not *of itself* lead to an understanding of that person's experience. Understanding is built of three elements: observation and hypothesis, knowledge incorporated from the worker's earlier work experience, and the inferences he draws about what the client is experiencing. It is necessary to be aware of the relative importance one ascribes to each of these three elements: over-emphasis on the first may produce theoretically brilliant hypotheses, but a client exhausted by enquiry and fast moving beyond help; over-emphasis on the second may tend towards categorical generalizations—'people like that need....'; over-emphasis on the third may promote over-identification with the client or unfortunate statements like 'If I were in your shoes, I would....' Reference has been made therefore to the need for intellectual detachment with emotional involvement, and to the paradox of 'disinterested sympathy'.

Particular attention is now paid to the notion of *empathy* as the process or ability by which this paradox is made sensible and useful. Empathy is the *volitional* capacity to experience within oneself the feelings of another. In this it differs from sympathy, which is an emotion based on finding analogies between one's own feelings and those of the other person. Empathy heightens direct awareness of the other's feelings; sympathy heightens awareness of one's own. Empathy therefore assists diagnosis by enabling the worker to infer the *unique* elements in the client's experience which cannot be derived from the generalizations of theories. It is not an alternative to intellect in diagnosis; neither is its use opposed to the use of intellect. The worker seeks to alternate in his use of each so that their different insights become complementary: sometimes experiencing in himself the client's experiences; at other times within the same interview becoming an 'impartial observer' of his client's responses and of his own. (See Katz (1963) for a fuller discussion of the source and nature of empathy.)

Some distortions in diagnosis

The subject of empathy cannot be left without reference to the ways in which it may become distorted. A worker may achieve this sharing of experience in only one aspect of the client's life or with only one member of a family. In the case of the adolescent boy who drew maps, it would be possible for the boy's repetitive preoccupation with his family and with his isolation from it to be transmitted to the caseworker with such intensity that the worker lost sight of the boy's activities and behaviour at school, and of the reality of other members of the family.

A further problem arises in diagnosis if the worker's anxiety to promote change contributes too much of the motivation in his attempt at empathy. He may assume a closer relationship with the client than the latter actually experiences, or may empathize with a client-ideal—with the client as he might be rather than as he is. In diagnosis this would lead to an unquestioning assumption of the highest motives in every action the client performs, tantamount to collusion with the client's rationalizations of his behaviour.

Empathy is necessary to diagnostic understanding. It provides a safeguard against the possibility of a remotely 'clinical' rationality by allowing *controlled* (willed) emotional involvement with the client and by finding a place in diagnosis for spontaneity and intensity of feelings. But, as we have seen, it may contain emotional risks for both worker and client which will affect the making of plans and the setting of goals. Furthermore it confronts the worker, because of his direct experience of the intensity of the client's feelings, with some basic problems about the nature of moral values in individual life; for example, 'If my client feels as strongly as this about such-and-such, do his feelings justify what he does?' The worker may be led into a position of extreme moral relativism which both vitiates his role as a representative of a social agency and may also, possibly, disturb the personal moral stability upon which some of his clients rely as a source of support.

Distortions of a different order may arise in the intellectual aspects of diagnosis. Richmond (1917) and Davison (1965) have drawn attention to four:

1. reliance upon an inadequate general rule about behaviour, in which the worker overlooks the fact that particular patterns of events may not *necessarily* lead to particular results. For example, hypotheses about the likely effectiveness of certain treatment procedures or plans should not lead the worker to assume, six months later, that these procedures have necessarily been effective in the way envisaged;
2. assuming false causal relationships in a situation. This may take two forms: first, assuming a consequential relationship in historical sequences of events in the client's life; and second, an oversimplification of such theories as, for example, the effects of maternal deprivation in early childhood;

3. drawing a mistaken analogy: assuming, for example, that two clients behaving in the same way have the same motives; or that they feel the same way because they do the same things;

4. jumping to the wrong conclusions about the client's actions: it must not be assumed, for example when a client misses an appointment, that the reason for his doing so is always as simple as he suggests; but neither must the opposite assumption be made that the reason lies in a complexity of feelings about his relationship with the worker.

These four possible distortions draw attention to the risk that the worker may not be prepared to look beyond a *personally* satisfying diagnostic formulation. Information which the worker gains during his association with a client will necessarily suggest patterns, hypotheses and theories selected, in part, according to the worker's pre-dilections. It is necessary therefore, in discussions with colleagues or in personal review of a diagnosis, to consider all the alternative theories and explanations available to a complex situation; even considering what—in the future of the case—are the *least* likely outcomes, and why these appear to the worker as 'least likely'.

David Fanshel (1958) has drawn attention to further distortions arising from a worker's expectations of the 'treatment-potential' of certain categories of cases. He found, for example, that many workers view parent-child conflicts as more probably amenable to help than marital problems; that reopened cases are assumed to be less promising than new cases; that the higher the socio-economic class of the client, the higher the expectations that help will be effective. It is probable, on this basis, that the worker's expectations of success and failure will influence the care he takes in diagnosis, and thus the relevance of the plans devised in work with certain clients.

Selecting the procedures of helping

We have seen how the assessment of a client's strengths indicates the quality of relationship necessary to achieve a goal of help and enhances the client's resources as a contributor to the plan. The presence or absence of these strengths will determine whether the client will benefit most (i.e. achieve a level of social functioning compatible with his own needs and with the demands of his social situation) by a relationship which is essentially supportive (whether of a protective or authoritative kind) or is based on the examination and identifying of inner motives and drives. The availability of external supports (in family or neighbourhood) and the client's capacity to use these in constructive ways, will affect whether—in a supportive relationship—greater or less activity is required of the worker in coping with crises. The quality of relationship which the client makes with the worker will suggest the quality of his other relationships, and the extent to which others in his environment may themselves need support, or need help in modifying and adapting their responses to the client.

Diagnosis prepares the caseworker for the ways in which he may be helpful. It reminds him of the various explanations of human behaviour available to his use; it increases his emotional sensitivity to the client's needs; it enhances his capacity for objective evaluation of the different individual and social demands made of him; and it helps him to evaluate his attitudes in his work. Diagnosis, like treatment, relies on the maintenance of relevance and purpose in relationship; the process of enabling a client to describe and define his needs, and to evaluate his impressions against those of the worker, can be a major part of the help provided.

Relationships vary in the extent to which they provide the individual with the feeling of being understood, of being recognized as he is, and of being supported. A 'good' treatment relationship is one which achieves a high degree of these qualities. But relationships vary also in the extent to which the participants are aware of each other as *observers*, or are aware of the observer positions of others external to the relationship. Families may open or close their ranks in response to an awareness of neighbours as observers. Marriages may be helped or destroyed by the partners' inferences of what others are saying or thinking about each of them. Worker-client relationships are influenced by an awareness (in one or the other) of outside observers (lay committees, senior colleagues, clients in the waiting room, the client's family and neighbours, etc.). Some relationships see their observers as threatening or persecuting, others as supportive and approving; an over-protective parent or an over-protective caseworker probably does not *feel* over-protective, for his behaviour is geared to his perception of external opposition to the interests of the child or client. The caseworker as diagnostician is a participant observer in, or attached to, these various kinds of relationships. The 'good' diagnostic relationship, therefore, is one in which the worker is aware of himself both as observer and as being observed by others in the whole work environment, and seeks, as his personal goal in diagnosis, to make this awareness as realistic as possible. The more realistic this awareness, the more his plans of help are likely to meet the actual location and source of stress for the client; the more likely also that goals will be based upon what the client is *really* capable of achieving and presented as neither too challenging nor too undemanding.

A note about diagnostic typologies

Whatever goals are established, the recurrent diagnostic question is: What *precise* actions are indicated in *this* situation to achieve *this* goal? The traditions of casework reject the categorizing of people and the attempt to view social problems in isolation from personalities; individuality in understanding and helping people is at the core of casework practice, and this book has been written in this tradition. Yet all caseworkers at some time think, 'I wish I knew what to do with this *type* of person in this *type* of situation.' Not surprisingly, categories of emotional response and of social situation have been borrowed from psychological medicine and sociology, and categories of treatment procedures have been devised and refined, notably by Hamilton and Hollis. But as Selby has pointed out (1958, 1966), there is as yet no diagnostic typology *specific* to social work, no *distinctive* professional system of thinking. Perhaps there never will be; perhaps social work will remain a field of study, in which various disciplines are related together, rather than become a discipline in its own right. It need not be any less professional for that. Various authors have suggested diagnostic typologies based on classification of need, motivation and capacity; on the concept of role; on the quality of family interaction. There are, as we have seen, so many diagnostic factors to be considered in the practice of casework within a wide range of social agencies that a precise yet comprehensive typology would demand more detail than a worker with a large caseload could cope with. Selby suggests that a typology might be developed on the basis of three broad variables: classifications of personality, of family and environment, and of crisis/problem. Whether these are discrete variables is a dilemma referred to earlier. But this kind of willingness among caseworkers to explore ways of classifying their diagnostic material is essential to the development of social work research and could also promote greater relevance and purposefulness in the help offered to clients.

Suggestions for further reading

In this book casework has been described sometimes as if it were akin to psychotherapy, and sometimes as a method of solving administratively defined social problems. Caseworkers, according to their individual inclinations and the function of their agencies, may be therapists, problem solvers or both. The subject of diagnosis has, therefore, been approached as far as possible from both points of view; the book attempts a compromise based on the idea that, however objectively a problem is defined as lying in the environment or in one small area of behaviour, the person with the problem has feelings about it, and that the caseworker has a responsibility of some kind towards these feelings. He helps to solve the problem in ways which meet the emotional needs of the client; he tries to effect changes in social situations while at the same time attempting to enhance the client's feeling of individual well-being. But as Chapter 2 suggests, the compromise is uneasy because of the difficulties of defining the purpose of social work either specifically or in general, and those who write as observers rather than practitioners tend to run to extremes in their support of one view or the other. Compare, for example, the purpose of casework implied by Wootton's chapter on the subject (1959) with that suggested by Halmos (1965); the one sees casework as practical problem-solving, the other as psychotherapy. Less dramatically, this variety of views can be detected in the writings of caseworkers; for example, Perlman (1953 and 1956) writes more from the problem-solving position. Hamilton (1951) and Hollis (1965) more from the viewpoint of effecting changes in emotional responses. Compare also Foren and Bailey (1968), whose subject (Authority) requires an emphasis on agency function, with Ferard and Hunnybun (1962), whose subject (Relationship) emphasizes the therapeutic aspect of casework. Other writers such as Davison (1965), Forder (1966) and Timms (1962 and 1964) achieve a middle course appropriate to their more comprehensive studies. These various approaches need not be incompatible in the practice of casework providing the worker's approach is pragmatic and eclectic in applying theory to each problem and need as these are presented. More detailed discussion of this dilemma will be found in Moffett (1968) and Timms (1968).

Each of the following books have clearly marked sections on diagnosis, and together provide a basic framework for further study: Davison (1965), Forder (1966), Hollis (1965), Perlman (1953 and 1956), and Timms (1962 and 1964).

In discussing the historical shifts in the meaning and purpose of social diagnosis, reference has been made in Chapter 1 to Timms (1961). This is usefully supplemented by Garrett's brief study of the evolution of casework (1949). Purpose in diagnosis cannot be divorced from the wider purpose of casework help in the context of formal and informal systems of social resources—the resources in the personal environment and in the provisions of the social services; neither can it be defined without reference to uncertainties about ends and means in welfare. These issues are briefly debated in Chapter 2, and discussed more fully by Nokes (1967) who, though not directly concerned with social work, provides a stimulating analysis of the problems of defining purpose in welfare by reference to the activities of teaching, hospital psychiatry and correctional work. His preface and first chapter aim to define welfare objectives by examining what workers actually do rather than what they say they do. For social workers, diagnostic purpose is related to the concept of agency function. This is discussed by Britton (1964) and Studt (1966) and by Foren and Bailey (1968) who, in addition, consider the worker's right to intervene in the lives of others and provide a useful guide to further reading on this topic.

Three further matters must be considered in defining the purpose of diagnosis: first, the problem of describing complex human needs in a precise form; second, the worker's intellectual imprisonment in his own language patterns and use of concepts; and third, the extent to which the worker embraces particular theories of explanation of human behaviour and responses to the exclusion of others. As these three issues influence *content* as well as purpose, reference is made to them at various points. The first is highlighted by Timms' (1968) study of homeless girls in London; the presence of human needs in his case studies is dramatically apparent, but they are not needs which as yet could be readily defined. The second issue can be studied in the work of Leonard (1966) and of Rickman (1967), who deals particularly with the difficulty of achieving objectivity, and whose book therefore has a bearing on discussions about the nature and use of empathy. On the third issue (purpose and content in relation to theories of explanation), a useful beginning can be made by comparing the diagnostic implications of the work of Jehu (1967) on learning theory, Reiner and Kaufman (1959) on psychoanalytic theory, Berne (1967) on games theory, Laing (1967 and 1969) on communication, and Caplan (1961) and Parad (1965) on crisis. Scheff (1966) provides a theoretical framework which goes some way towards reconciling aspects of these various theories, and draws attention to some common but as yet unproven assumptions about the explanations of human behaviour. He, Laing and Goffman (1961 and 1963) are usefully provocative about the dangers of diagnostic labels and categories, and of using words like 'abnormal'.

A brief comment is made in Chapter 3 about Hollis's (1965) three categories of the sources of problems and needs. The third category includes distortions in *conscience*, and as this is a word which tends to blanket a variety of meanings, reference should be made to Stephenson's study of the development of conscience (1966).

Many books have been written about marital difficulties and how they may be helped by casework, and it is not easy to make a selection from them. The work of the Family Discussion Bureau has been influential in this country, and its development can be studied in their two publications (1955 and 1962). Ackerman (1954) and Dicks (1967) demonstrate how psychodynamic insights can be employed in understanding marital problems and formulating plans of help, and Dicks' work is particularly well illustrated by case material. In recent years, Ackerman and others have experimented with whole-family interviews in both marital and parent-child relationship difficulties, and Ackerman (1966) is worth studying. Not all caseworkers would feel able to use his methods, but he records interviews verbatim with a parallel commentary of diagnostic thinking, and demonstrates how the process of diagnosis is concurrent with helping. Reference should be made also to Lowe's study (1969) of the effects on family relationships of psychological disorders in one member.

In attempting to understand family life and needs, a major problem for caseworkers is how to relate sociological and psychological systems of description and explanation. Both disciplines contribute to diagnosis but have independent conceptual frameworks. Bott's study of family and social relationships (1957) comes near to being interdisciplinary in approach. Handel's (1968) collection of essays is a useful sourcebook for further study of the relationship between disciplines. There are three aspects of casework theory and practice in which this relationship is of special importance: the concept of role, the quality of communication between worker and client, and the nature of transference and of ego defence mechanisms. On the concept of role, the works of Bott, Handel, Timms (1967) and Ruddock (1969) should be studied. Irvine's article on transference and reality (1956) links the theories of role and transference. Specifically on the topics of transference and ego-defence, one chapter in Zald (1965) provides sociological explanations, and complements the psychoanalytic explanations of Ferard and Hunnybun (1962). Bott (1957) contains some interesting descriptions of the displacement of feelings studied from the sociological viewpoint. All these works contribute to the worker's understanding of worker-client communication. This is studied in a lively way by Wilson (1965) from the standpoint of the philosopher and logician (pp. 79-86; 117-153), and in the context of social attitudes to moral questions about sexual behaviour.

In Chapter 5 we have been concerned with three basic issues in formulating plans of helping: the client's right of self-direction, empathy as a means of understanding need, and the possible sources of distortion in diagnosis. The first of these can be studied further in the works of Davison (1965), Biestek (1961), and Katz and Kahn (1966). Katz's (1963) work on empathy, to which reference is made in the text, is a detailed study which can be helpfully preceded by reference to Ferard and Hunnybun (1962) and Keith-Lucas (1966). Davison (1965) and Richmond (1917) have written sections on distortions in diagnosis, and there is a reference in the text to a useful article by Fanshell (1958). These authors all draw attention to the dangers of oversimplifying general theories of behaviour. One such theory particularly favoured by caseworkers is that concerned with the effects of maternal deprivation in early childhood, and for this reason as well

112

as for its intrinsic interest the WHO Report of 1962 is worth studying.

In writing a diagnostic statement one hopes to achieve something of immediate relevance to the process of helping, and, at the same time, something which will enhance the study of differential methods in casework and contribute to wider research into the nature of human problems and needs. Precision in the use of words is the first essential, and reference should be made to Timms' (1968) study of the language of casework. Weiss and Munroe (1959), Selby (1966) and Stockbridge (1968) suggest various ways of ordering material to enhance its usefulness in further study. The place of records in research into problems and needs is variously exemplified in the works of Kogan and others (1953), Parker (1964 and 1966) and the most recent study by the Cambridge Institute of Criminology (1969).

Bibliography

ACKERMAN, N. W. (1954) 'Diagnosis of Neurotic Marital Interaction', *Social Casework*, April 1954.
(1966) *Treating the Troubled Family*, New York and London: Basic Books.

BERNE, E. (1967) *Games People Play*, London: Penguin Books.

BIESTEK, F. (1961) *The Casework Relationship*, London: Allen & Unwin.

BOTT, E. (1957) *Family and Social Network*, London: Tavistock Publications.

BRITTON, C. (Winnicott) (1964) *Child Care and Social Work*, London: Codicote Press.

CAMBRIDGE INSTITUTE OF CRIMINOLOGY (1969) *Present Conduct and Future Delinquency*, London: Heinemann.

CAPLAN, G. (1961) *An Approach to Community Mental Health*, London: Tavistock Publications.

DAVISON, E. H. (1965) *Social Casework*, London: Baillière, Tindall & Cox.

DICKS, H. V. (1967) *Marital Tensions*, London: Routledge & Kegan Paul.

FAMILY DISCUSSION BUREAU (1955) *Social Casework in Marital Problems*, London: Tavistock Publications.
(1962) *The Marital Relationship as a Focus for Casework*, London: Codicote Press.

FANSHELL, D. (1958) 'A Study of Caseworkers' Perceptions of their Clients', *Social Casework*, December 1958.

FERARD, M. L. and HUNNYBUN, N. K. (1962) *The Case-worker's Use of Relationship*, London: Tavistock Publications.

FORDER, A. (1966) *Social Casework and Administration*, London: Faber & Faber.

FOREN, R. and BAILEY, R. (1968) *Authority in Social Casework*, London: Pergamon Press.

GARRETT, A. (1949) 'A Historical Survey of the Evolution of Casework', *Social Casework*, June 1949.

GOFFMAN, E. (1961) *Asylums*, New York: Doubleday; and London: Penguin Books.

(1963) *Stigma*, New Jersey: Prentice-Hall, Inc.; and London: Penguin Books.

GOTTLIEB, W. and STANLEY, J. H. (1967) 'Mutual Goals and Goal Setting', *Social Casework*, October 1967.

HALMOS, P. (1965) *The Faith of the Counsellors*, London: Constable.

HAMILTON, G. (1951) *Theory and Practice of Social Case-work*, New York: Columbia University Press.

HANDEL, G. (ed.) (1968) *The Psychosocial Interior of the Family*, London: Allen & Unwin.

HOLLIS, F. (1965) *Casework—A Psychosocial Therapy*, New York: Random House.

(1968) 'A Profile of Early Interviews in Marital Counselling', *Social Casework*, January 1968.

IRVINE, E. (1956) 'Transference and Reality in the Case-work Relationship', *British Journal of Psychiatric Social Work*, Vol. III No. 4, 1956.

(1964) 'The Right to Intervene', *Social Work U.K.*, April 1964.

JEHU, D. (1967) *Learning Theory and Social Work*, London: Routledge & Kegan Paul.

KATZ, R. L. (1963) *Empathy: its Nature and Uses*, New York: Free Press of Glencoe.

KATZ, R. C. and KAHN (1966) *The Social Psychology of Organisations*, New York: Wiley & Sons.

KEITH-LUCAS, A. (1957) *Some Casework Concepts for the*

Public Welfare Worker, University of North Carolina Press.

(1966) 'The Art and Science of Helping', *Case Conference*, September 1966.

KOGAN, HUNT and BARTELME (1953) *A Follow-up Study of the Results of Social Casework*, New York: Family Service Association of America.

LAING, R. D. (1967) *The Politics of Experience*, London: Penguin Books.

(1969) 'How Best to Intervene?', *New Society*, 11 September 1969.

LEHRMAN, L. J. (1954) 'The Logic of Diagnosis', *Social Casework*, May 1954.

LEONARD, P. (1966) *Sociology in Social Work*, London: Routledge & Kegan Paul.

(1966) 'Scientific Method in Social Work Education', *Case Conference*, September 1966.

LOWE, G. R. (1969) *Personal Relationships in Psychological Disorders*, London: Penguin Books.

MARSHALL, T. A. (1965) *Welfare in the Context of Social Policy*, University of Toronto Press.

MOFFETT, J. (1968) *Concepts in Casework Treatment*, London: Routledge & Kegan Paul.

NOKES, P. (1967) *The Professional Task in Welfare Practice*, London: Routledge & Kegan Paul.

PARAD, H. J. (ed.) (1965) *Crisis Intervention*, New York: Family Service Association of America.

PARKER, R. (1964) *Research in Social Work*, London: National Institute for Social Work Training.

(1966) *Decision in Child Care*, London: Allen & Unwin.

PERLMAN, H. H. (1953) 'Social Components in Casework Practice' in *Social Welfare Forum 1953*, Cleveland Press, Ohio.

(1956) *Social Casework—A Problem-Solving Process*, Chicago University Press.

REINER, B. and KAUFMAN, J. (1959) *Character Disorders in*

Parents of Delinquents, New York: Family Service Association of America.

RICHMOND, M. (1917) *Social Diagnosis*, New York: Free Press.

RICKMAN, H. P. (1966) *Understanding and the Human Sciences*, London: Heinemann.

RUDDOCK, T. J. (1966) *Roles and Relationships*, London: Routledge & Kegan Paul.

SCHEFF, T. J. (1966) *Being Mentally Ill*, London: Weidenfeld & Nicolson.

SELBY, L. G. (1966) 'Typologies for Caseworkers', in YOUNGHUSBAND, E. *New Developments in Casework*, London: Allen & Unwin.

STEPHENSON, G. M. (1966) *The Development of Conscience*, London: Routledge & Kegan Paul.

STOCKBRIDGE, M. E. (1968) 'Social Case Recording', *Case Conference*, December 1968.

STUDT, E. (1966) 'Worker-Client Authority Relationships', in YOUNGHUSBAND, E. *New Developments in Casework*, London: Allen & Unwin.

TIMMS, N. (1961) 'Historical Development of Social Work', *Case Conference*, April and May 1961.

(1962) *Casework in the Child Care Service*, London: Butterworth.

(1964) *Social Casework*, London: Routledge & Kegan Paul.

(1967) *A Sociological Approach to Social Problems*, London: Routledge & Kegan Paul.

(1968) *Language of Social Casework*, London: Routledge & Kegan Paul.

(1968) *Rootless in the City*, London: National Council of Social Service, for the National Institute for Social Work Training.

WEISS, V. W. and MUNROE, R. R. (1959) 'A Framework for Understanding Family Dynamics', *Social Casework*, January-February 1959.

BIBLIOGRAPHY

WILSON, J. (1965) *Logic and Sexual Morality*, London: Penguin Books.

WOOTTON, B. (1959) *Social Science and Social Pathology*, London: Allen & Unwin.

ZALD, M. N. (ed.) (1965) *Social Welfare Institutions*, New York: Wiley & Sons.

WORLD HEALTH ORGANISATION (1962) *Deprivation of Maternal Care*, Public Health Papers No. 14, United Nations.

SPEAKING
Of
Success

INSIGHT PUBLISHING
SEVIERVILLE, TENNESSEE

SPEAKING
Of Success

© 2007 by Insight Publishing Company.

Disclaimer: This book is a compilation of ideas from numerous experts who have each contributed a chapter. As such, the views expressed in each chapter are of those who were interviewed and not necessarily of the interviewer or Insight Publishing.

Published by Insight Publishing Company
P.O. Box 4189
Sevierville, Tennessee 37864

10 9 8 7 6 5 4 3 2

Printed in the United States of America

ISBN: 978-1-60013-111-5

Table of Contents

A Message from the Publisher

When we decided to do a series of books on success, we searched long and hard to find just the right combination of authors who were not only a success in business but were successful in their personal life as well.

The authors we found had personal stories to tell that revealed their inner values—values that contributed to the achievements they have made and the positive influence they have on others. These authors are people whom others revere as persons of integrity. They are winners.

Everyone wants to be a winner. I have never met anyone who wants to be a loser. And I'm sure you haven't either. That's why we found some of the best motivational/inspirational speakers and authors in the country to contribute to this series. Some of these men and women are household names. Others are rising stars. All of them have achieved the kind of success all of us want—the kind that sparks enthusiasm in others and leaves an indelible, positive impression.

The road to success is one of hard work and persistence. *Speaking of Success* can help you unlock your potential and inspire you to realize the many possibilities awaiting you as you learn how to remove any mental blocks you might have to the success you deserve.

If you're already well on your way down the success highway, the stories and experiences of these authors will encourage you, inform you, and I guarantee that you will learn something.

It is with great pride that we Insight Publishing present this series, *Speaking of Success.* We think you will discover that you will find something new each time you read through these books.

The chapters in this series are real page-turners, so get ready to be inspired. Get ready to be delighted. Get ready to learn. And remember, *you* are the author of your own success journey. Others can shine a light on the path but you must do the walking.

Interviews conducted by:
David E. Wright
President, International Speakers Network

Chapter 1

DEANNE DEMARCO

THE INTERVIEW

David Wright (Wright)

Today we're talking with Deanne DeMarco, MA, RCC. She is a business coach and communications master who partners with executives and provides insight on how to motivate employees for productivity, increased morale, and to create a more supportive corporate culture where people like to work.

Deanne has won numerous national and international public speaking and professional awards, including recognition by *Training* magazine's "Top 100." Her multicultural training and communication research extends across twenty-eight countries and fifty-two cultures. She was a conflict mediator during the first Gulf War Crisis.

Deanne is author of four books, numerous workbooks, and she has been published in more than fifty trade and professional journals. She is a member of the National Communication Association, The National Speakers Association, The Worldwide Association of Business Coaches, and is certified as a Corporate Coach Instructor.

Deanne, welcome to *Speaking of Success*.

Deanne DeMarco (DeMarco)
Thank you.

Wright
As a business coach and corporate trainer, what is one secret of success you could share with our readers?

DeMarco
One secret of success is the realization that as we travel down the road of life we sometimes need to rebuild the road on which we are traveling. When you drive your car sometimes you will observe a construction crew digging up the old road. The crew will first dig up the old road, lay a new foundation, and then they will resurface the road.

The same is true in our lives. If you want to find personal or professional success you sometimes have to tear up the old road and lay a new foundation before you resurface. Just as in our lives, a quick-fix patch job just doesn't work.

Wright
Will you share with our readers some examples of when you need to "repair the road"?

DeMarco
An example is a manager who may want to improve performance with either an employee or a team, improve team synergy, or build stronger employee relationships. On an individual basis, you may want better work-life balance in your life, more fulfillment in your career, or you may want to develop stronger personal relationships. In each of these situations, you may need to evaluate the road of your life and rebuild that road.

Wright
How can managers improve employee performance by replacing the road?

DeMarco
One way is to develop the skill-set of a coach-manager. In the world of sports, athletes hire personal coaches to fine-tune their skills and break through the boundaries to improve performance and achieve goals. In the business world, managers need solid coaching skills to fine-tune individual and team performance in delivering bot-

tom line results. The manager who is able to coach has the ability to make profound improvement in the performance of employees while keeping them motivated.

Coaching is a results-oriented approach that has a completely different skill-set than training, mentoring, managing, or counseling. There is a fine line that separates the interrelated process of coaching, providing feedback, performance appraisals, and managing. Coaching is a goal-centered approach that involves a more dynamic interaction between the coach and the coachee or in this case, the coach-manager and the employee.

Coaching others is an unnatural process for many managers. As a coach-manager you are more centered on asking powerful questions that will help drive performance solutions and improve personal accountability. This process aids the coachee in achieving the ultimate goal. As managers we tend to utilize more of a "telling" rather than an "asking" approach. An asking or non-directive approach is a new skill for most managers. As a manager, one of the most difficult aspects of the job is that balance between using both directive and non-directive approaches with our employees.

Wright

In your seminars and workshops you teach managers the skills to be an effective coach-manager. What are some the advantages that benefit corporations in training their managers to also be a coach?

DeMarco

Numerous studies of Fortune 500 companies have clearly shown that correctly coaching employees improves both productivity and job quality. Additionally, organizations that have paired training and coaching together are experiencing outstanding bottom line profitability. For example, stand-alone training may improve productivity by 22 percent while training coupled with coaching increased productivity by as much as 88 percent. Typically, a company can see bottom line results such as:

- Improved productivity—53 percent
- Improved quality—48 percent
- Improved customer satisfaction—39 percent
- Employee retention—32 percent
- Cost reductions—23 percent

In addition, employees who are coached are reporting a number of additional benefits. For example, they are reporting the following:

- Relationships are improved with their direct reports and their managers—70 percent
- Improved teamwork—67 percent
- Improved job satisfaction—61 percent
- Conflict reduction—52 percent
- Improved organizational commitment—44 percent

I have worked with numerous companies implementing coach training initiatives and these managers have reported to me that their actual numbers are statistically higher than the ones I just mentioned. For example, one Fortune 500 manager informed me that conflict in his department had been reduced by over 75 percent and that the morale and teamwork skyrocketed in his department. He acknowledged that prior to the coaching and training initiative, mediating conflict between two of his work groups consumed a great deal of his time. Immediately after the coaching and training initiative the conflict between these two groups almost completely disappeared. He thought it was remarkable that for the first time members of these two conflicting groups were now working together to achieve company objectives without having a referee or without his intervention. He conveyed that the initiative improved work quality, morale, and the harmony within his department was a welcomed bonus.

It has been impressive what companies are experiencing with this coach-manager model.

Wright

You said that the coach is centered on asking powerful questions. Would you explain the skill and perhaps give us some examples?

DeMarco

The ability to ask powerful questions is probably one of the most important tools the coach-manager has in his or her toolbox. This form of communication is often referred to as the Socratic approach. Through the use of both open- and close-ended questions the coach-manager can help the coachee or employee determine his or her blocks to success, what resources are needed to break through the barriers, and how to reach specific goals and corporate objectives.

The coach-manager utilizes an asking approach instead of a telling approach. For example, let's say a manager has just delegated a project to an employee who is new to project management. The coach-manager might ask questions such as:

- What are some of the goals of this project?
- What are the necessary subtasks that will need to be completed?
- What are the due dates for each project task?
- What are the milestones?
- What barriers do you see with this project?
- What resources do you need in order to be successful in this project?

By asking a series of open-ended questions, the coach-manager-helps the employee think through the complete project.

All too often the manager assumes that the employee understands what is required or the manager tells the employee a string of facts that the employee may not completely grasp.

I heard one horror story about a manager who delegated a complex project to an inexperienced project manger and then expected the employee, on her own, to figure out the process and the tasks to be completed. When the project was not completed to the manager's satisfaction he blamed the employee for poor work. The manager would have been more effective using a coach-manager style rather than a directive approach.

Let me give another example. A manager may want to ask some questions about project goals. Some powerful questions might include:

- What do you want to achieve?
- What is the ideal outcome?
- How are you going to accomplish this goal?
- What steps are necessary in order to achieve this project goal?

If the manager observed some possible barriers hindering the progress of a project, the coach-manager might ask some questions about hindrances such as:

- What barriers are you experiencing?

- What are your options?
- What is wrong with the way you have been approaching this project so far?
- What could prevent you from achieving the project goal?
- What obstacles do you envision? What do you think should be your steps to overcome them?
- What resources do you need?

By asking powerful questions the manager as coach has the employee think through the problem. This process enables the employee to come up with some of the solutions, move forward with the project, and successfully achieve the goal that he or she seeks.

Wright

Would you share a success secret on how a manager could be more effective as a coach-manager?

DeMarco

The ability to adapt one's communication style to the preferred style of the coachee maximizes our effectiveness. Failure to modify your own personal communication style may often result in conflict-prone personal and professional relationships.

Throughout industry, politics, and sports we have seen successful coaches and leaders who exhibit all sorts of behavioral styles. Although there are many different personalities, communication styles can be narrowed down to four major behavioral approaches. These four styles are grounded in the original research that was conducted two thousand years ago by Hippocrates who is known as the "Father of Medicine." In the late 1920s Dr. William Marston, a Harvard-trained psychologist, continued the research that is widely recognized and accepted today.

Over the years, consultants have given these categories their own names, however, they parallel the original distinctions and research made by Hippocrates and Marston. The four styles defined by Marston are: dominance, influence, steadiness, and conscientiousness.

Employees who exhibit the dominance communication style are direct, opinionated, want the bottom line, seek immediate results and enjoy challenges. Communicators who use this style like to win, are risk-takers, and will work hard to get desired results.

To be effective as a coach-manager, show them the simplest and quickest way to be productive. Be firm, direct, and clearly define the limits of their authority. They like public recognition for creating results that make a difference.

The influence style communicators prefer to interact with people; they are fast-paced, animated, enthusiastic, and like to express their thoughts and feelings. These outgoing employees desire results, however, they are very sociable in their interaction. They are excellent communicators and can literally chat with you at length on just about anything.

An effective coach-manger needs to avoid overwhelming details and should request specific feedback to check on the employee's understanding of how to complete a project. Use public praise and provide opportunities for them to interact with others.

Employees who exhibit the steadiness communication style are very accepting of others and are known as the peacemakers. They like cooperation, harmony, and are very good at calming others. This employee likes security, being part of a team, and stability. These people dislike change and are not risk-takers.

With this communicator, the coach-manager needs to use a step-by-step plan for development. Provide one-on-one, hands-on instruction and regular informal feedback on improvements. These are loyal employees who respond positively to group achievements.

Conscientious communication style employees thrive on details and they demand quality. They like to work under known conditions and prefer to follow written standards and procedures. This employee is neat and orderly; he or she values accuracy and has a perfectionist nature.

When managing this communicator, be specific and detailed. Before a meeting, prepare information to be discussed prior to the conversation. The employee exhibiting this communication style will ask many questions, so allow extra time for your meeting.

A work group that has all four styles can be an effective team. Each style brings different strengths to the team. However, it is important for the coach-manager to set a positive tone by demonstrating mutual respect, trust, and acceptance for each style. If the manager can create the right environment and allow the group to motivate themselves, this team can achieve outstanding results.

Wright
How does the coach-manager deal with an employee who is a poor performer?

DeMarco

There are several schools of thought on this issue. The old school of management states that you should continually eliminate the bottom 10 percent of the workforce. However, I would like to tell you a true story of a young man by the name of Bobby.

Bobby was born with physical limitations. Doctors were all in agreement that Bobby would never be able to run. However, Bobby had another opinion. Bobby wanted to learn how to run.

In sixth grade Bobby joined the track team. Bobby knew the challenges and that the chance of winning a race was slim, however, he showed up every day for practice and he showed up for every track meet. The coach could have easily cut Bobby from the track meets since he clearly was not physically able to compete with the other boys. Instead, this coach embraced Bobby's goal and encouraged him to keep trying.

I will never forget the day when I witnessed this young man run. Bobby was in tenth grade at the time—a sophomore in high school. It was the last race and the last meet of the school year. The boys were all lined up when the gun went off. The boys quickly took off from the starting gate. The event was one lap around the track.

Well, the runners exploded off the starting line and in no time they reached the quarter mark. Bobby was just barely off the starting line. He was running—well, sort of. Bobby's gait was awkward in appearance and clearly not like that of the other boys.

The pack of runners was at the halfway mark and Bobby was far behind. As Bobby crossed the halfway mark all the other boys had finished the race. Three teammates dashed across the field and walked about fifteen feet behind Bobby in the grassy area inside the track field. I wasn't sure what I was watching or what these boys were up to. They shadowed Bobby all the way to the finish line.

I don't think anyone in the bleachers was prepared for what followed. When Bobby crossed the line these three boys made a mad dash toward him. There was massive commotion on the field with students everywhere. There were cheers and screams coming from the crowd. These boys grabbed Bobby and lifted him high above their heads. There was a massive roar from the students who were on the field and in the stands; they crowded around Bobby as he was carried off the field. The students were all cheering for him. You would have thought that Bobby had won the race instead of coming in dead last. Bobby was treated as a hero that day.

I couldn't understand why the boys carried him off so I asked the coach afterward. He told me that because of Bobby the track team ranked first and was impossible to beat. They had won every single race and every single event they had ever competed in during the whole year. The coach told me that Bobby was not fast and he may not win any races but he was a determined competitor. Bobby's encouragement and persistence challenged everyone. Because of Bobby each team member improved his performance one or two seconds at a time—steadily, persistently, everyone improved.

"As a team," the coach said, "we won every event at every meet." Sometimes the team would take first, second, and third place. He said, "A record like ours is unheard of in high school track. Because of Bobby this has been the best team for this or any high school. Normally, the boys are very competitive with each other, but by his example, Bobby showed us how to be a team and how to help each other. Trust formed within the team and encouraging each other was part of the norm." The coach concluded by saying that it had been an incredible year and he had never experienced anything like it.

I think there is a lesson here in Bobby's story. Bobby did not win and he always came in dead last, but because of his desire to improve the team also improved. In business, the accomplishments of the team are greater than the accomplishments of any one person. In order for a manager to be successful, he or she needs a coach-manager mindset to lead a good team. The coach-manger has a skill-set that is supportive of his or her employees. For many managers that will require eliminating the old mindset of power, control, dominance, and leading by threat. That old style of management went out the door with the traditionalists—those born between 1900 and 1945—and definitely with the Baby Boomers—those born between 1946 and 1964.

This Generation X workforce is independent, resilient, adaptable, and technically literate. This group does not respond to the old management styles that worked well in the past. Successful corporations need a productive and loyal workforce and turnover is costly. If companies want to retain their talent the manager needs to re-evaluate his or her managerial style through a whole new filter.

Bobby switched schools and his new coach worked with Bobby using more progressive techniques. He was very effective with Bobby. By the time Bobby graduated from high school, just two years later, Bobby ran a marathon and finished in second place in his age group.

If managers and companies want to be effective with this new workforce, they need to tear up and discard that old road of management and move forward in more progressive techniques by being a coach-manager.

Wright

You mentioned earlier that individuals also could benefit from digging up the road before laying a new foundation and a new road. Would you explain?

DeMarco

On an individual basis, people who are unhappy with how their life is going—whether they want more work-life balance, happiness in a career, or stronger personal relationships—need to take a realistic look at the road they are presently traveling.

I coached a woman who worked for years as a marketing broker-buyer for an independent grocery store chain. She was successful but wanted a change. Through the discovery process she determined that she wanted to be a paralegal. This is a tough field to enter. Most paralegals prepare for this profession right out of high school. In order for her to reach this dream she needed to tear up her old road and acquire new skills and the education needed for the foundation of her dream. Her persistence paid off. After graduating from paralegal school she got temporary work at one law firm, which led to additional temporary work at another firm. In just over a year she gained considerable experience and secured a full-time job as a paralegal.

Today she is living in the career of her dreams.

Wright

What steps do you think are necessary in order to be successful?

DeMarco

I think there are basically six steps that we need to look at in rebuilding our road. You can apply these steps in business as well as in personal life. First, people need to identify their dream or their goal and answer two questions: "What would give my life meaning?" What would make my life take on the radiance of a glow stick?"

Watching a construction crew reminds us that the layering of a new road is a process and not a quick fix. Rebuilding a new road or achieving a dream is completed one step at a time, one layer at a time. Both, however, start with the requirement of identification.

Just as the construction worker needs to know which road to tear up, you need to identify your dream!

Second, it is important to visualize what the results are going to look like. This involves clarifying your dream or goal with details. It does not matter how many people believe in your dream or goal, it only takes one person—you—to believe.

If we look at Bobby's story, no one believed that Bobby would be able to run. His parents, doctors, and teachers all agreed that Bobby would never be able to run like a normal child. Yet Bobby believed that he was going to learn how to run.

When clarifying your dream, answer the following two questions: First, what will your dream or goal allow you to do better or more of? Second, how would you describe success? When answering these two questions it is important not to ask friends or family for their thoughts. Often the well-meaning intentions of others don't parallel the desires of our hearts.

The third step is to be committed to rebuilding your road. This is a critical step. Again, the construction crew provides us with the answer. What would our roadways look like if construction crews left roads unfinished? I don't think we would be able to drive anywhere because we would have all these unfinished roads everywhere. The same is true with our own personal success road. We need to commit to the dream; we need to commit to rebuilding our road.

In my coaching practice I have heard many excuses: I'm too old, I'm too young, I'm not clever enough, etc. Yes, it is risky to start down a new path, and to start rebuilding takes courage and a willingness to get off the safe sofa of life and move forward. I truly believe that we can have a more fulfilling life, career, and the relationships of our dreams if we are willing to get involved and be committed to the desires of our hearts and minds.

I once read that success is not measured in dollars but by the quality and quantity of personal satisfaction that it brings. Look at Bobby's story one more time. Bobby showed up for every practice and every track meet. He did not win any race. However, he showed up every day. Every day he made the choice to keep moving forward.

Like Bobby, the choice is ours to make. We can sabotage ourselves with the attitudes and beliefs of our fears. We can sabotage ourselves by listening to the discouraging words of others. We have a clear choice to make. That choice is to either hold back or to move forward. If success is what you desire, then you must make that step of commitment every single day.

Step four is one of discovery—discovering what is possible. Your dream will open new doors, new adventures, and you will meet new people. Possibilities will begin to emerge as you begin to live your dream. In Bobby's story Bobby switched schools and a new coach embraced his dream and started to coach Bobby in a new way. Bobby started to run longer distances and his coach helped him to build upper and lower body strength so that he could start running 5K and 10K races. The coach helped Bobby see new possibilities, which led to his marathon victory. The same is true for our dreams. We need to look for those possibilities that come knocking at our door and look for the opportunities our dream might offer us.

The fifth step is to design a blueprint for success. In step two we looked at where we wanted to go. In this step we need to determine how we are going to get there. What resources are we going to need? What barriers do we need to overcome? Sometimes it is rather painful to develop this to-do list, and the action steps needed to accomplish the tasks.

The last step—step six—is persistence. Every day of every week we need to work toward our dream. In my upcoming book, *Stop Spinning, Start Winning: Strategies for achieving personal and professional success*, I discuss how one needs to do a minimum of two activities every day that will bring value to our dreams. I call it making WOW deposits. WOW stands for "Within One Week." If a person can do at least two activities every day toward his or her dream, then within a week that WOW deposit slip will have at least fourteen line items on it. With every WOW deposit we get closer to realizing our dream and achieving the desires of our hearts.

I think that if we are going to rebuild our road we need to put energy into our dream every day of every week. Bobby never stopped. He showed up for practice. He showed up for every meet. By the time he graduated high school he ran and finished a marathon. I think that in order for us to find success we need to follow that same model. Bobby's story is a powerful metaphor to communicate some important lessons like the power of perseverance and daring to dream big!

Wright

What do you think prevents people from becoming successful or realizing their dream?

DeMarco

I think the answer to that lies in conquering our fear and developing a courageous attitude. Without the courage to actively pursue our dreams and goals, our dreams can pass us by like clouds carried off by the wind. I think it takes courage to try something new. No dream is realized without persistence and hard work.

According to Webster's Dictionary, courage is that "quality or state of mind or spirit enabling one to face danger or hardship with confidence or resolution." Unfortunately, I think friends and neighbors and family members are great at telling us what we can't do and what we can't accomplish. These well meaning friends are often negative because being negative is easy. If you want to be successful, don't listen to the negative talk of others who try to prevent you from moving forward.

I think my son, Bobby, teaches us the lesson of courage. I will never forget the day he came home telling me he wanted to join the track team. He announced, "Mom, Mom, guess what I found out! I found out I can join the track team. They can't kick me off as long as I show up for every practice and every meet. I don't have to win. I just have to show up!" You know, it took a lot of courage for that young sixth grader. He could barely walk and yet he wanted to join the track team.

How many people have dreams and then fears kick in and they become unwilling to try? I think that to move forward you must show up. Bobby didn't allow anything to get in his way. Bobby showed courage when he joined that track team knowing that he would not win any races. It was clear that Bobby did not have the talent or basic skills to participate on a track team and it took courage to keep showing up day after day, year after year. It would have been easy for him to listen to his peers—"You will never win; you can't run; you can barely walk; you won't be able to contribute anything to the team; you will be the laughing stock of the school; everyone will think you are a fool; people will call you retard." Bobby had the courage to move forward toward his dream even through the cruel and negative comments of his peers.

Moving forward toward your dream requires you to show up every single day of every single year.

Wright

What a great conversation. I have learned a lot here today and I am sure that our readers have. I really appreciate your taking all this time with me to answer all these questions. It has really been informative.

DeMarco

Thank you. This has been enjoyable.

Wright

Today we have been talking with Deanne DeMarco. She is a business coach and communication master. She works with high-level executives and provides insight on how to motivate employees for productivity, increased morale, and to create a more supportive corporate culture where people like to work.

Deanne, thank you so much for being with us today on *Speaking of Success*.

About the Author

According to a January 2006 article in *Fortune 500* magazine, Generation X workers—those born between 1964 and 1977—require a different management approach than previous generations. Bringing out the best in others, inspiring loyalty, and increasing job satisfaction among members of this elusive group has been the hallmark of Deanne DeMarco's career. Deanne employs a set of strategies aligned with her GenXer Factor™ Management Model to inspire more productivity, passion, and enthusiasm with the younger, Gen-X workforce. This proven approach helps corporations of all sizes create an enthusiastic corporate culture where people achieve more and love to work.

Deanne's unique style and penchant for results has been most affected by her son Bobby's amazing story. "Six months after we brought our son home from the hospital, we started planning for his funeral. Medical tests led doctors to believe that he wouldn't live beyond his first birthday. And, if by some miracle he did survive, he would never walk."

With Deanne's encouragement, Bobby believed he could learn to run and eventually achieved his dream. It was Bobby's example that taught Deanne some of the most powerful lessons that fuel her work with corporations and individuals today.

Deanne's successful training programs are nationally recognized by *Training Magazine's* Top 100. An author, speaker, corporate trainer, and coach, Deanne has written four books, numerous workbooks, and her articles have been published in more than fifty trade and professional journals. Her multicultural training and research extends across twenty-eight countries and fifty-two cultures, including a stint as a conflict mediator during the first Gulf War Crisis.

Deanne DeMarco, MA, RCC
Breaking-Boundaries International, Inc.
3013 South Wolf Road, #730
Westchester, Illinois 60154
Phone: 866.91.COACH
E-mail: info@Breaking-Boundaries.com
www.Breaking-Boundaries.com
www.DeanneDeMarco.com

Chapter 2

DR. KEN BLANCHARD

THE INTERVIEW

David E. Wright (Wright)

Few people have created a positive impact on the day-to-day management of people and companies more than Dr. Kenneth Blanchard, who is known around the world simply as Ken, a prominent, gregarious, sought-after author, speaker, and business consultant. Ken is universally characterized by friends, colleagues, and clients as one of the most insightful, powerful, and compassionate men in business today. Ken's impact as a writer is far-reaching. His phenomenal bestselling book, *The One Minute Manager*®, co-authored with Spencer Johnson, has sold more than thirteen million copies worldwide and has been translated into more than twenty-five languages. Ken is Chairman and Chief Spiritual Officer of the Ken Blanchard Companies. The organization's focus is to energize organizations around the world with customized training in bottom line business strategies based on the simple, yet powerful principles inspired by Ken's bestselling books.

Dr. Blanchard, welcome to *Speaking of Success*!

Dr. Ken Blanchard (Blanchard)
Well, it's nice to talk to you, David. It's good to be here.

Wright
I must tell you that preparing for your interview took quite a bit more time than usual. The scope of your life's work and your business, the Ken Blanchard Companies, would make for a dozen fascinating interviews. Before we dive into the specifics of some of your projects and strategies, will you give our readers a brief synopsis of your life—how you came to be the Ken Blanchard we all know and respect?

Blanchard
Well, I'll tell you, David, I think life is what you do when you are planning on doing something else. I think that was John Lennon's line. I never intended to do what I have been doing. In fact, all my professors in college told me that I couldn't write. I wanted to do college work, which I did, and they said, "You had better be an administrator." So I decided I was going to be a Dean of Students. I got provisionally accepted into my master's degree program and then provisionally accepted at Cornell, because I never could take any of those standardized tests.

I took the college boards four times and finally got 502 in English. I don't have a test-taking mind. I ended up in a university in Athens, Ohio, in 1966 as an Administrative Assistant to the Dean of the Business School. When I got there he said, "Ken, I want you to teach a course. I want all my deans to teach." I had never thought about teaching because they said I couldn't write, and teachers had to publish. He put me in the manager's department.

I've taken enough bad courses in my day and I wasn't going to teach one. I really prepared and had a wonderful time with the students. I was chosen as one of the top ten teachers on the campus coming out of the chute!

I just had a marvelous time. A colleague by the name of Paul Hersey was chairman of the management department. He wasn't very friendly to me initially because the Dean had led me into his department, but I heard he was a great teacher. He taught organizational behavior and leadership. So I said, "Can I sit in on your course next semester?"

"Nobody audits my courses," he said. "If you want to take it for credit, you're welcome."

I couldn't believe it. I had a doctoral degree and he wanted me to take his course for credit, so I signed up.

The registrar didn't know what to do with me because I already had a doctorate, but I wrote the papers and took the course, and it was great.

In June 1967, Hersey came into my office and said, "Ken, I've been teaching in this field for ten years. I think I'm better than anybody, but I can't write. I'm a nervous wreck, and I'd love to write a textbook with somebody. Would you write one with me?"

I said, "We ought to be a great team. You can't write and I'm not supposed to be able to, so let's do it!"

Thus began this great career of writing and teaching. We wrote a textbook called *Management of Organizational Behavior: Utilizing Human Resources*. It came out in its eighth edition October 3, 2000 and the nineth edition will be out June 15, 2007. It has sold more than any other textbook in that area over the years. It's been over forty years since that book came out.

I quit my administrative job, became a professor, and ended up working my way up the ranks. I got a sabbatical leave and went to California for one year twenty-five years ago. I ended up meeting Spencer Johnson at a cocktail party. He wrote children's books—a wonderful series called *Value Tales for Kids including*. He also wrote *The Value of Courage: The Story of Jackie Robinson and The Value of Believing In Yourself: The Story Louis Pasteur.*

My wife, Margie, met him first and said, "You guys ought to write a children's book for managers because they won't read anything else." That was my introduction to Spencer. So, *The One Minute Manager* was really a kid's book for big people. That is a long way from saying that my career was well planned.

Wright

Ken, what and/or who were your early influences in the areas of business, leadership and success? In other words, who shaped you in your early years?

Blanchard

My father had a great impact on me. He was retired as an admiral in the Navy and had a wonderful philosophy. I remember when I was elected as president of the seventh grade, and I came home all pumped up. My father said, "Son, it's great that you're the president of the seventh grade, but now that you have that leadership position, don't ever use it." He said, "Great leaders are followed because people respect them and like them, not because they have power." That was a wonderful lesson for me early on. He was just a great model for me. I got a lot from him.

Then I had this wonderful opportunity in the mid 1980s to write a book with Norman Vincent Peale. He wrote *The Power of Positive Thinking*. I met him when he was eighty-six years old and we were asked to write a book on ethics together, *The Power of Ethical Management: Integrity Pays, You Don't Have to Cheat to Win*. It didn't matter what we were writing together, I learned so much from him, and he just built from the positive things I learned from my mother.

My mother said that when I was born I laughed before I cried, I danced before I walked, and I smiled before I frowned. So that, as well as Norman Vincent Peale, really impacted me as I focused on what I could do to train leaders. How do you make them positive? How do you make them realize that it's not about them, it's about who they are serving. It's not about their position, it's about what they can do to help other people win.

So, I'd say my mother and father, then Norman Vincent Peale, all had a tremendous impact on me.

Wright

I can imagine. I read a summary of your undergraduate and graduate degrees. I assumed you studied business administration, marketing management, and related courses. Instead, at Cornell you studied government and philosophy. You received your master's from Colgate in sociology and counseling and your PhD from Cornell in educational administration and leadership. Why did you choose this course of study? How has it affected your writing and consulting?

Blanchard

Well, again, it wasn't really well planned out. I originally went to Colgate to get a master's degree in education because I was going to be a Dean of Students over men. I had been a government major, and I was a government major because it was the best department at Cornell in the Liberal Arts School. It was exciting. We would study what the people were doing at the league governments. And then, the Philosophy Department was great. I just loved the philosophical arguments. I wasn't a great student in terms of getting grades, but I'm a total learner. I would sit there and listen, and I would really soak it in.

When I went over to Colgate and got in these education courses, they were awful. They were boring. The second week, I was sitting at the bar at the Colgate Inn saying, "I can't believe I've been here two years for this." It's just the way the Lord works—sitting next to me in the bar was a young sociology professor who had just gotten his PhD at Illinois. He was staying at the Inn. I was moaning and groaning about what I was doing, and he said, "Why don't you come and major with me in sociology? It's really exciting."

"I can do that?" I asked.

He said, "Yes."

I knew they would probably let me do whatever I wanted the first week. Suddenly, I switched out of education and went with Warren Ramshaw. He had a tremendous impact on me. He retired some years ago as the leading professor at Colgate in the Arts and Sciences, and got me interested in leadership and organizations. That's why I got a master's in sociology.

The reason I went into educational administration and leadership? It was a doctoral program I could get into because I knew the guy heading up the program. He said, "The greatest thing about Cornell is that you will be in a School of Education. It's not very big, so you don't have to take many education courses, and you can take stuff all over the place."

There was a marvelous man by the name of Don McCarty, who eventually became the Dean of the School of Education, Wisconsin. He had an impact on my life; but I was always just searching around. My mission statement is: to be a loving teacher and example of simple truths that help myself and others to awaken the presence of God in our lives. The reason I mention "God" is that I believe the biggest addiction in the world is the human ego; but I'm really into simple truth. I used to tell people I was trying to get the B.S. out of the behavioral sciences.

Wright

I can't help but think, when you mentioned your father, that he just bottomed lined it for you about leadership.

Blanchard

Yes.

Wright

A man named Paul Myers, in Texas, years and years ago when I went to a conference down there, said, "David, if you think you're a leader and you look around, and no one is following you, you're just out for a walk."

Blanchard

Well, you'd get a kick; I'm just reaching over to pick up a picture of Paul Myers on my desk. He's a good friend, and he's a part of our Center for FaithWalk Leadership where we're trying to challenge and equip people to lead like Jesus. It's non-profit. I tell people I'm not an evangelist because we've got enough trouble with the Christians we have. We don't need any more new ones. But, this is a picture of Paul on top of a mountain. Then there's another picture below that of him under the sea with stingrays. It says, "Attitude is everything. Whether you're on the top of the mountain or the bottom of the sea, true happiness is achieved by accepting God's promises, and by having a biblically positive frame of mind. Your attitude is everything." Isn't that something?

Wright

He's a fine, fine man. He helped me tremendously. In keeping with the theme of our book, *Speaking of Success,* I wanted to get a sense from you about your own success journey. Many people know you best from *The One Minute Manager* books you coauthored with Spencer Johnson. Would you consider these books as a high water mark for you, or have you defined success for yourself in different terms?

Blanchard

Well, you know, *The One Minute Manager* was an absurdly successful book, so quickly that I found I couldn't take credit for it. That was when I really got on my own spiritual journey and started to try to find out what the real meaning of life and success was.

That's been a wonderful journey for me because I think, David, the problem with most people is they think their self-worth is a function of their performance plus the opinion of others. The minute you think that is what your self-worth is, every day your self-worth is up for grabs because your performance is going to fluctuate on a day-to-day basis. People are fickle. Their opinions are going to go up and down. You need to ground your self-worth in the unconditional love that

God has ready for us, and that really grew out of the unbelievable success of *The One Minute Manager.*

When I started to realize where all that came from, that's how I got involved in this ministry that I mentioned. Paul Myers is a part of it. As I started to read the Bible, I realized that everything I've ever written about, or taught, Jesus did. You know, He did it with the twelve incompetent guys He "hired." The only guy with much education was Judas, and he was His only turnover problem.

Wright

Right.

Blanchard

It was a really interesting thing. What I see in people is not only do they think their self-worth is a function of their performance plus the opinion of others, but they measure their success on the amount of accumulation of wealth, on recognition, power, and status. I think those are nice success items. There's nothing wrong with those, as long as you don't define your life by that.

What I think you need to focus on rather than success is what Bob Buford, in his book *Halftime,* calls significance—moving from success to significance. I think the opposite of accumulation of wealth is generosity.

I wrote a book called *The Generosity Factor* with Truett Cathy, who is the founder of Chick-fil-A. He is one of the most generous men I've ever met in my life. I thought we needed to have a model of generosity. It's not only your treasure, but it's your time and talent. Truett and I added *touch* as a fourth one.

The opposite of recognition is service. I think you become an adult when you realize you're here to serve rather than to be served.

Finally, the opposite of power and status is loving relationships. Take Mother Teresa as an example; she couldn't have cared less about recognition, power, and status because she was focused on generosity, service, and loving relationships; but she got all of that earthly stuff. If you focus on the earthly, such as money, recognition, and power, you're never going to get to significance. But if you focus on significance, you'll be amazed at how much success can come your way.

Wright

I spoke with Truett Cathy recently and was impressed by what a down-to-earth, good man he seems to be. When you start talking about him closing on Sunday, all of my friends—when they found out I had talked to him—said, "Boy, he must be a great Christian man, but he's rich and all this." I told them, "Well, to put his faith into perspective, by closing on Sunday it cost him $500 million a year."

He lives his faith, doesn't he?

Blanchard

Absolutely, but he still outsells everybody else.

Wright

That's right.

Blanchard

According to their January 25, 2007, press release, Chick-fil-A is currently the nation's second-largest quick-service chicken restaurant chain in sales. Its business performance marks the thirty-ninth consecutive year the chain has enjoyed a system-wide sales gain—a streak the company has sustained since opening its first chain restaurant in 1967.

Wright

The simplest market scheme, I told him, tripped me up. I walked by his first Chick-fil-A I had ever seen, and some girl came out with chicken stuck on toothpicks and handed me one; I just grabbed it and ate it, it's history from there on.

Blanchard

Yes, I think so. It's really special. It is so important that people understand generosity, service, and loving relationships because too many people are running around like a bunch of peacocks. You even see pastors who measure their success by how many in are in their congregation; authors by how many books they have sold; businesspeople by what their profit margin is—how good sales are. The reality is that's all well and good, but I think what you need to focus on is the other. I think if business did that more and we got Wall Street off our backs with all the short-term evaluation, we'd be a lot better off.

Wright

Absolutely. There seems to be a clear theme that winds through many of your books that have to do with success in business and organizations—how people are treated by management and how they feel about their value to a company. Is this an accurate observation? If so, can you elaborate on it?

Blanchard

Yes, it's a very accurate observation. See, I think the profit is the applause you get for taking care of your customers and creating a motivating environment for your people. Very often people think that business is only about the bottom line. But no, that happens to be the result of creating raving fan customers, which I've described with Sheldon Bowles in our book, *Raving Fans*. Customers want to brag about you, if you create an environment where people can be gung-ho and committed. You've got to take care of your customers and your people, and then your cash register is going to go ka-ching, and you can make some big bucks.

Wright

I noticed that your professional title with the Ken Blanchard Companies is somewhat unique—Chairman and Chief Spiritual Officer. What does your title mean to you personally and to your company? How does it affect the books you choose to write?

Blanchard

I remember having lunch with Max DuPree one time, the legendary Chairman of Herman Miller, who wrote a wonderful book called *Leadership Is An Art.* "What's your job?" I asked him.

He said, "I basically work in the vision area."

"Well, what do you do?" I asked.

"I'm like a third grade teacher," he replied. "I say our vision and values over, and over, and over again until people get it right, right, right."

I decided from that, I was going to become the Chief Spiritual Officer, which means I would be working in the vision, values, and energy part of our business. I ended up leaving a morning message every day for everybody in our company. We have twenty-eight international offices around the world. I leave a voice mail every morning, and I do three things on that as Chief Spiritual Officer: One, people tell me who we need to pray for. Two, people tell me who we need to praise—

our unsung heroes and people like that. And then three, I leave an inspirational morning message. I really am the cheerleader—the Energizer Bunny—in our company. I'm the reminder of why we're here and what we're trying to do.

We think that our business in the Ken Blanchard Companies is to help people lead at a higher level, and to help individuals and organizations. Our mission statement is to unleash the power and potential of people and organizations for the common good. So if we are going to do that, we've really got to believe in that.

I'm working on getting more Chief Spiritual Officers around the country. I think it's a great title and we should get more of them.

Wright

So those people for whom you pray, where do you get the names?

Blanchard

The people in the company tell me who needs help, whether it's a spouse who is sick, or kids who are sick, or they are worried about something. We've got over five years of data about the power of prayer, which is pretty important.

One morning, my inspirational message was about my wife and five members of our company who walked sixty miles one weekend—twenty miles a day for three days—to raise money for breast cancer research.

It was amazing. I went down and waved them all in as they came. They had a ceremony, and they had raised 7.6 million dollars. There were over three thousand people walking, and a lot of the walkers were dressed in pink; they were cancer victors—people who had overcome it. There were even men walking with pictures of their wives who had died from breast cancer. I thought it was incredible.

There wasn't one mention about it in the major San Diego papers. I said, "Isn't that just something." We have to be an island of positive influence because all you see in the paper today is about Michael Jackson and Scott Peterson and Kobe Bryant—celebrities and their bad behavior—and here you get all these thousands of people out there walking and trying to make a difference, and nobody thinks it's news.

So every morning I pump people up about what life's about, about what's going on. That's what my Chief Spiritual Officer job is about.

Wright

I had the pleasure of reading one of your releases, *The Leadership Pill.*

Blanchard

Yes.

Wright

I must admit that my first thought was how short the book was. I wondered if I was going to get my money's worth, which by the way, I most certainly did. Many of your books are brief and based on a fictitious story. Most business books in the market today are hundreds of pages in length and are read almost like a textbook.

Will you talk a little bit about why you write these short books, and about the premise of *The Leadership Pill?*

Blanchard

I really developed my relationship with Spencer Johnson when we wrote *The One Minute Manager.* As you know, he wrote, *Who Moved My Cheese*, which was a phenomenal success. He wrote children's books, and is quite a storyteller.

Jesus taught by parables, which were short stories.

My favorite books are, *Jonathan Livingston Seagull* and *The Little Prince.*

Og Mandino, author of seventeen books, was the greatest of them all.

I started writing parables because people can get into the story and learn the contents of the story, and they don't bring their judgmental hats into reading. You write a regular book and they'll say, "Well, where did you get the research?" They get into that judgmental side. Our books get them emotionally involved and they learn.

The Leadership Pill is a fun story about a pharmaceutical company who thinks that they have discovered the secret to leadership, and they can put the ingredients in a pill. When they announce it, the country goes crazy because everybody knows we need more effective leaders. When they release it, it outsells Viagra. The founders of the company start selling off stock and they call them Pillionaires. But along comes this guy who calls himself "the effective manager," and he challenges them to a no-pill challenge. If they identify two non-performing groups, he'll take on one and let somebody on the pill take another one, and he guarantees he will out-perform that person by the end of the year. They agree, but of course they give him a drug test every week to make sure he's not sneaking pills on the side.

I wrote the book with Marc Muchnick, who is a young guy in his early thirties. We did a major study of what this interesting "Y" generation, the young people of today, want from leaders, and this is a secret blend that this effective manager uses. When you think about it, David, it is really powerful on terms of what people want from a leader.

Number one, they want integrity. A lot of people have talked about that in the past, but these young people will walk if they see people say one thing and do another. A lot of us walk to the bathroom and out into the halls to talk about it. But these people will quit. They don't want somebody to say something and not do it.

The second thing they want is a partnership relationship. They hate superior/subordinate. I mean, what awful terms those are. You know, the "head" of the department and the hired "hands"—you don't even give them a head. "What do you do? I'm in supervision. I see things a lot clearer than these stupid idiots." They want to be treated as partners; if they can get a financial partnership, great. If they can't, they really want a minimum of psychological partnership where they can bring their brains to work and make decisions.

Then finally, they want affirmation. They not only want to be caught doing things right, but they want to be affirmed for who they are. They want to be known as a person, not as a number.

So those are the three ingredients that this effective manager uses. They are wonderful values when you think about them.

Rank-order values for any organization is number one, integrity. In our company we call it ethics. It is our number one value. The number two value is partnership. In our company we call it relationships. Number three is affirmation—being affirmed as a human being. I think that ties into relationships, too. They are wonderful values that can drive behavior in a great way.

Wright

I believe most people in today's business culture would agree that success in business has everything to do with successful leadership. In *The Leadership Pill*, you present a simple but profound premise, that leadership is not something you do to people, it's something you do *with* them. At face value, that seems incredibly obvious. But you must have found in your research and observations that leaders in today's culture do not get this. Would you speak to that issue?

Blanchard

Yes. I think what often happens in this is the human ego. There are too many leaders out there who are self-serving. They're not leaders who have service in mind. They think the sheep are there for the benefit of the shepherd. All the power, money, fame, and recognition moves up the hierarchy; they forget that the real action in business is not up the hierarchy; it's in the one-to-one, moment-to-moment interactions that your front line people have with your customers. It's how the phone is answered. It's how problems are dealt with and those kinds of things. If you don't think that you're doing leadership *with* them—rather, you're doing it to them—after a while they won't take care of your customers.

I was at a store once (not Nordstrom's, where I normally would go) and I thought of something I had to share with my wife, Margie. I asked the guy behind the counter in Men's Wear, "May I use your phone?"

He said, "No!"

"You're kidding me," I said. "I can always use the phone at Nordstrom's."

"Look, buddy," he said, "they won't let *me* use the phone here. Why should I let you use the phone?"

That is an example of leadership that's done *to* employees not *with* them. People want a partnership. People want to be involved in a way that really makes a difference.

Wright

Dr. Blanchard, the time has flown by and there are so many more questions I'd like to ask you. In closing, would you mind sharing with our readers some thoughts on success? If you were mentoring a small group of men and women, and one of their central goals was to become successful, what kind of advice would you give them?

Blanchard

Well, I would first of all say, "What are you focused on?" If you are focused on success as being, as I said earlier, accumulation of money, recognition, power, or status, I think you've got the wrong target. What you need to really be focused on is how you can be generous in the use of your time and your talent and your treasure and touch. How can you serve people rather than be served? How can you develop caring, loving relationships with people? My sense is if you will focus on those things, success in the traditional sense will come to you. But if you go out and say, "Man, I'm going to make a fortune, and I'm going to do this," and have that kind of attitude, you might get some of those numbers. I think you become an adult, however, when you realize you are here to give rather than to get. You're here to serve not to be served. I would just say to people, "Life is such a very special occasion. Don't miss it by aiming at a target that bypasses other people, because we're really here to serve each other." So that's what I would share with people.

Wright

Well, what an enlightening conversation, Dr. Blanchard. I really want you to know how much I appreciate all the time you've taken with me for this interview. I know that our readers will learn from this, and I really appreciate your being with us today.

Blanchard

Well, thank you so much, David. I really enjoyed my time with you. You've asked some great questions that made me think, and I hope my answers are helpful to other people because as I say, life is a special occasion.

Wright

Today we have been talking with Dr. Ken Blanchard. He is the author of the phenomenal best selling book, *The One Minute Manager*. The fact that he's the Chief Spiritual Officer of his company should make us all think about how we are leading our companies and leading our families and leading anything, whether it is in church or civic organizations. I know I will.

Thank you so much, Dr. Blanchard, for being with us today on *Speaking of Success.*

Blanchard

Good to be with you, David.

About The Author

Few people have created more of a positive impact on the day-to-day management of people and companies than Dr. Kenneth Blanchard, who is known around the world simply as "Ken."

When Ken speaks, he speaks from the heart with warmth and humor. His unique gift is to speak to an audience and communicate with each individual as if they were alone and talking one-on-one. He is a polished storyteller with a knack for making the seemingly complex easy to understand.

Ken has been a guest on a number of national television programs, including *Good Morning America* and *The Today Show*. He has been featured in *Time, People, U.S. News & World Report*, and a host of other popular publications.

He earned his bachelor's degree in government and philosophy from Cornell University, his master's degree in sociology and counseling from Colgate University, and his PhD in educational administration and leadership from Cornell University.

Dr. Ken Blanchard
The Ken Blanchard Companies
125 State Place
Escondido, California 92029
Phone: 800.728.6000
Fax: 760.489.8407
www.kenblanchard.com

Chapter 3

DUSTIN HILLIS

THE INTERVIEW

David Wright (Wright)
Today we're talking with Dustin Hillis. He is an expert on sales fundamentals, and through his teaching he provides people with tools and techniques for improving execution. His foundation was forged from his years of direct sales with The Southwestern Company, a 150-year-old sales training company with over 3,500 salespeople worldwide. Dustin finished number one in his first year with Southwestern, then he eclipsed the all-time company record making a profit of over $100,000 in fourteen weeks. During that time he was also a junior in college. Mr. Hillis is a top sales professional and as a product of Southwestern, he is now a founding partner in the Southwestern Seminars division known as Success Starts Now!™ He is a motivational speaker, professional trainer, and confidence coach.

Dustin, welcome to *Speaking of Success!*

Dustin Hillis (Hillis)
Thank you for having me.

Wright

What were the three toughest challenges you have ever had to overcome?

Hillis

I don't look at a challenge as a problem, but instead as an opportunity to grow in the three main areas of my life: personal, physical, and business. I am thankful for the challenges in my life and the character developed from those challenges.

In my personal life, I would say that the number one challenge was convincing my wife, Kyah, to marry me—that was the best sale I've ever made!

A physical challenge was in high school when I was the state finalist in wrestling. Making the state finals was a big challenge and an exciting goal to achieve. It really helped my confidence in the long run.

Another challenge I have faced is in my business endeavors. I set a goal to break the Southwestern all-time company sales record. You know that turn you sometimes feel in your stomach—those butterflies? That's the feeling I had when I set that goal. I was going into my third year of working with Southwestern and wanted to break the company record! When I set that goal it was refreshing to have something I knew would challenge me that I could put my mind to and work through.

Those were my top three challenges.

Wright

As a professional sales trainer, motivational speaker, and confidence coach for Success Starts Now!™, what motivated you to choose the field of professional speaking?

Hillis

My speaking and sales training career started at Southwestern. After breaking the company record in my third year, I participated in a lot of the sales training throughout the company, both on a national and global scale. My first big keynote speech was the European Great Recruiter's Seminar in London. Prior to this speaking event, I hadn't thought of training or coaching; I was just focusing on being a top producer. After my first presentation, a new passion built up inside of me. Before I walked out on stage I felt as though I was about to go and play a football game! The company made a CD out of that speech—and then asked me to make the same speech at the Great Recruiter's Seminar in the United States in front of more than 1,000 people.

After those two speaking events, I received a lot of great feedback regarding the techniques for increasing belief levels and doubling production. Students and managers shared success stories that they had after listening to my CD—and hearing that was all I needed. It helped those people reach and achieve their personal goals. Then I decided to give as much help as possible and started booking myself with any sales manager who wanted to have me speak to his or her group.

Southwestern and Success Starts Now!™ asked me to be one of the founding partners and bring the philosophies of The Southwestern Company to the professional sales world. It's something I love; it's exciting talking about selling and helping people reach their goals both personally and professionally!

Wright

Southwestern's Success Starts Now!™ sales training division teaches the execution of fundamentals. What does that mean?

Hillis

We don't teach tricks. We don't talk about gimmicks that get people to buy product. We focus on techniques and principles that have been proven to work time and time again. Southwestern is a 150-year-old direct sales company. Every year 3,500 college students work out of state going door-to-door to sell educational reference books, software, and CDs to help students save time on homework.

Anyone who has forged his or her success principles in door-to-door selling will hear other sales managers and sales professionals say, "If you can do direct sales and you can sell books door-to-door, you can sell anything."

Execution of the fundamentals is our focus and we provide techniques or tools on how to be successful. The principles that Southwestern teaches are hard work, positive mental attitude, and how to work like a true sales professional by following the cycle of the sale.

Southwestern provides training on how to execute the cycle of the sale, which is something every salesperson does consciously or subconsciously when a sale is made. Sales professionals know the psychology behind why the selling cycle is important. It is designed to save time and increase production by following these seven steps:

1. Prospecting/Pre-Approach
2. Initial Contact
3. Qualifying
4. Presentation
5. Answering Objections
6. Closing
7. Referrals/Follow up

Wright

What's the difference between a top producer and an average producer?

Hillis

The common thread of all top producers is the combination of habits they form and act out every single day. In the book *The Common Denominator of Success,* Albert Gray relates that, "The common denominator of success—the secret of success of every man who has ever been successful—lies in the fact that he formed the habit of doing things that failures don't like to do." Top producers believe in that, and if you form the right habits you will become a top producer much faster.

All top producers form three common habits regardless of the industry:

1. They focus on being a student of the game. They always want to learn and expand their knowledge base. They are willing to be impacted with that knowledge and internalize it to use it. They never stop learning.

2. Top producers are competitive and always believe that the difference between being an average producer and a top producer is that you have to have a competitive edge. Being competitive is not necessarily a gift or innate, but the key is conditioning yourself to be competitive with everything you do. This doesn't mean only being competitive with others—it can also mean self-competition that will drive you to success.

   At Success Starts Now!™, we talk about techniques for setting goals designed for hitting your Maximum Earning Potential (M.E.P.). We teach about taking incremental steps to hit a large goal; we call this "The Slight Edge." It's defined as doing an activity a little bit more than the competition every single day. This results in a huge difference that will separate you from the competition. For example: A marksman is shooting at a bull's-eye a mile away. If he adjusts his sights one click, it will result in a major change in the direction of the bullet and whether or not it hits the bull's-eye. If the marksman clicks his sight more than one click he could be completely off the target!

3.   Top producers are goal oriented. They review their goals daily and have action items to achieve their goals. They are also accountable to those goals. My business partner, and one of our motivational speakers, Gary Michels, has developed what's called "The Ideal Wheel." You set goals through the seven different quadrants of your life and put action items on how to hit your goal. You share your action items with an accountability partner who can help you get there.

The difference between average producers and top producers are these three habits:

1. Be a student of the Game. Be like a sponge and absorb knowledge all the time. No matter what your production level is, you can always do better.

2. Cultivate a competitive edge with yourself and others by using The Slight Edge theory.

3. Set goals daily and focus on action items that help you hit the goal.

That is the Southwestern winning formula.

Wright

What are the factors needed to reach Maximum Earning Potential and finish number one?

Hillis

The reason people do not reach their true potential is because they subconsciously build barriers that cause self-doubt. They don't believe they can hit high goals. The three most important characteristics for breaking belief barriers are commitment, control, and confidence.

1. Commitment is doing the work—putting in the effort with no excuses! Top producers do not make excuses; they stay committed.

   When I think of commitment I am reminded of a time when I was working in Southwest Missouri in McDonald County. I was selling books door-to-door. While in Missouri, I had over ten flat tires in three months! I had so many flat tires I started timing myself with a stopwatch as if I were on a NASCAR pit crew. So I find myself in the middle of nowhere, on a mile-long driveway (scenery common to that area). The driveway passed through a canopy of trees.

   As I was changing the tire trying to beat my pit crew record time, I noticed my arm looked like my skin was crawling. Upon further inspection I realized I was completely covered in ticks! I don't know about you, but when people ask me what my favorite critter is I don't say ticks. So what did I do? I reacted the same way any other rational human being would—I flipped out! I stripped down buck naked and threw my clothes in a plastic bag so ticks would not get in the car. Then I drove to the nearest gas station. I hopped out, but realized I'd better put my pants back on. So after that embarrassing incident, I ran into the gas station with no shirt and no shoes.

   An older lady looked at me and said "Son, what's wrong with you?" I replied "I've got *ticks!*" So I grabbed a razor and ran to the bathroom. Now as I was looking at myself in the mirror and trying to pick the ticks off, I had a deep sense of doubt. I wanted to quit what I was doing, go home, and use this as a reason why I didn't hit my goal. But, something inside of me said No. I had committed to my sales manager, my friends, parents, and (more importantly) to myself I was not going to quit on a single day, week, or month. So I shaved the ticks off one by one. I went on and finished my day. That day was not my most productive day, but it was my most important because after that experience I knew nothing would stop me from fulfilling my commitments from then on.

2. There are certain things in life that we cannot control, such as death, natural disasters, flat tires, ticks, or even who buys from us. Top producers realize this so they focus

on controlling the controllable factors. Those factors are the number of hours we work, the amount of calls or prospecting we do in a day, and our attitude.

Now you're probably saying "that sounds good, but how am I supposed to do this?" We teach a technique called R.A.F.T. This helps harness emotion from an uncontrollable event and creates a positive outcome. R.A.F.T. is an acronym that stands for:

Realize an event is occurring.

Accept the situation.

Focus on the controllable (hours, calls, and attitude).

Transform the negative emotion into positive momentum.

I came up with this technique when I was working in Fairbanks, Alaska—the only place on earth you will see a sign that says "North Pole, next exit." One day I received a call from my teenage brother.

"Hello."

"Dude, we have to talk . . . it's about Mom and Dad."

My parents had been married for twenty-five years and on that day I found out they were getting a divorce. I felt mad, frustrated, confused, and worst of all, I couldn't find the number for Dr. Phil—my head was out of the ballgame. So I applied the R.A.F.T. technique:

- Realized an event was occurring—by my productivity stopping.
- Accepted the situation—even though I didn't want to.
- Focused on my hours and calls. My attitude was hard to control so I was using positive phrases to keep my Positive Mental Attitude (P.M.A.) right. (More about P.M.A. later.)
- Transformed the negative energy into positive momentum by putting on the blinders and going to work.

In spite of how I felt emotionally, this technique helped me focus professionally. Everyone has moments fraught with personal conflict or hardship, but it doesn't need to be an excuse that hinders you in the workplace. My parents' situation was out of control, but by applying the R.A.F.T. technique, I focused on what I could control. As a result, I made more commission that week than anyone in the history of The Southwestern Company. As a junior in college, in one week I made over $15,000 and had over sixty customers selling books door-to-door!

3. The last factor in breaking belief barriers and becoming number one in your industry is unconditional confidence. Why is unconditional confidence important? People are attracted to it, it evokes trust, and people will be led to take action by unconditional confidence.

Wright

What is Unconditional Confidence and how is it defined?

Hillis

There are three types of confidence: False, Conditional, and Unconditional.

- False Confidence is saying you can do something, but deep down inside you think there is no way you can actually do the task. It's negative self-talk. A good example is someone who, when with their group of friends talks and acts as though they were superman or superwoman, but when put into an unfamiliar selling situation, they change from superman to super-scared. False confidence comes from F.E.A.R. which is defined by Tony Robbins as False Evidence Appearing Real.

- Conditional Confidence is why this job can be frustrating. The job of sales can be emotional. Why do you think that is? It's because we attach our self-worth to whether or not we make a sale. Many people have made one, two, or three sales in a row and their confidence goes way up. Then they go a day, a week, or a month with no sales and what happens to their confidence? Right! It hits peaks and valleys like a roller coaster. This confidence is conditional on the outcome.

- The last and most important factor that separates all top producers from average producers is *unconditional confidence.*

Top Producers who strive for unconditional confidence have that something special—charisma, or what Austin Powers would call it: "mojo."

Unconditional confidence is based on knowing that you do have skills. The key is that your self-worth is not attached to how much you produce; your self-worth is based on effort.

A good positive affirmation to use when forming unconditional confidence is saying to yourself every day when you look into the mirror:

"I do not expect success all the time, but due to the belief in my own abilities and acquired skills I can be fearless in the moment. In reality, self-worth has nothing to do with the outcome. So when the pressure comes, I cannot hesitate. Knowing sometimes I will do well and sometimes I won't, regardless, I know failure is temporary and success will happen with perseverance."

Wright

How did you finish number one out of 3,500 salespeople at the Southwestern Company year after year, and even finish number one your first year?

Hillis

People are only as successful as the people with whom they choose to associate. How anyone can become a top producer starts with the mentors and influences surrounding them.

Some good examples are the role models I have chosen to learn from and who helped instill the belief and the drive that it takes to consistently be a top producer.

To start with, my grandfather taught me to never back down. When adversity comes, always stand up for what you believe and walk tall with the presence of someone who knows what he wants. So even if it's your first year of going into a business where a lot of people might be better than you are, if you believe in yourself then you can do anything you set your mind to do.

Then my dad taught me honesty, integrity, and faith. The reason people buy from you is because they like you and trust you. If you are honest and never misleading, they will trust you. Trust is instilled when your customer knows you want to do what's right for the betterment of the group you are working with, and they will like you and trust you in return. I always remember my dad saying, "I don't care *who* is right, I care about *what* is right." Adopting that philosophy engenders respect and trust.

My role models in athletics were wrestling and football coaches. They helped instill in my character a good work ethic and they helped infuse mental toughness within myself. To be the number one top producer in the field of sales you have to be mentally tough. You have to have a competitive edge and you have to have confidence. You have to know that anything is possible as long as you work hard and you are determined. I think I got that from my athletic coaches.

And then finally, what really forged all of this together and refined my techniques was working with The Southwestern Company. They took everything that I had gained from the past and then taught me techniques and systems that focused my energy into something productive.

For parents who have kids in college, or for those who are college age, The Southwestern Company of Nashville, Tennessee, is the best opportunity—not only to make a good amount of money while you're in college and during the summertime—but it's also the best opportunity for future employment and for developing the skills it takes to be a top producer upon entering the career arena of sales. At The Southwestern Company, you will find mentors and coaches to help guide you in the direction of success.

Wright

What skills did you develop working with Southwestern?

Hillis

The Southwestern Company's philosophy is "We build people, and people build companies." The coaches and trainers at Southwestern helped me develop traits I did not naturally have, such as attention to details. Being detail oriented is not a natural gift for many people, however, when one follows through on a daily detailed plan, a great deal of satisfaction and accomplishment results. People can become successful by doing the little, often mundane things that it takes to be successful. Being detail oriented in sales means two things:

One is focusing on the Cycle of the Sale as previously outlined. By making sure that every customer is qualified, getting objections out on the table, and eliminating procrastination by asking questions such as, "If we were to meet your needs, would this be something we could move forward with today, or should somebody else be involved in the decision-making process?" By asking questions this way, focus is on details and the small steps it takes to make a big difference in increasing personal production—The Slight Edge.

Another example of focusing on details is after meeting sales prospects, make sure to touch base with them six times. Send thank-you cards, make them feel important and special. Doing that will encourage people to like you and trust you—that's why they buy from you.

The second detail on which top producers focus is using positive affirmations and having a Positive Mental Attitude (P.M.A.). The techniques used in conditioning a P.M.A. are using positive affirmations and telling yourself what you are going to do before you do it, and then believing that you can do what you told yourself. Through positive affirmation your belief level is raised and you expect that whatever you're telling yourself over and over is going to happen. For example, if you call your customers and you are having negative thoughts about whether they will buy, then they're probably not going to buy. But if you're telling yourself all day long, "Everyone's getting them; this is going to be great," your reality is probably going to be success with your sales.

Focusing on those two things will be the difference between average producers and top producers.

Wright

When you broke the 150-year-old Southwestern Company sales record, you made a personal profit of over $100,000 in a matter of fourteen weeks and you did this while you were a junior in college. How did that feel?

Hillis

As a junior in college, it was great! To be honest, that summer it was more of a relief to just reach my goal and break the company record—I was not even concerned with the amount of money I was making. That's how focused I was on doing what I said I was going to do and hitting my goal. At Southwestern we keep track of production in units. With the goal to sell 20,000 units and after having sold 9,000 units the summer before (which was a really good year), my goal was to double my production. Then when I came out of the summer, and I actually hit the goal, I wasn't even focused on the fact that I had just made a hundred thousand dollars, I was more focused on being excited that I had hit my goal. That was great! Returning to college life with over $100,000 in the bank was a lot of fun!

Needless to say, we did a couple of trips and I did what any normal college student would do. The next year I needed to go back to work and break some more company records and make that money back. But it was great, it really was.

Wright

You achieved so many accomplishments at such an early age. What would you suggest for others to reach their goals quickly?

Hillis

Unconditional confidence and accountability for reaching goals are how people get a fast start and reach goals quickly.

Unconditional confidence is something that can be taught and it can be transferred from one person to another. To have confidence one has to have a passion for focusing on what can be controlled and know that it can be done—and then just find the way to make that happen.

Everyone should have a business coach to hold him or her accountable just as Olympic athletes have coaches to hold them accountable and serve as guides to winning the gold medal. To reach goals quickly and develop unconditional confidence, people need to find someone to help them get there. Those who are qualified to be accountability coaches are (ideally):

1. Those who have been where you want to go. Why is that? They know the path to success. Learn from the mistakes of others and don't take chances that are not necessary.

2. Those who have the same goal as you have. Why is that? Competition! A good example of two people who developed competition through sharing the same goal is Mark McGwire and Sammy Sosa who had the same goal—to break the homerun record for baseball. Mr. McGwire ended up on top and broke the record, but in the end Mr. Sosa and Mr. McGwire developed a deep respect for each other and helped each other get further than they ever would have on their own.

Wright

You played college football for two years. How did that help with your career in sales?

Hillis

The first time I experienced the passion I now have for doing sales training and being a motivational speaker was when I was the team captain in football and gave a motivational speech to the team before a big game. It was such a great feeling to get the whole team energized and ready to go out on the "battlefield." That was the first time I really felt the effects of what motivation can do, and saw the difference motivation can make in a player in a game.

If you have a football player who has all the talent in the world, but he's not motivated and not excited to do what he's out to do, he will not perform at optimal level. But you take that same player, get him playing with every bit of passion he has, and motivate him by getting him to understand what it means to win the game, he's going to produce and he's going to play or perform at a higher level. He will be motivated and inspired.

That's something I took away from playing football.

Wright

So what's up next for Dustin Hillis? What are your goals for the future?

Hillis

My goal is to help our company, The Southwestern Company and its sales training division Success Starts Now!™, be the number one sales training company in the world. Right now we have sales training in London, Scotland, and all throughout Europe. Here in the United States we are concentrating on big events and sales training conferences. Our next step is to focus on growing our training and coaching programs.

Right now I'm working on confidence coaching and helping people get to the next level of unconditional confidence and having consistency in their production.

We also want to provide customized training for businesses. We'll do three-day workshops (or longer if needed) and work with salespeople on a one-on-one basis.

The three services we want to provide are sales training and motivational events, personal coaching, and sales and leadership training through customized workshops to help businesses increase production.

Wright

What a great conversion. Dustin, I really appreciate your taking all this time with me today to answer all these questions. Sales is always on my mind all the time. I'm engaged in sales, as is almost everybody in one aspect or another. I think our readers will get a lot from what you are saying!

Hillis

This has been terrific and I'm looking forward to meeting each and every reader and each and every person who comes to our sales training conferences.

Wright

Today we have been talking with Dustin Hillis who is an expert on sales fundamentals. He teaches people tools and techniques for improving, as he calls it, "execution." He talks a lot about forming positive habits and using positive affirmations to get where we want to go. I don't know about you, but I'm going to listen to him. I think he knows what he is talking about.

Dustin, thank you so much for being with us today on *Speaking of Success.*

Hillis

Thank you and God bless.

About the Author

DUSTIN HILLIS has worked with The Southwestern Company since 2002. The company has a 150-year-old sales training program and has trained hundreds of thousands of sales professionals to do direct selling. Dustin finished number one out of 3,500 salespeople worldwide during his first year with The Southwestern Company. He then finished number one every year after that and eclipsed The Southwestern Company's all-time sales record for the most product sold in a single selling season. He is a founding partner in the Southwestern Seminars professional sales training division known as Success Starts Now!™, striving to help other sales professionals break records and reach goals of their own.

Dustin Hillis
Southwestern Seminars (Success Starts Now!™)
2451 Atrium Way
Nashville, Tennessee 37214
Phone: 615.260.0182
E-mail: dhillis@ssnseminars.com
www.ssnseminars.com

Chapter 4

Barbara Sexton Smith

THE INTERVIEW

David Wright (Wright)

Today we're talking with Barbara Sexton Smith. She has helped raise more than $181 million during the past twenty years for the Fund for the Arts, Metro United Way, Louisville Olmsted Parks Conservancy, the National Conference for Christians and Jews, and the West Louisville Boys and Girls Choirs. She also founded Quick Think Inc. whose vision is, "To teach you how to get others to do what you want!" Her clients include General Electric, Nissan, Alcoa, Humana, Norton Healthcare, Brown-Forman, Steel Technologies, and Kentucky Fried Chicken. In 1996 she was nominated for the Ernst & Young Entrepreneur of the Year Award. Along the way she has also helped raise seven children and managed to make sure that 450,000 schoolchildren have an arts experience every year.

As regional manager for Wendy's International in the early eighties she was selected from 3,000 managers worldwide as Wendy's Employee of the Year. She went on to become the National Franchise Director for the Fresher Cooker.

Barbara was appointed by Mayor Jerry Abramson to serve on the Metro Louisville Air Pollution Control District Board of Directors. Her other volunteer roles include:

- President, Voter Outreach Program
- President, Downtown Police Advisory Board
- Alcoa Community Advisory Board
- Simmons College of Kentucky Board of Trustees
- Chair, Interfaith Community Hunger Project

As a member of the International Speakers Network and the National Speakers Association, Barbara is a highly sought-after speaker who inspires every audience, every time.

Barbara, welcome to *Speaking of Success.*

Barbara Sexton Smith (Sexton Smith)
Thanks, David. I'm glad to be here.

Wright
Barbara, let's get right to it. What is the most success-defining moment of your life?

Sexton Smith
I survived an armed robbery—successfully!

Wright
What happened?

Sexton Smith
When I was twenty-three years old I was in all my glory working as a newly hired assistant manager for Wendy's and it was almost midnight. Four teenagers were cleaning up while I was completing the nightly paperwork.

All of a sudden the place went wild—loud noises, screaming, and someone pounding on the office door screaming as loud as he could, "Open the door or I'll blow her brains out!"

I had no choice. I opened the door and there he stood. The robber who had broken into the restaurant was interested in taking whatever money we had but he was also threatening to kill the sixteen-year-old girl he was holding if I didn't do exactly everything he said. Immediately, four teenagers were on the floor as he grabbed me and began to beat the daylights out of me, screaming for the money, and telling me to open the safe.

When he hit me on the back of the head with his sawed-off shotgun, blood went everywhere and I couldn't see anything. I couldn't see the numbers on the safe and I thought, "What in the world am I going to do?"

There was a child lying on the floor next to me (I'll never forget this) who was a young Catholic boy. He was saying "Our Fathers" (repeating the Lord's Prayer) and "Hail Marys" as fast as he could go.

"What are my own beliefs?" I wondered. At the time I had no idea. To tell you the truth, David, I hadn't given it much thought. But something told me that if I didn't figure out what to do right then and get help from somebody or something not in that room, those four teenagers were going to die. I wasn't worried about myself, I was worried about them.

I placed my hand on the safe and closed my eyes and I said, "If there's a God out there somewhere, if you'll move in here and open this safe and help me do the right things and get this guy out of here, I will follow you all the days of my life." I had not turned the dial on the safe because I couldn't see clearly. I lifted my arm and the safe opened! It was a miracle.

I handed that guy the money. He had hit me twenty-two times in the back and on the head. He yanked my ponytail around one last time and made me stare right down the barrel of his shotgun. He was getting ready to pull the trigger. But then he let go and left. There are now five people living to tell that story. And that was the moment I first believed! Talk about being successful!

Wright

So how do you define success?

Sexton Smith

In my opinion, success is simply a state of mind that you achieve by enriching the lives of others every day.

Wright

Speaking of enriching the lives of others, I heard an amazing story about how you brought your community together to help an impoverished boys' choir. Tell us about that.

Sexton Smith

In August 2000 I led the journey that took the West Louisville Boys Choir to London, England, and Paris, France, to perform six concerts in spring 2001. Upon their return to America we hosted a reception for the Choir members to thank the 400 plus people who contributed money to make the trip a reality. The University of Louisville became so impressed with the project that they promised full college scholarships to every choir member who stays in the Choir through high school, meets the minimum college entrance requirements, and stays out of trouble with the law! To most of these children "college" was just a word in the dictionary!

Wright

Who are these children and where do they come from?

Sexton Smith

We're talking about thirty-one young African-American men, ages eight to eighteen, living in the poorest neighborhoods of Louisville with 80 percent coming from single parent homes.

Wright

How did you find out about them?

Sexton Smith

I'll never forget the day I met Mr. McDaniel Bluitt, founder and director of the Choir. He looked right at me and said, "Barbara, it's more than music, it's sounds of hope. We try to instill hope in the hearts of these young men, and as a child 'thinketh in his heart, so is he.'" I thought, "Oh my gosh, I know those words!" They are from the book of Proverbs—Proverbs 23:7.

Wright

When did Mr. Bluitt start this program?

Sexton Smith

The program began in 1989 as part of the Moore Temple Boys Choir. However, in 1990 he sought new ways to expand the Choir's mission by using music to reach children from Louisville's inner city. He wanted to get young African-American men off the streets after school and give them something positive to do—keep them out of harm's way. This became a crime prevention program. It wasn't long before he realized they needed school tutors as well as etiquette coaching for putting their best foot forward during concerts.

Wright

How often and where do they perform?

Sexton Smith

They perform fifty to sixty concerts every year. They have performed at the Governor's Mansion in Frankfort, Kentucky, for the Kentucky Derby Breakfast. President Bill Clinton, when in office, heard of the West Louisville Boys Choir and asked that they perform in Washington, D.C., at the unveiling of the National African-American Civil War Monument, sculpted by Ed Hamilton, another one of Louisville's heroes. When that happened, Europe called. Ed is one of the many angels on this journey!

Wright

What did you do after hearing Mr. Bluitt's story?

Sexton Smith

Lacey (my husband) and I started raising money from every corner of the community but we were still about $20,000 short when the travel agency called for final payment. I asked for forty-eight more hours and they just laughed! Lacey told me to call Bob Hill, a columnist for the *Courier-Journal,* and ask him to write about the Boys Choir's plight. When I got Bob on the phone I introduced myself and said, "Sir, I have the second greatest story to ever be told and I want to share it with you to see if you'll write about it in tomorrow's paper. How 'bout it?"

Wright

Are you saying you were able to get this story in the newspaper?

Sexton Smith

Yes. Bob's article, which appeared February 27, 2001, was titled *Sounds of Hope* and ended with his quoting me, quoting McDaniel, "If you want to help instill hope in the hearts of these young men, send money to Barbara Sexton Smith," and he put our home address on the front page of the newspaper! I'm not kidding!

Wright

Did anyone send money to help the cause?

Sexton Smith

Did they ever! The postman delivered ninety-four envelopes the next day and eighty-eight the following day. Bob forwarded an e-mail to me from the president of the University of Louisville. The e-mail said, "Bob, I've only lived here for six years and I've never heard of the West Louisville Boys Choir but this is the best article you've ever written! Call that woman and ask her to call me."

When he answered his phone I said, "Sir, this is *that woman* in the newspaper."

He proceeded to tell me that he would raise the final $20,000 we needed if I would bring the Choir to sing two songs at his next Board of Trustees meeting. Not knowing exactly how this was going to work, we showed up at Papa John's Cardinal Stadium at the appointed time.

Wright

Now, just how did it work?

Sexton Smith

Well, I told the kids if they would go in there and sing two songs those folks would give them $20,000 and save the trip. I asked them if they knew what that meant. Cormac Parker said, "Sure! That means they're paying us $10,000 a song!"

Wright

I guess you're telling me that the trip was saved and a good time was had by all!

Sexton Smith

Yes. The kids sang, the Trustees wrote checks, and 218 more envelopes arrived in our mailbox in just one week. Thirty-one young men representing Louisville, Kentucky, USA, sang their hearts out in the Louvre, at Notre Dame Cathedral, and at the church where Princess Diana and Charles were married. Thirty-one young men's lives were changed forever.

Wright

Barbara, you mentioned something earlier about college scholarships for these kids. How did that work?

Sexton Smith

When the choir returned to Louisville the president of the University was so taken with the boys' spirit that he guaranteed every one of them full scholarships to the University of Louisville. That gave us the courage to start the West Louisville Girls Choir with the same scholarship opportunities. In spring 2006, O'Farrell Head will graduate from the University of Louisville as our first choir member to do so.

These children have literally changed my life. I'll be forever grateful to each and every one of them. The greatest reward of all is not in the having but in the doing.

Wright

This is an amazing story of hope but something tells me you navigated the ship every step of the way on your path to success.

Sexton Smith

I appreciate your vote of confidence but I think first and foremost you have to believe in a greater power. To be successful you must have a vision supported by your personal mission and a set of values that you live by every day. Then you must communicate that vision while embracing humility. You then have to share your testimony and display integrity at all times. You have to be honest with yourself and others at all times. I know it's not an easy list but it's a list worth doing.

I don't think I've mentioned fun. You've got to have fun in what you're doing!

The paths we choose in life are simply vehicles through which we will accomplish our real missions. These things we call jobs are simply vehicles in which we travel to accomplish a much greater mission. Think about it.

Wright

Looking out for others seems to be a big theme in your life. Do you think serving others is necessary to becoming successful?

Sexton Smith

Absolutely! I call this servanthood.

Wright

What do you mean by servanthood?

Sexton Smith

First you have to understand that it's not about you, it's about serving others. A servant-leader is someone who leads with his or her head, heart, and hand. You must think it, feel it, and do it. You've got to put feet to your feelings.

Wright

How do you do that?

Sexton Smith

Think about what's important—what you want to be remembered for, and what kind of legacy you want to leave. Feel that in your heart with passion and take action! To sum it up, you could say that thoughts without passion are simply figments of your imagination and passion without action is simply a dream. Action changes lives.

Wright

How does a leader turn this into success?

Sexton Smith

Leaders must hire the right people. Develop them. Then race to the bottom of the pyramid to lift them up and cheer them on to greatness.

Wright

What does this do to the typical organizational chart?

Sexton Smith

Turns it upside-down! This is where the *V-Factor* comes in—V as in victory. The *V-Factor* is simply a pyramid turned upside down with a value-driven leader at the bottom. Think about that for a minute. Take the typical organizational chart with the leader standing at the top. Turn it upside down and put your hands in the air. Down at the point is your heart—that's right where you as a leader stand with all your values. A value-driven leader with a vision will be right there pushing and catching and cheering everybody else on to victory—the *V-Factor!*

Wright

This sounds great but how do you convince an ego-driven leader to do this?

Sexton Smith

Servanthood requires a huge dose of humility. Pride has no place on the path to success because "Pride goeth before destruction, and an haughty spirit before a fall" (Proverbs 16:18). Fear and pride are on opposite sides of the coin. Fear is pride's first cousin and together they'll beat you every time. Your best defense is humility and confidence.

Wright

Is servanthood your favorite word?

Sexton Smith

No, my favorite word is "hope."

Wright

So why hope?

Sexton Smith

I think one enriches the lives of others by instilling hope in their hearts. Remember, it's not about you—a heart filled with hope is a powerful thing. "As a man thinketh in his heart, so is he" (Proverbs 23:7). Hope breeds an attitude of possibility, which in turn breeds self-confidence.

Wright

So you think self-confidence is critical to success?

Sexton Smith

Absolutely!

Wright

Why?

Sexton Smith

Self-confidence is the power within that gives you the will to achieve a greater purpose. I believe we were all put on this earth to leave it a little better than how we found it. That's the universal vision.

My personal mission (everyone should have one) is to instill hope in the hearts of everyone I meet. Hope breeds confidence. A self-confident person filled with hope is someone who has only positive expectations. The word hope stands for:

Having
Only
Positive
Expectations

Wright

How can someone instill hope in the heart of someone else?

Sexton Smith

To be successful you have to be able to connect with the emotional centers of the people you are leading. Find out where they are coming from and what is important to them. It's not about you. Communicate your vision/dream in a way that reflects your understanding of their interests. Successful leaders communicate their vision in a way that makes people feel connected to the dream.

Wright

What do you mean by "their interests"?

Sexton Smith

You have to find out what their hopes and fears are. You have to show them how they can be part of something that is much bigger than they are—that's the vision. I believe people see themselves in relation to others; that's how it was all planned to be. You have to help each other develop a sense of belonging—a sense of purpose. A purpose-driven life is a life worth living.

Wright

How do you get this confidence you have talked so much about?

Sexton Smith

I think you get self-confidence by taking a chance and making it; by having faith in a greater power. Fear and confidence are opposite sides of a coin. You've got to release that fear within and replace it with self-confidence.

Wright

So how do you know when you're successful?

Sexton Smith

People define success in many different ways. When you spend most if not all your time trying to catch other people doing the right thing instead of looking for what they're doing wrong, you are successful—you get it. I learned this when I worked at Wendy's.

Many people want to evaluate success based on monetary gain and material possessions. I never did. I probably felt most successful when the president of an organization I was working for stood up and introduced me to everyone as "God's Cheerleader." I felt pretty darn good that day. That's real success in my book!

Wright

So who are the successful people you've known and why do you think they're successful?

Sexton Smith

I've been very fortunate. I have had a number of really good mentors, some of whom I will always remember. The first is Brad Ray, Chairman of the Board, Steel Technologies, a $1.3 billion company. Brad placed his employees and their families at the top of his organizational chart. When asked what he loses sleep over, he looked out over the audience and said, "Making sure that our employees and families are provided for." Brad gets it.

Wright

What about folks you have worked with? Has anyone been successful according to your definition?

Sexton Smith

The best example would be Rob Reifsnyder who served as president of Metro United Way. I got to see a real CEO in action. "CEO" in my opinion stands for Chief Expectation Officer. Rob never demanded anything. He always expected exceptional performance from everyone every day. From the maintenance crew to the senior management team, he expected everyone to surpass their goals.

As a result, Metro United Way led the nation three years in a row in highest percentage increase in dollars raised for our community and we were judged against 2,600 United Way organizations. Each year we achieved 12 percent increases. Did we enrich the lives of others? We were able to help more than 300,000 people every year, not to mention the 100,000 donors who became part of something much greater themselves.

Wright

Sounds like Rob played a key role in your career path. Are there any women who have influenced you along the way?

Sexton Smith

Sure. In 1999, Minx Auerbach asked me to take the lead and help her raise money to preserve and protect our precious Olmsted Park system. Minx had a reputation for asking a lot of others but you knew she was always right in there giving it her all every step of the way! As a result the Olmsted Outrageous Halloween Party has become one of the community's most highly attended events each year. It has raised more than $800,000! Hats off to Minx and all of her followers!

Joan Riehm is another one. As Deputy Mayor, Joan has been one of Louisville Mayor Jerry Abramson's greatest assets in running our great city. Joan is successful because she is the quintessential listener. She always makes time to listen to people. She immediately starts connecting people who can add value to one another.

I'll never forget the day I was waiting in the mayor's lobby for a meeting with Joan. As she came through the door she said, "Oh my gosh, Tom, you have to meet Barbara. She can really help you and you can help her." Well, Dr. Thomas Crawford, Chemistry Professor Emeritus at the University of Louisville was standing there. He had stopped by to drop off information for a program the city was co-funding with the University of Louisville.

Later that afternoon Dr. Tom called me and asked if I would help him identify fifteen dynamic people who would become the Stephen Covey certified trainers for the *Seven Habits of Highly Effective Teens.* I agreed to help him and so together, thanks to Joan's introduction, Dr. Tom and I recruited fifteen folks who are now certified Covey trainers. Through this program we have enriched the lives of more than 700 African-American youth in our community with many more to follow.

Wright

I'm pretty impressed with the number of well-known, successful businesses headquartered in Louisville. How about some of those folks?

Sexton Smith

You must be talking about David Novak, Chairman of the Board of Yum! Brands Inc., the largest restaurant company in the world with more than 33,000 restaurants. Many outside the company don't realize that Yum! is an acronym and stands for You Understand Me!

David believes that if management can understand the needs of their employees, only then can they treat each employee as though he or she is the most important person in the world. He believes that employees will in turn treat customers as though they're the most important people in the world. You can read all about it in *Customer Mania,* one of Ken Blanchard's bestselling books.

Wright

This all sounds great but do you think the folks at Yum! really walk the talk?

Sexton Smith

I witnessed David walking his talk during the Fund for the Arts Employee Campaign. I was asked to host *Yum! Idol,* fashioned after the ever-so-popular *American Idol* television show. The contest lasted five days. David was seen on the front row more than once. Why? Because this event was important to his employees and he wanted them to know they were important to him. He moved the senior management team meeting across town to the service center so they could experience the excitement alongside the employees.

Successful leaders reach out to their followers. They're not afraid to meet them in their comfort zones. David is enriching the lives of others—all 804,000 plus employees worldwide.

Wright

Some people might say it's easy to be considered successful when you run a company that big. Can you think of someone you consider successful who is running a small company in Louisville?

Sexton Smith

One unsung hero is Cathy Zion. Cathy is President and Publisher of *Today's Woman,* one of the most successful women's magazines in America. Cathy publicly and privately gives all credit consistently to her staff. It's amazing! She says they're the real heroes behind the magazine's success and she's enriched their lives by trusting in their talents and lifting them up. Cathy is a good example of the *V-Factor:* Vision. Values. Victory. (Remember the upside-down pyramid?)

Wright

When I hear you mention vision it reminds me of those framed vision statements I see hanging on people's walls. Will you give us an example of someone who really puts it into action?

Sexton Smith

Sure. Steve Williams is President and CEO of Norton Healthcare in Louisville, Kentucky. Steve has done the very thing Stephen Covey teaches—to "begin with the end in mind." During his senior year in college, Steve served as my husband's legislative aide in the Kentucky State Senate.

As the story goes, one day Steve walked into Lacey's office and said, "Hey Senator, I'm going to have a career in the healthcare industry and someday I'm going to be the administrator of a major hospital. Can you give me any advice?" Steve now enriches the lives of more than 9,800 employees and their families not to mention the thousands of satisfied patients every year. Lacey must have said some pretty powerful words that day!

Wright

I've met a number of very motivated young people during my life. Can you think of someone just starting out who measures up to your definition of success?

Sexton Smith

Bristol Lansman (Coach). At twenty-one years old Bristol was named the youngest varsity field hockey coach in America at Atherton High School. As a ninth-grader she formed the first girls' high school crew team in Kentucky at the Collegiate School. Following that, as a junior at Assumption High School, she helped form the first girls' high school ice hockey team in Kentucky. She gets it. Bristol understands the power of Title IX, the federal legislation requiring sports opportunities for female athletes. She learned the importance of this from Lacey, her step-dad.

While in the State Senate, Lacey worked on the legislation that brought funding to sports programs for girls in Kentucky high schools. We have college scholarships going to female athletes all across Kentucky. These young women would have never had a chance before had it not been for Lacey and Bristol.

Wright

Once people become successful, are they always successful?

Sexton Smith

Absolutely not. Success starts over each morning when you get the wake-up call. We all play the most important sport—it's the game of life. There is only one coach. When I get the wake-up call, it's the same one you get—I don't question a thing. I get up and say, "Send me in, coach! I'm ready to play!"

Of course you have to have game rules when you're in sports. The game rules in the game of life are very simple: (1) you have to have faith and believe in yourself; (2) hope for the best; (3) you have to love yourself; and (4) you have to have rhythm—you have to be a rhythm-maker.

Wright

Rhythm-maker—is this how you motivate yourself to be successful every day?

Sexton Smith

Yes. I use the rhythm method! Now don't be misled. I'm talking about the rhythm method of *worth* control. I developed this system and anyone can follow it (everyone *should* follow it). I believe you determine your self-worth by the rhythm you choose every day. It's just that simple. You may not be able to choose what happens throughout the day but you have complete power over choosing how you will feel about it and what you will do about it.

Success is a state of mind that you choose, which is directly related to your self-worth. So you have to have a rhythm others can't knock—this is your R-O-C-K—your foundation. If you build a house on sand, it's going to end up in the sea. If you build it on a rock, it's going to stand forever. Successful people are rhythm-makers and unsuccessful people are rhythm-breakers. Your R-O-C-K is a state of mind. It's all in the big A—your attitude. Attitude is a choice.

Wright

So how does having a R-O-C-K help you achieve success?

Sexton Smith

I believe people want to follow a leader who has a strong foundation. It communicates to others that you have a vision. You're committed, you'll make tough decisions, and you have the confidence it takes to let the followers shine and share the glory when you all cross the finish line together.

This is a good place to mention *"followership"*—another one of my favorite words. You have to understand how to follow in order to be a successful leader. Leaders should constantly be helping their followers understand how what they are doing as followers fits into the vision as presented by the leader. Maybe we need to teach classes in followership. Heaven knows there are many more followers than there are leaders.

Wright

Is adversity important to becoming successful? If so, what role does it play?

Sexton Smith

I love adversity because I know that when it comes knocking, therein lies a rich opportunity for growth. You must have growth opportunities to become successful and I call these the tests we take in life. The eagle stirs up the nest so the young might learn to fly. My experience has shown that the harder the test, the greater the testimony. We really are transformed by trouble.

Wright

So how do you handle adversity?

Sexton Smith

My first reaction is to embrace it with my eyes and my ears wide open. I see opportunity in every problem, whereas a pessimist is going to see a problem in every opportunity. I also tend to look for differences among the parties because that is where the real opportunities exist. I think you have to develop a mindset to build on these differences to make the pie bigger.

Wright

So, who has influenced your life the most?

Sexton Smith

Mom and Dad. You can't ever forget where you came from, never. That's where I get grounded. I watched every move they made and hung onto every word they said. My dad taught me the importance of a strong work ethic and effective followership. He called it "towing the company line." And Mom always said, "Barbara Ann, if you don't have anything nice to say, don't say anything at all. Just remember, you made your bed, now sleep in it!" Mom had a way with words; that was her way of telling me to be decisive, be committed, and lift others up along the way.

My mom was living in Eastern Kentucky near Fightin' Holler when her daddy died in the coal mining camp. This caused my grandmother to send four children under the age of nine to an orphanage in Lexington. Mom and Aunt Cleta ended up at the Kentucky Baptist Orphanage in Louisville. When Mom met Dad, he was studying engineering at Virginia Polytechnic Institute on a diving scholarship. His father, who had been in charge of purchasing for Westinghouse, had just passed away. Dad came to Louisville as a young man in college to visit an older brother who had moved here to work in the ammunition plant during World War II. Uncle Stuart told Dad, "There are many beautiful orphans to pick from down here!"

Uncle Stuart chose Flossie, Dad chose Mom, and when two worlds collide great things can happen!

Wright

We all know you cannot be successful by yourself. How have you engaged others along the way?

Sexton Smith

Throughout the years I have recruited, trained, and motivated thousands of volunteers who have come on board with whatever project I was working on. It's all about negotiation—it's a matter of getting others to do what you want.

Wright

I understand that you teach the Street-Smart Principled Negotiation Program in businesses all over the country. Who benefits the most?

Sexton Smith

Anyone who tries to get others to do what they want.

Wright

So what makes your program different?

Sexton Smith

Street-Smart Principled Negotiation is different because our program goal is to actually modify the negotiation behavior of the participants so as to produce increases in revenue and profitability and to produce improvements in productivity for their companies. We teach interest-based negotiation, which moves the parties away from polarization caused by positional bargaining. The parties jointly seek solutions to the issues between them. This prevents the negotiation process from becoming a contest of wills.

The program teaches ways to identify the interests of both parties and how to generate options to meet those interests. We then teach how to use standards to craft solutions that are legitimate and fair. We teach both parties how to frame positions so they can have an optimal opportunity of being agreed to.

At the end of the day participants walk away with techniques they can use immediately to become better negotiators.

Wright

How will they benefit? What's in it for them?

Sexton Smith

First of all they will use the R.E.A.L. ROI system of measurement to improve results that we've developed. They will:

1. Own a practical framework to negotiate with every day,
2. Grow their business and increase their productivity,
3. Sharpen their negotiation skills,
4. Master change and catapult effectiveness,
5. Build better relationships,
6. Learn how to solve their own toughest problems, and
7. Make more durable deals.

Wright

What a great conversation. I have learned a lot here today and I really do appreciate this time you have spent with me here answering all these questions. I've been taking copious notes and I'm really learning.

Do you have any final thoughts?

Sexton Smith

Yes. Success is a state of mind that you achieve by enriching the lives of others. It's not about you. You define your own success. The feeling and thinking—that's the easy part, but it is what we finally choose to do that makes all the difference, not just for those whom we serve but for ourselves. Our actions define who we are and what we think is important.

We must get and give hope. We were all put on this earth to leave it a little better than how we found it. Now, go do it and do it today!

Wright

Today we've been talking with Barbara Sexton Smith. Over the past twenty years she has been responsible for helping to raise more than $181 million for the arts, education, health and human services, and the never-ending fight against racism, bias, and bigotry. In all of her pursuits—civic as well as business—she is a team-builder, a team leader, a motivator, an innovator, and it could be argued that she personifies entrepreneurship.

Barbara, thank you so much for being with us today on *Speaking of Success.*

About the Author

BARBARA SEXTON SMITH is among the top ten speakers for the International Speakers Network and is a nominee for the 2007 Woman of Achievement Award. She was named the 2003 Community Angel by *Today's Woman*. She and her husband, Lacey, received the 2006 McDaniel Bluitt Hope Award for instilling hope in the hearts of so many young people.

Barbara Sexton Smith
Quick Think Seminars
711 West Main Street
Louisville, Kentucky 40202
Phone: 502.583.0467
E-mail: barbara@barbarasextonsmith.com
www.barbarasextonsmith.com

Chapter 5

DR. STEPHEN R. COVEY

THE INTERVIEW

David Wright (Wright)

We're talking today with Dr. Stephen R. Covey, cofounder and vice-chairman of Franklin Covey Company, the largest management company and leadership development organization in the world. Dr. Covey is perhaps best known as the author of *The 7 Habits of Highly Effective People* which is ranked as a number one best seller by the *New York Times*, having sold more than fourteen million copies in thirty-eight languages throughout the world. Dr. Covey is an internationally respected leadership authority, family expert, teacher, and organizational consultant. He has made teaching principle-centered living and principle-centered leadership his life's work. Dr. Covey is the recipient of the Thomas More College Medallion for Continuing Service to Humanity and has been awarded four honorary doctorate degrees. Other awards given Dr. Covey include the Sikh's 1989 International Man of Peace award, the 1994 International Entrepreneur of the Year award, *Inc.* magazine's Services Entrepreneur of the Year award, and in 1996 the National Entrepreneur of the Year Lifetime Achievement award for Entrepreneurial leadership. He has also been recognized as one of *Time* magazine's twenty-five most influential Americans and one of Sales and Marketing Management's top twenty-five power brokers. Dr. Covey earned his undergraduate degree from the University of Utah, his MBA from Harvard, and completed his doctorate at Brigham Young University. While at Brigham Young he served as assistant to the President and was also a professor of business management and organizational behavior.

Dr. Covey, welcome to *Speaking of Success!*

Dr. Stephen Covey (Covey)

Thank you.

Wright

Dr. Covey, most companies make decisions and filter them down through their organization. You, however, state that no company can succeed until individuals within it succeed. Are the goals of the company the result of the combined goals of the individuals?

Covey

Absolutely, because if people aren't on the same page, they're going to be pulling in different directions. To teach this concept, I frequently ask large audiences to close their eyes and point north, and then to keep pointing and open their eyes and they find themselves pointing all over the place. I say to them, "Tomorrow morning if you want a similar experience, ask the first ten people you meet in your organization what the purpose of your organization is and you'll find it's a very similar experience. They'll point all over the place." When people have a different sense of purpose and values, every decision that is made from then on is governed by those. There's no question that this is one of the fundamental causes of misalignment, low trust, interpersonal conflict, interdepartmental rivalry, people operating on personal agendas, and so forth.

Wright

Is that mostly a result of the inability to communicate from the top?

Covey

That's one aspect, but I think it's more fundamental. There's an inability to involve people—an unwillingness. Leaders may communicate what their mission and their strategy is, but that doesn't mean there's any emotional connection to it. Mission statements that are rushed and then announced are soon forgotten. They become nothing more than just a bunch of platitudes on the wall that mean essentially nothing and even create a source of cynicism and a sense of hypocrisy inside the culture of an organization.

Wright

How do companies ensure survival and prosperity in these tumultuous times of technological advances, mergers, downsizing, and change?

Covey

I think that it takes a lot of high trust in a culture that has something that doesn't change—principles—at its core. There are principles that people agree upon that are valued. It gives a sense of stability. Then you have the power to adapt and be flexible when you experience these kinds of disruptive new economic models or technologies that come in and sideswipe you. You don't know how to handle them unless you have something you can depend upon. If people have not agreed to a common set of principles that guide them and a common purpose, then they get their security from the outside and they tend to freeze the structure, systems, and processes inside and they cease becoming adaptable. They don't change with the changing realities of the new marketplace out there and gradually they become obsolete.

Wright

I was interested in one portion of your book *The 7 Habits of Highly Effective People* where you talk about behaviors. How does an individual go about the process of replacing ineffective behaviors with effective ones?

Covey

I think that for most people it usually requires a crisis that humbles them to become aware of their ineffective behaviors. If there's not a crisis the tendency is to perpetuate those behaviors and not change. You don't have to wait until the marketplace creates the crisis for you. Have everyone accountable on a 360 degree basis to everyone else they interact with—with feedback either formal or informal— where they are getting data as to what's happening. They will then start to realize that the consequences of their ineffective behavior require them to be humble enough to look at that behavior and to adopt new, more effective ways of doing things. Sometimes people can be stirred up to this if you just appeal to their conscience—to their inward sense of what is right and wrong. A lot of people sometimes know inwardly they're doing wrong, but the culture doesn't necessarily discourage them from continuing that. They either need feedback from people, or they need feedback from the marketplace, or they need feedback from their conscience. Then they can begin to develop a step-by-step process of replacing old habits with new, better habits.

Wright

It's almost like saying, "Let's make all the mistakes in the laboratory before we put this thing in the air."

Covey

Right; and I also think what is necessary is a paradigm shift, which is analogous to having a correct map, say of a city or of a country. If people have an inaccurate paradigm of life, of other people, and of themselves it really doesn't make much difference what their behavior or habits or attitudes are. What they need is a correct paradigm—a correct map—that describes what's going on. For instance, in the Middle Ages they used to heal people through bloodletting. It wasn't until Samuel Weiss and Pasteur and other empirical scientists discovered the germ theory that they realized for the first time they weren't dealing with the real issue. They realized why women preferred to use midwives who washed rather than doctors who didn't wash. They gradually got a new paradigm. Once you've got a new paradigm then your behavior and your attitude flows directly from it. If you have a bad paradigm or a bad map, let's say of a city, there's no way, no matter what your behavior or your habits or your attitudes are—how positive they are—you'll never be able to find the location you're looking for. This is why I believe that to change paradigms is far more fundamental than to work on attitude and behavior.

Wright

One of your seven habits of highly effective people is to begin with the end in mind. If circumstances change and hardships or miscalculation occurs, how does one view the end with clarity?

Covey

Many people think to begin with the end in mind means that you have some fixed definition of a goal that's accomplished and if changes come about you're not going to adapt to them. Instead, the "end in mind" you begin with is that you are going to create a flexible culture of high trust so that no matter what comes along you are going to do whatever it takes to accommodate that new change or that new reality and maintain a culture of high performance and high trust. You're talking more in terms of values and overall purposes that don't change, rather than specific strategies or programs that will have to change to accommodate the changing realities in the marketplace.

Wright

In this time of mistrust between people, corporations, and nations for that matter, how do we create high levels of trust?

Covey

That's a great question and it's complicated because there are so many elements that go into the creating of a culture of trust. Obviously the most fundamental one is just to have trustworthy people. But that is not sufficient because what if the organization itself is misaligned? For instance, what if you say you value cooperation but you really reward people for internal competition? Then you have a systemic or a structure problem that creates low trust inside the culture even though the people themselves are trustworthy. This is one of the insights of Edward Demming and the work he did. That's why he said that most problems are not personal; they're systemic. They're common caused. That's why you have to work on structure, systems, and processes to make sure that they institutionalize principle-centered values. Otherwise you could have good people with bad systems and you'll get bad results.

When it comes to developing interpersonal trust between people, it is made up of many, many elements such as taking the time to listen to other people, to understand them, and to see what is important to them. What we think is important to another may only be important to us, not to another. It takes empathy. You have to make and keep promises to them. You have to treat them with kindness and courtesy. You have to be completely honest and open. You have to live up to your commitments. You can't betray them behind their back. You can't badmouth them behind their back and sweet-talk them to their face. That will send out vibes of hypocrisy and it will be detected. You have to learn to apologize when you make mistakes, to admit mistakes, and to also get feedback going in every direction as much as possible. It doesn't necessarily require formal forums; it requires trust between people that will be open with each other and give each other feedback.

Wright

My mother told me to do a lot of what you're saying now, but it seems like when I got in business I simply forgot.

Covey

Sometimes we forget, but sometimes culture doesn't nurture it. That's why I say unless you work with the institutionalizing—that means formalizing into structure, systems, and processes the values—you will not have a nurturing culture. You have to constantly work on that. This is one of the big mistakes organizations make. They think trust is simply a function of being honest. That's only one small aspect. It's an important aspect, obviously, but there are so many other elements that go into the creation of a high trust culture.

Wright

"Seek first to understand then to be understood" is another of your seven habits. Do you find that people try to communicate without really understanding what other people want?

Covey

Absolutely. The tendency is to project out of our own autobiography—our own life, our own value system—onto other people, thinking we know what they want. So we don't really listen to them. We pretend to listen, but we really don't listen from within their frame of reference. We listen from within our own frame of reference and we're really preparing our reply rather than seeking to understand. This is a very common thing. In fact very few people have had any training in seriously listening. They're trained in how to read, write, and speak, but not to listen.

Reading, writing, speaking, and listening are the four modes of communication and they represent about two-thirds to three-fourths of our waking hours. About half of that time is spent listening, but it's the one skill people have not been trained in. People have had all this training in the other forms of communication. In a large audience of

1,000 people you wouldn't have more than twenty people who have had more than two weeks of training in listening. Listening is more than a skill or a technique so that you're listening within another frame of reference. It takes tremendous courage to listen because you're at risk when you listen. You don't know what's going to happen; you're vulnerable.

Wright

Sales gurus always tell me that the number one skill in selling is listening.

Covey

Yes—listening from within the customer's frame of reference. That is so true. You can see that it takes some security to do that because you don't know what's going to happen.

Wright

With our *Speaking of Success!* talk show and book we're trying to encourage people in our audience to be better, to live better, and be more fulfilled by listening to the examples of our guests. Is there anything or anyone in your life that has made a difference for you and helped you to become a better person?

Covey

I think the most influential people in my life have been my parents. I think that what they modeled was not to make comparisons and harbor jealousy or to seek recognition. They were humble people. I remember my mother one time when we were going up in an elevator and the most prominent person in the state was in the elevator. She knew him, but she spent her time talking to the elevator operator. I was just a little kid and I was so awed by this person and I said to my mom, "Why didn't you talk to the important person?" She said, "I was. I had never met him." They were really humble, modest people who were focused on service and other people rather than on themselves. I think they were very inspiring models to me.

Wright

In almost every research paper that anyone I've ever read writes about people who influenced their lives, in the top five people, three of them are teachers. My seventh grade English teacher was the greatest teacher I ever had and influenced me to no end.

Covey

Would it be correct to say that she saw in you probably some qualities of greatness you didn't even see in yourself?

Wright

Absolutely.

Covey

That's been my general experience that the key aspect of a mentor or a teacher is someone who sees in you potential that you don't even see in yourself. They treat you accordingly and eventually you come to see it in yourself. That's my definition of leadership or influence— communicating people's worth and potential so clearly that they are inspired to see it in themselves.

Wright

Most of my teachers treated me as a student, but she treated me with much more respect than that. As a matter of fact, she called me Mr. Wright in the seventh grade. I'd never been addressed by anything but a nickname. I stood a little taller; she just made a tremendous difference. Do you think there are other characteristics that mentors seem to have in common?

Covey

I think they are first of all good examples in their own personal lives. Their personal lives and their family lives are not all messed up—they come from a base of good character. They also are usually very confident and they take the time to do what your teacher did to you—to treat you with uncommon respect and courtesy.

They also, I think, explicitly teach principles rather than practices so that rules don't take the place of human judgment. You gradually come to have faith in your own judgment in making decisions because of the affirmation of such a mentor. Good mentors care about you— you can feel the sincerity of their caring. It's like the expression, "I don't care how much you know until I know how much you care."

Wright

Most people are fascinated with the new television shows about being a survivor. What has been the greatest comeback that you've made from adversity in your career or your life?

Covey

When I was in grade school I experienced a disease in my legs. It caused me to use crutches for a while. I tried to get off them fast and get back. The disease wasn't corrected yet so I went back on crutches for another year. The disease went to the other leg and I went on for another year. It essentially took me out of my favorite thing—athletics—and it took me more into being a student. So that was kind of a life-defining experience which at the time seemed very negative, but has proven to be the basis on which I've focused my life—being more of a learner.

Wright

Principle-centered learning is basically what you do that's different from anybody I've read or listened to.

Covey

The concept is embodied in the far-eastern expression, "Give a man a fish, you feed him for the day; teach him how to fish, you feed him for a lifetime." When you teach principles that are universal and timeless, they don't belong to just any one person's religion or to a particular culture or geography. They seem to be timeless and universal like the ones we've been talking about here: trustworthiness, honesty, caring, service, growth, and development. These are universal principles. If you focus on these things then little by little people become independent of you and then they start to believe in themselves and their own judgment becomes better. You don't need as many rules. You don't need as much bureaucracy and as many controls and you can empower people.

The problem in most business operations today—and not just business but non-business—is that they're using the industrial model in an information age. Arnold Toynbee, the great historian, said, "You can pretty well summarize all of history in four words: nothing fails like success." The industrial model was based on the asset of the machine. The information model is based on the asset of the person—the knowledge worker. It's an altogether different model. But the machine model was the main asset of the twentieth century. It enabled productivity to increase fifty times. The new asset is intellectual and social capital—the qualities of people and the quality of the relationship they have with each other. Like Toynbee said, "Nothing fails like success." The industrial model does not work in an information age. It requires a focus on the new wealth, not capital and material things.

A good illustration that demonstrates how much we were into the industrial model, and still are, is to notice where people are on the balance sheet. They're not found there. Machines are found there. Machines become investments. People are on the profit and loss statement and people are expenses. Think of that—if that isn't blood-letting.

Wright

It sure is.

When you consider the choices you've made down through the years, has faith played an important role in your life?

Covey

It has played an extremely important role. I believe deeply that we should put principles at the center of our lives, but I believe that God is the source of those principles. I did not invent them. I get credit sometimes for some of the Seven Habits material and some of the other things I've done, but it's really all based on principles that have been given by God to all of His children from the beginning of time. You'll find that you can teach these same principles from the sacred texts and the wisdom literature of almost any tradition. I think the ultimate source of that is God and that is one thing you can absolutely depend upon—in God we trust.

Wright

If you could have a platform and tell our audience something you feel would help them or encourage them, what would you say?

Covey

I think I would say to put God at the center of your life and then prioritize your family. No one on their deathbed ever wished they spent more time at the office.

Wright

That's right. We have come down to the end of our program and I know you're a busy person, but I could talk with you all day Dr. Covey.

Covey

It's good to talk with you as well and to be a part of this program. It looks like an excellent one that you've got going on here.

Wright

Thank you.

We have been talking today with Dr. Stephen R. Covey, co-founder and vice-chairman of Franklin Covey Company. He's also the author of *The 7 Habits of Highly Effective People,* which has been ranked as a number one bestseller by the *New York Times*, selling more than fourteen million copies in thirty-eight languages.

Dr. Covey, thank you so much for being with us today on *Speaking of Success!*

Covey

Thank you for the honor of participating.

About The Author

Stephen R. Covey was recognized in 1996 as one of Time magazine's twenty-five most influential Americans and one of Sales and Marketing Management's top twenty-five power brokers. Dr. Covey is the author of several acclaimed books, including the international bestseller, The 7 Habits of Highly Effective People. It has sold more than fifteen million copies in thirty-eight languages throughout the world. Other bestsellers authored by Dr. Covey include First Things First, Principle-Centered Leadership (with sales exceeding one million), and The 7 Habits of Highly Effective Families.

Dr. Covey's newest book, The 8th Habit: From Effectiveness to Greatness, which was released in November 2004, rose to the top of several bestseller lists, including New York Times, Wall Street Journal, USA Today, Money, Business Week, and Amazon.com and Barnes & Noble. The 8th Habit . . . has sold more than 360,000 copies.

Dr. Covey earned his undergraduate degree from the University of Utah, his MBA from Harvard, and completed his doctorate at Brigham Young University. While at Brigham Young University, he served as assistant to the President and was also a professor of business management and organizational behavior. He received the National Fatherhood Award in 2003, which, as the father of nine and grandfather of forty-four, he says is the most meaningful award he has ever received.

Dr. Covey currently serves on the board of directors for the Points of Light Foundation. Based in Washington, D.C., the Foundation, through its partnership with the Volunteer Center National Network, engages and mobilizes millions of volunteers from all walks of life—businesses, nonprofits, faith-based organizations, low-income communities, families, youth, and older adults—to help solve serious social problems in thousands of communities.

Dr. Stephen R. Covey

www.stephencovey.com

Chapter 6

KIRK WEISLER

David Wright (Wright)

Are you looking for insights that magnify your power to inspire your people and *invite* them to move to higher ground? Then meet Kirk Weisler, an amazingly creative and insightful corporate sage, speaker, and author whose contagious energy and passion jumps off the stage—and the pages of his books—straight into your heart. His life mission is to imbue organizations with deeper meaning, greater purpose, passion and, *fun!*

Author of the best *smelling* book, *Dog Poop Initiative,* Kirk Weisler is *the* Chief Morale Officer and expert in creating outrageously cool, committed, company cultures.

So let's get started.

I have heard—and heard of—some of Kirk's, presentations: "The How and the Wow and the Flight of the Cow," "It's all about the Love," "Motivator in Black," and "Little Big Leadership."

Are we expecting a normal interview? Nope. In fact, Kirk has already told me that we will discover how level five business leaders are dramatically enhancing the power and effectiveness of their company cultures with "Milk and Cookie Management" and "Love Note Leadership." We will also explore other fun things leaders can do *right now* to create a more positive, connected, and outrageously cool company culture.

I can tell you're ready, Kirk, so let's go!

Kirk Weisler (Weisler)

That's right, David. My goal is that your listeners and readers will leave this interview with at least three things they can implement right now—no additional tools to buy, no consultants to hire, and best of all *no permission needed.* In other words, no excuses for not making our world of work better right now—for our people and ourselves.

Wright

The context is culture and the mission is to nurture it, improve it, and inspire the people who sustain it and in the process, create cool, connected, company cultures, right?

Weisler

Right on, David. I call it cultural leadership.

Wright

In a sentence or two, would you define organizational culture for our readers?

Weisler

Sure thing. It's what really happens around here and what that feels like. It's what *really is,* not what we hope or pretend that it is.

Wright

"It's what it really is." Hum, I like that.

Weisler

Our organization's culture is that feeling that comes from what we really do around here *and the spirit in which it is done.* It supersedes what we say we are and reflects who we really are. It eclipses our pithy posted mission statements and validates or voids our vision statements. It is what our company feels like. It is what our company sounds like. It is manifest in our prevailing attitudes and behaviors. It is in the language we use, the types of stories we tell; it is the real *spirit* of the place. This feeling—this spirit—is as felt by those outside the company as it is experienced and felt by those inside the company.

Even more important than what culture is, is what it does. It affects every measurable outcome.

Visualize, David, a sliding scale. At one end is joy, emotional commitment, camaraderie, connection, engagement, all the good stuff that good leaders are always striving for, and on the other end is disengagement, discontent, discord and disconnection—even despair—the bad stuff good leaders are always striving against. Every organization's culture is somewhere on this scale, passively moving down the scale in response to circumstances or actively moving up the scale as a result of the focused, deliberate attention their leaders give their company culture. One employee called it "retention guided by intention." I call it Cultural Leadership.

Wright

So you're either headed from "Good to Great" or—

Weisler

Or sliding from "Good to Grey."

Wright

Okay then Kirk, how about taking us to "great" with some things leaders can do—today—to transform their corporate culture and keep them growing in the right direction.

Weisler

Yes. There are a dozen things that really work—and begin to work immediately. In fact, today I will give you three of my top ten favorite activities that help leaders create and nurture outrageously cool cultures. Number one: serve milk and cookies. Number two: write love notes. And number three: read to your people.

Wright

Read to them? Read what to them?

Weisler

David, the "what" doesn't matter nearly so as the "how." Certainly you should read something that is relevant and inspiring. Read them something you know and love and want to share because it moved you emotionally, energetically, or creatively. It doesn't need to be overtly connected to their daily tasks; in fact, it doesn't necessarily need to be linked to their work at all. Remember, you aren't reading to them to try to fix them, you are reading to awaken or nurture the seeds of greatness inside them and inspire their initiative and creativity.

I often read books to my teams at work or corporate audiences that you would never find in the business section of the bookstore—or even the self-help section, for that matter.

Wright

What kind of books are we talking about then?

Weisler

I prefer reading children's stories like, *Sneetches, Sir Kevin of Devin,* and *Oh, the places you'll go . . .*

Wright

Sounds like fun, how do adult executives react to that?

Weisler

They absolutely love it. Whether it is at a corporate executive re-treat, a conference keynote with hundreds of people, or a ten-person weekly staff meeting, adults love to be read to. You can count on your team cynics and naysayers to roll their eyes when you first start read-ing a Dr. Seuss book, but you can also count on the majority of your people loving it. In many cases they will demand that it be done more often. Furthermore, I can promise that when you consistently do this, your cynics will be the first to complain if you were to stop.

Wright

Wow! Reading a children's book is easy. I could do that.

Weisler

Exactly. But will you? I don't mean to sound blunt, but the road to poor culture is paved with good intentions of things that could have been done but were not. There are so many things that *could* be so easily done, but it is developing the habit of doing it that actually gets it done. Cultural leadership requires us to invite people to actually commit to doing these new things, engage in new behaviors, and grow in the process.

The direct nature of the "will you?" question helps to immediately assess someone's willingness and faith in you and your leadership. So it's not a question of if you *can;* rather, it is a question of if you *will.*

So, David, *will you* take two to seven minutes and read to the wonderful people you work with—and *will you* do it in your next staff meeting?

Wright

You got me. And, yes, I will. I am actually excited to. Does it need to be a children's book?

Weisler

It could be; but remember, the *how* is more important that the *what.* Some of the favorite books I read to my team at home, and to audiences abroad, are "grown-up books" that are fun quick reads but also have depth and inspiration—books like *Raving Fans, The Big Moo, Q B Q, Who Moved My Cheese,* and even from those big, fat intimidating books such as *The Goal, Good to Great, Leadership Challenge,* we can easily find exciting vignettes loaded with insights that uplift, inform, and inspire. Remember, read your selections with the same excitement you felt when you first "got it"—with the same enthusiasm you would share any exciting discovery. When you do, I promise you that great things will happen.

Wright

Great things like—?

Weisler

Like what happened to my friend and client, Brenda. Brenda shifted her company culture in one day. Here's what happened. She walked into her weekly staff meeting and said, "Listen to this! I have been reading this really cool book on change. Before we jump into today's agenda, I just have to read this to you."

She opened the book *Who Moved my Cheese,* and enthusiastically began to read. In moments, her team knew the characters and could identify with them. They listened intently as she read right up to a "cliffhanger spot" then, looking at her watch, she stopped abruptly. "Well, that's all we have time for right now, but it's a great story. I loved it, thanks for letting me share a bit of it with you."

A member of the team pled with her to finish the story, or at least tell them what happens when the character re-enters the scary maze.

Brenda declined, but said that anyone who wished to could stop by and borrow the book. She told them she even had an extra copy they could borrow. What do you think happened?

Wright

Someone came and borrowed the book?

Weisler

More than that. By noon, *seven* people came and borrowed the book.

Wright

How do seven people borrow one book?

Weisler

I had told Brenda what to expect and she had the extra copies waiting in her desk drawer.

Wright

Ah ha, smart lady (smart Kirk). Here's another question. I might know the answer, but let me ask it anyway. How did reading that book shift the company culture in one day?

Weisler

Well, obviously, this didn't move her culture from one end of the scale to other, but this did invite and move it in the right direction. The cumulative effect of consistently doing what Brenda did is where the power is. By reading to her team, and inspiring them to read she gave them something in common. You see, cultures are established and maintained by the things they have in common, things like stories—true stories, legends, histories, fables, parables—stories that illustrate and prove values, behavioral standards, and a shared and common language—especially a common language. These stories can be intentionally installed into your culture from books, the experiences from your cultural leaders, or from inspiring, internal examples. However it happens, and the principles they illustrate, they must be told deliberately and repetitiously to drive these stories into the heart of your culture. You will know you have succeeded, and your culture has shifted, when you hear echoes of those stories coming back to you in the everyday language of your company.

The next day someone on Brenda's team was wandering around the office looking for something he had misplaced and a co-worker walked up and said, "Are you looking for your cheese?"

Immediately, another called out from the next cubicle, laughing, "Too bad, I moved it!"

Bingo! Their shared and common experience and values had shifted to a different level and style of thinking. The office culture had shifted and their language immediately reflected that shift. By the way, their humor indicated a certain level of acceptance and adoption of the change in culture and language.

Wright

Yes. I get it. The culture immediately shifted through stories. Like the one you just told me. But I would assume it could shift right back once the novelty of the story wore off, right?

Weisler

Right. Absolutely. Good catch. But this wasn't a one-time experience. Brenda kept up the practice—she made it a tradition. And remember, it went beyond just reading to them. Brenda read to them with passion and purpose. You have to let your enthusiasm for your favorite books become contagious so that you inspire them to want to read more themselves—and share what they read with each other.

No one would argue that it is more fun to work with someone who is in a state of growth and development than it is to work with someone who is stagnant. Green wood is more flexible and much less likely to burn (out) than deadwood.

Gallup's wonderful research in the area of "employee engagement" clearly indicates that a key element that must be present for employee engagement to be at its zenith is personal and professional development.

The greatest single thing supervisors and CEOs can do to get their people into a state of growth and development is to be in one themselves. One of the best ways I know of to accomplish this is to read what great and inspiring authors like Dr. Seuss or Jim Collins have to say and then share those thoughts and ideas, not by preaching your new discoveries and ideas, but by simply doing what Brenda did—reading to your team.

Wright

I love it Kirk, share another example with us.

Weisler

I have hundreds of e-mails and letters from company leaders like Brenda telling me how they made it happen; but let me tell you a story about how it *didn't* work.

It is also a true story and tragically it is one of many. A particular company had some big changes coming. (Who doesn't?) In a well in-tended but poorly executed attempt to prepare their people for this change, they decided it would be good to have everyone read the aforementioned best selling book on change, *Who Moved My Cheese?*

Wright

Like Brenda did—

Weisler

No, not quite. This company's idea was awesome, but their imple-mentation was awful. Like so many companies, they lacked the per-sonal buy-in that is inherent in the kind of contagious cultural lead-ership that Brenda demonstrated when she read to her people.

This other company just handed out the book and expected their people to read it. They purchased hundreds of copies and laid them on people's keyboards so they would discover them when they arrived at work the next morning.

Wright

So, everyone got a book, right?

Weisler

Yes, but the objective wasn't for them to get the book. The objec-tive was for them to get the message—the message that was in the book. The company wanted and needed to get their people to *read* the book to get the book's powerful message. It wasn't just to get the books into their hands but to get the book's message into their hearts—and their minds—so it would affect their language and be-havioral responses thereby producing measurable, positive effects. That's how cultural leaders create cultural change.

Wright

I can see why they didn't read it. They show up, find it on their keyboard, and most likely view it as another task on their plates that are already too full or as another stumbling attempt by management to "improve morale around here" or maybe even some kind of subtle criticism that they needed to be more "positive" or something like that.

Weisler

Exactly right, David; and, well, their positive intent to get their people to start reading uplifting and inspirational books didn't happen. They spent thousands of dollars on books that few even opened and even fewer read. The book simply got moved from their desktops to their shelf tops—to be read later, if ever. The company didn't affect the mindset of their culture, let alone the heart-set. They totally failed to help their people prepare for change.

Wright

Okay. Here's what I've got so far. You can shift your company culture upward in one day—or at least start the process—by reading to your people, not by reading just anything, but by reading something that matters. Read with passion so you entice them to read it themselves—and maybe even to each other—so it sinks into the heart and shows up in an enhanced company culture. Do I have it right?

Weisler

Yes; and what else did you get out of this, David?

Wright

What do you mean?

Weisler

Knowing is not enough, we must—

Wright

Oh yes, *act*. I will read to my people at our next staff meeting here at Insight Publishing.

Weisler

Great, they'll love you for it.

Wright

Really, I'm going to do it. Heck, I'm excited to do it. It's such a simple idea, yet obviously effective. But we aren't done, yet. You said you had *three* ideas you would share with us that would make an immediate change. Do you have time for a couple more? Actually, I'm not letting you leave here until you do anyway. You said something about love notes and milk and cookies. What is that all about, oh sage of simplicity? Are these also things I can do right here, right now, with my own staff?

Weisler

You sure can David; in fact, anyone can. We'll end with the cookies and milk. Let's go first to the love because it's all about the love. Are you feelin' the love?

Wright

Yes, I'm feeling it!

Weisler

David, one very easy, yet incredibly effective thing any leader can do right now is to simply write a "love note."

Wright

A love note? Well, this is a business book so obviously you're not talking romance. I am sure you're talking cultural context, right?

Weisler

Of course. Company culture is the crucible of production and profit; the birthplace of all desired organizational results—particularly long-range results. Culture is the heart of the organization. People are the heart of the culture and, well, the heart is the heart of the people—their emotions and their feelings are what drive them and keep them going over the long-haul.

If you operate with the understanding that culture drives your company and at the core of culture is the individual and at the core of the individual is the heart, then you must realize that if you are going to change your company culture you must start with the heart of the individual. Love notes are an easy, quick, and powerful way to get you closer to the heart of the individual—the heartbeat of your culture.

A love note in the context of our discussion is simply a handwritten note of appreciation written by anyone in the culture to anyone else in the culture. The key elements of the note are: first, that someone cares enough to write it; second, that it is descriptive or specific as it conveys what or who is appreciated and why; and third, that it is given in the spirit of genuine appreciation. Oh, and the signature, that's important too.

Wright

The signature?

Weisler

Some notes are powerful if they are left anonymously, some are more effective if they are signed by the entire team, and others are better if they are signed individually. It depends on the situation.

Wright

How does a person know what is best?

Weisler

You usually just know. Follow your instincts. You see, David, love notes are important because of the power they have to meet one of the greatest human needs we know of: the need to feel loved, recognized, and appreciated—the feeling that I matter, that I make a difference, and that what I *do* is worthwhile and worth noticing and therefore *I* am worthwhile and worth noticing.

This is a very important principle or truth and we each have the ability to use its power to bless more lives, more often. We can start *right now* by simply taking a few moments to write a genuine note of appreciation for someone in our world or work—or our world in general.

My editor proudly told me he has a box of really classy thank-you notes in his top desk drawer. I asked him why? He said "so I can give them to people." I asked him how long they had been in his desk drawer. He gulped in embarrassment and said, "Oh, I guess I haven't been giving them out enough."

Wright

Well, that put him on the spot.

Weisler

My question was spontaneous and was not meant to put him on the spot and while I didn't mean to embarrass him (he is tough he can take it), it was on target. He told me the next day that he got them out immediately and used them to thank several people for their contributions and support.

When discussing this principle in trainings and keynotes, I commonly ask my audiences if they have ever received a handwritten note of appreciation from a co-worker or supervisor. Usually there are a good number who raise their hands, but there are far too many who do not.

I then ask how many have received such notes have kept them for more than one year, five years, ten years. Most of the hands that were raised remain so. It's common to find people who have kept these "love" notes for over twenty years. One lady told me she kept one of hers tucked away in a desk drawer for over twenty-seven years—almost her entire professional life.

Not only do people keep these notes, they treasure these genuinely written *specific* words of appreciation as though they are written in gold. They keep them in special folders and boxes and re-read them again and again. These notes seem to get sweeter with each reading.

Wright

There is a lot of power in this, isn't there?

Weisler

There sure is, David; because matters of the heart such as genuine gratitude and recognition are almost sacred. Gallup's research tells us that for a company culture to be at its optimum, most positive and productive level, meaningful recognition on a personal level must occur every seven days.

Wright

What? Every week? What company can do that? That's an awful lot!

Weisler

It is a lot, but it is worth a lot. And you are also right, few companies do it—and that is a sad thing. Love notes are such an easy, inexpensive way to immediately enhance morale and productivity and practically no one does it. Many organizations have annual recognition events where a few select employees are acknowledged. Some have quarterly events; but none of these events even begin to fill the need that we human beings have for acknowledgement, not just "attaboys," but real constructive recognition of specific things we do or specific traits we have that enhance others.

Wright

So what kind of event should a company have and how often?

Weisler

"Events" aren't going to solve the problem. The fact is, the need for acknowledgement that Gallup describes cannot be met at an institutional level. It can only be met at a personal level—the intimate individual level. It does not need to be formal. In fact, informal works better anyway. At this interpersonal level, meaningful recognition doesn't need to come from a particular person or place, it just needs to happen. And the recognition doesn't need to be public; in fact, most people prefer personal, handwritten notes over the more showy but less meaningful organizational certificates and plaques.

Wright

What do you say to the people in your audiences who have never received any love notes at all?

Weisler

That's easy. I remind them of a couple of important truths. First, it's not about them, it's about others. Second, you get what you give. There is a close correlation between what we sow and what we reap.

Wright

The law of the harvest?

Weisler

Exactly. As cultural leaders our mission is to invite them and commit them in the strongest terms possible to improve their culture by taking action. We challenge them to do a very simple thing: ask themselves what would it feel like for them to find a genuine, specific, and heartfelt handwritten note or e-mail waiting for them at the beginning of a workday. If the answer is, "It would make me feel great," or "energized" or "more focused" or "more productive," then I suggest that they let that answer inspire them to action so they can give that great feeling to someone else and watch—and *feel*—what happens.

Wright

I know I'd love to get one . . .

Weisler
So—

Wright
So I'd better get to writing them if I expect to get any.

Weisler
Good, but be sure to write them to bless lives, not so you will receive one for yourself. It is far more powerful when we are doing it with no thought of what we might get from the experience ourselves.

Wright
Got it. You are right, of course. And the great thing, Kirk, about what you are suggesting is that the times we serve in the spirit you describe are among the most personally rewarding times of our lives.

Weisler
Exactly. So David, will you commit to writing at least one note of recognition for three members of your staff this week?

Wright
I will!

Weisler
I promise you that when you do, your culture will shift to higher ground.

Wright
I believe it.

Weisler
Now, are you now ready for "milk and cookies"?

Wright
Are you kidding? I'm always ready for milk and cookies!

Weisler
With chocolate chips? Good. I have a couple dozen wonderful stories about how leaders have used milk and cookies to enhance their culture building efforts. Nearly every one of those stories was inspired by the following story.

It was just something I accidentally did right one day as a fairly young supervisor. Our company was growing quickly—from two employees to a thousand in less than two years. As the second person hired, I was privileged to be along for a wonderful, challenging, highly educational ride. As our headcount pushed passed 600, I became aware that we hadn't taken the time lately to pull the troops together and have some meaningful connection.

We were already a fun company and there was nothing identifiably wrong, but I just felt the need to really connect and check in with the people in a way we hadn't really been doing lately. Morale was good. People liked each other. There was no real dissention in the ranks, and in the area of retention and recruitment we were leaders in our industry.

Still, I had the feeling that we needed to do something fun—something that would create a special memory for every employee, something that would give each of them a story to tell; not just a story, but a very fun happy ending type of story. An idea involving milk and cookies came to mind, so I scheduled the CEO for a four-hour meeting that read in his appointment schedule: "Urgent meeting. Subject: Milk and Cookies."

Wright
What was his reaction when he saw that on his calendar?

Weisler
He called me immediately. "Hey, Kirk, I see you've got me signed out for most of next Tuesday. What am I going to be doing?"

"Don't worry," I said. "Trust me. It will be great." Somehow, I really believed it would be.

I made arrangements with a local bakery for extra-large freshly baked chocolate chip cookies to be delivered in batches of 200 every two hours all day on the next Tuesday. I also contacted the local dairy and found out where I could get those little kindergarten sized milk carton drinks, the kind that we had when we had milk and cookie time when we were in kindergarten.

When my CEO came in on Tuesday morning, I had a cart loaded with still warm, freshly baked cookies and a couple of cases of cold milk. I threw on some napkins for good measure.

For an extra touch of home—and mostly to have fun—I dressed our oh-so-macho CEO in a pink, frilly apron.

He grimaced, then grinned and said, "Okay. Now that you've dressed me like my mother, what's my mission?"

"Your mission," I said, "is to go out there and share the love. Our people are out there on the phones trying to provide great customer service for the companies who hired us to do that, and to be a delight to everyone who calls us.

"Your mission is simply to go out there, show our people that you know they are there, and have fun as you connect with them. You will do that by giving each of them some of these big warm chocolate chip cookies, a couple of cartons of milk, and a big smile—and let them 'feel the love'!"

He smiled and said, "If this is about helping our people feel the love, I'd better start with our chief financial officer because I'm guessing you haven't yet told him he was paying for these cookies."

Then, decked out in a pink, frilly apron, and pushing a cart of warm cookies and cold milk, he headed down the executive hallway to our most grumpy person—our CFO and Controller who, in fact, didn't know that he would soon be getting a bill for well over a thousand cookies.

As I said, there was no real plan for all this. At the time I didn't understand the powerful potential of this exercise; but the results were really exciting. I wish I could tell you that I had planned very deliberately and executed it brilliantly and that I had known great and miraculous things would happen as a result of my incredible brilliance. But that wasn't the case. Of course I hoped something good would happen—I guess all leaders hope for that—but what happened far exceeded my expectations.

The CEO went out there and began to pass these cookies out to our employees, mostly young adults—technicians. I figured he would last a few hours at best, and then I would have someone take over for the evening shift. But I was wrong. Our CEO would not give up that cookie cart to save the world. You couldn't get it away from him. He was having so much fun. He delivered cookies and milk all day, and stayed for the night shift as well. He got engaged. The more engaged he got in this activity of visiting and serving and touching the hearts of his people—well, it was just contagious.

Our already good company morale shot through the ceiling. Our already fun place to work became a warmer and friendlier and an even more fun place to work. But there were other really cool results of "Milk & Cookie Day." Applicants waiting for an open position went from 30 to 300. At the same time that our competitors and peers were actually complaining to the Governor of our state about their difficulty in finding qualified people, we had hundreds of qualified applicants waiting for an opening.

Our next four or five hiring groups were standing room only. Remember, we were in the outsource call center/customer service profession. Companies in this industry are not usually considered employers of choice and turnover is typically pretty severe. But our company was considered a great employer, and with Milk & Cookie Day our social capital in the community went up even more.

One of the things we did during new employee orientation was to ask how the new hires had heard about our company. More than half of them said they'd heard about Milk & Cookie Day and thought this would be a really cool company to work for. This little milk and cookie exercise turned out to be a huge recruiting tool, saving us tens of thousands of dollars in recruitment and retraining costs our competitors were required to spend because they would never do anything as elementary as buy everyone milk and cookies.

I was brilliant and I didn't even know it. How would I have known that this simple idea—that touched every soul in our company, that cost less than one-half the expenditure of replacing one employee lost to poor culture—would cause such an immediate, positive cultural reaction?

It proved how doing something as simple as giving your people chocolate chip cookies could so easily and "sweetly" shift your culture. It also spoke to that other principle I mentioned earlier, that principle I now teach cultural leaders. Leaders who desire to shift their culture need to give their people a story to tell—a "viral" message that will live a life of its own and spread like wildfire.

When our employees went home after Milk & Cookie Day (which, by the way, they insisted on having again and again every few months), they'd tell their friends that their CEO brings them milk and cookies. These friends would tell their friends and this story is still told nearly seven years later.

Milk & Cookie Day gave them a story to tell and helped them feel more emotionally connected to our company and our company's mission of providing great customer service.

Wright

This is an easy thing to do—it seems so simple. It seems pretty straightforward. Is there anything to watch out for?

Weisler

Sadly enough there is. It seems that no matter how simple or obvious the point, someone with the wrong attitude and approach can, and usually will, mess it up. There are some leaders of organizations who reported to me that they tried it and it was a total flop. When I asked for details I found that they missed the point entirely because they thought it was about the cookies, not the connection. Consequently, they ordered in a huge batch of cookies and several gallons of milk, plopped them down in a central location, and sent around an e-mail saying, "Come and get it." Good grief!

Wright

Yes, this idea works because of the principles of service and connection—a hands-on connection. This is something that is pretty rare even in small organizations. When you do it with the right attitude and spirit, and when you combine that with the element of surprise and a pink frilly apron, you also give your people a story to tell that will be told and retold like positive gossip you can never stop—not that you would ever want to.

Weisler

That's right. Think about it. Every day, when someone goes home from work or a conference or a meeting, someone—roommate, spouse, friend—is going to ask, "How was work today?" You know that each one of the people you work with is going to tell some kind of story. It might be just a terse "same ol' same ol'"—but if something unique happened (good or bad) they will tell that story—good or bad!

Cultural leaders give them a great response—something fun and interesting to say—a great story to tell. And the story they tell sets the tone and spirit for tomorrow.

Wright

That is really interesting. Creating a story like Milk & Cookie Day, that gets retold because it is so unique and also pre-sets the mood for the next day, is simple and inexpensive—yet profitable and fun. Wow.

Weisler

Our lives follow our language. What we say today we will get more of tomorrow. There is nothing new about that, but I began to learn that this principle was one you could intentionally harness and utilize as an effective cultural leader. So now I teach cultural leaders to understand that their people are going to be asked a question today—"how did it go at work?" They will either grunt and shrug or they will tell a story (actually a grunt and a shrug is a story, a not-so-good story, but they will tell a story), and if you don't give them a good one to tell, their story will probably sound like a war story or a horror story or just a slice of juicy but negative gossip, and you will have lost your opportunity for some incredibly powerful and positive press.

There are too many people out there telling war stories and exaggerating or horriblizing the day because their circle of friends is doing the same and they don't want to feel left out. So, since we know they are going to tell stories anyway, why not give them a great story to tell? Give them a story that says, "I work for a cool place. You ought to come and work with me."

One of the common themes inherent in the hundred best companies to work for in America is that when you ask an employee of one of these companies how work went on any specific day, they will say odd things like "glorious" and "wonderful." They also say strange things about their company like, "What a great place to work."

To the uninspired, these people are oddballs. They love what they do and they love how they get to do it. They love the people they work with and for, and they love the culture in which they get to work. What they've "got" to do they "get" to do, they are delighted to do it, and those are the stories they tell.

Their friends say, "Gosh, I wish I worked for your company," and that begins to perpetuate a sense of pride that employees get to work somewhere other people want to work. Cultural leaders can create this kind of positive press in a very simple way—give them some warm cookies to eat and a cool story to tell.

Wright

Wow. This is great. The idea of intentionally creating a moment that gives our people a story to tell can be accomplished with every activity you gave us. If someone read Dr. Seuss to me at work, I would surely go home and tell everyone about it. If someone let me know that I mattered to my company by writing me a "love note" all my friends and family would soon know about it.

Weisler

These ideas have worked again and again for hundreds of people who, on their journey of improving their workplace cultures, have now blessed tens of thousands of lives. Each idea easily adapts itself to the personality of the person delivering the service, and each idea is personally and culturally rewarding.

Wright

Kirk, I know you have to get going and that's too bad. I wish we had time to discuss the rest of your top ten list of ways to create outrageously cool company cultures. What I like is that they aren't complicated theories, just simple, fun, inexpensive little things that make a big difference.

Weisler

Most leaders don't want more leadership theory, they want action. They want insights, ideas, and activities that they can do, right now, to make a positive difference. Thank you, David, for our interview today; I've enjoyed our time together.

Wright

Me too Kirk, thank you for a fun and insightful experience and for some things I will be doing this week with and for the people I work with here at Insight Publishing.

We've been talking today with Chief Morale Officer Kirk Weisler who travels around the world giving experiential keynotes revealing *everyday* things leaders can do to build great company cultures. Kirk's unique background as a U.S. Army Ranger, his work with at-risk youth, and experience as a master storyteller and team-builder make him a fun, engaging, sought-after speaker.

He is the author of the best smelling book, *The Dog Poop Initiative,* which we have all read here at Insight, and we love it! In addition he has authored *The Cookie Thief, A Question-Able Culture*, and *A More Question-Able Culture*. He is a way out-of-the-box thinker, a make-it-happen guy.

Kirk, thank you again for being with us today on, *Speaking on Success*.

Weisler

My pleasure David, and to your readers I say, "Make it a great day. It's your choice!"

About the Author

In the low morale, high turnover world of outsource call centers with their churn and burn approach to management (creating 150–200 percent annual attrition—and astronomical related costs), a certain reasonably young man created his own title and began his own cultural revolution believing that "work—all work—matters."

While there he developed a full-scale corporate university with a full two-year curriculum, was a prime mover in the creation of over 700 jobs, created an award-winning customer service process, and created an industry-leading employee recognition program. His role as Chief Morale Officer (CMO) helped establish an attrition rate five times less than the industry norm and a 97 percent referral rate for new hires.

Since that day Kirk has been continually invited to share his evangelical cultural-changing message to audiences around the world encouraging, inspiring, and inviting them to create the culture they desire, to take ownership of their environment, and to stop having "a job" and start having a life! He is an expert on creating culture, change, community, and connections in the workplace. Considering how vital the culture issue is to our world of work today, Kirk's message is one that organizations seeking higher levels of employee involvement, engagements, and commitment want and need to hear. His passionate and evangelical delivery on Culture Building and Creating Community are needed more now than at any time in the history of corporate America.

Kirk lives in Atlanta, Georgia, with his, "Wonderful wife, Rebecca, and their five remarkable children who seem to have a fun way of showing up in nearly every presentation he does!"

Kirk Weisler, Chief Morale Officer
Team Dynamics, Inc.
100 Olivia Court, Suite 007
Fayetteville, GA 30215
Phone: 404.783.5661
E-mail: kirk@kirkweisler.com
kirkweisler.com
dogpoopinitiative.com
bowlingballonarope.com
givingpeopleastorytotell.com
morebetterbooks.com

Chapter 7

THE INTERVIEW

David Wright (Wright)

They say that hindsight is 20/20. With 20/20 hindsight we can look back and see exactly what we did wrong and what happened because of it. We can then accurately kick ourselves for all the things we did wrong.

With 20/20 hindsight we can see clearly what we should or shouldn't have done, and what we wished we had done right. But why can't we see forward as well as we can see backward? Why can't we have 20/20 foresight?

Chad Hymas says we can. At the age of twenty-seven, an accident that he could have prevented changed his life in an instant. The accident happened because Chad was in a hurry and didn't take a few minutes to do something he should have done. He would like to kick himself for not doing what he should have done; but he can't kick himself—he can't kick anything—because he is now paralyzed.

But he doesn't need to kick himself anyway. In the very few years following his accident, Chad has been recognized by the state of Utah as the *Superior Civilian of the Year.* A member of the National

Speakers Association, he travels 150,000 miles a year speaking to hundreds of professional and civic organizations. He is author of a regionally best-selling book, *Soaring to New Heights.*

Chad is a world-class wheelchair athlete—basketball, rugby, hang-gliding, and snow skiing. In July 2003, Chad set a world record by wheeling a 513-mile marathon from Salt Lake City, Utah, to Las Vegas, Nevada.

More important than any of those achievements, Chad and his wife, Shondell, are the proud parents of three children. They reside in Rush Valley, Utah, on a beautiful 5,100-acre private wildlife preserve.

Chad is many more times successful and happy since his "tragic" accident than he was before. Why? It's because of his focus. What is his focus? His focus is *Vision.* He calls it 20/20 vision. Not just 20/20 hindsight, but 20/20 foresight. As a professional speaker, Leadership, Teambuilding, Customer Service, and Mastering Change are his topics, but his focus is 20/20 foresight.

Chad, welcome to *Speaking of Success.*

Tell us more about this thing you call 20/20 foresight or vision and how you came up with that concept.

Chad Hymas (Hymas)

I was twenty-seven years old in the prime of my life. Everything I had ever desired was coming to me. Life couldn't have been better. I was hurrying to feed the elk on my ranch when the bucket of a tractor with which I was transporting a 2,000-pound bale of hay jerked spasmodically. It flipped the bale backwards and it crashed down on top of me.

I sat there with my neck shattered, my face forced into the steering wheel, totally paralyzed, fighting for my every breath, wondering what was next—if anything.

I wondered if anyone would find me. I wondered if I would be alive when they did. I also wondered how long it would have taken me to add the hydraulic fluid that would have prevented the accident in the first place!

During the time I lay pinned against the steering wheel, and throughout the following sixty-three days I spent in the hospital, I had a lot of time to figure it out. I calculated it would have taken me five to seven minutes to add the hydraulic fluid that would have prevented the accident.

Sure saved a lot of time, didn't I? It now takes me that long to put on one sock! Hindsight—ain't it great? They say hindsight is 20/20. I guess they are right.

My wife found me forty-eight minutes after the bale landed on me. I was air-lifted to LDS Hospital in Salt Lake City. As I lay in the hospital room alone in the dark, berating myself for the mistake that had caused my own accident, my dad came to my bedside and whispered something that changed my perspective—and my life.

He said, "Chad, it's not those who never make mistakes in this life who get ahead, it's those who do fail, accept it, and move on. In fact, son, the most successful are those who fail faster, accept it quicker, then get on with the next step sooner."

What was my next step? I wondered what it would look like since the one thing I couldn't do was "step." I was paralyzed, remember? My next step would be unlike any other I had ever taken. What would it look like? What would my life look like? Would I still have my family? Could I still be a dad? A husband? Well, of course I could. I would be back. I was going to get all better. I was going to walk again. I would be back! I would play ball, referee, run my ranch, and manage my landscaping business. I would be back! I could see it.

Wright

Tell our readers what it really takes to come back.

Hymas

Well, actually I was wrong about coming back. What I didn't realize was that I could never come back—I could only come forward. To do that was going to require something new—it was going to require 20/20 foresight—a special kind of vision. This vision would not only draw me forward into an incredible life but also draw forward those who looked to me for leadership—my family, my employees, and now my audiences.

Please, again, do not think I am speaking from ego. I am incredibly blessed, but so can every single person out there be blessed in the same or similar way if each of them will see as I see, with 20/20 vision—20/20 foresight—see clearly what they desire, and let that vision pull them into a beautiful future.

Wright

This could not have been easy, especially for a quadriplegic. But you imply that you have a simple formula that anyone can use to move ahead.

Hymas

I'm not trying to be clever or cute when I say, "I didn't come back—I went forward." Moving forward doesn't happen overnight, especially when dealing with what appears to be a disaster. It takes seconds for the change to happen, and months, sometimes years, to deal with it and move ahead.

And you don't get over it, you get on with it. That may sound philosophical, and it is. When your body is gone, philosophy, attitude, and vision, are almost all you have left. I say almost—I actually had a lot.

Wright

What was it that you had?

Hymas

Six years ago I was just like you. I was active physically, played on a basketball team, and had been married for six years to a very beautiful woman. We had two small boys—Christian, three and Kyler, one.

April 2, 2001, sticks out because my wife and I had had an argument. As we reflect back on some of the things we took for granted, we remember that day and how happy we are that we were quick to make up that evening, because the very next day was a changing day for both of us.

One night I was happily making up with my wife from an argument—my fault I'm sure—three nights later I woke up in the hospital, from the accident, not from the argument!

I was in a halo, a contraption that is not angelic by any means. It is a brace—a metal ring around your head, hooked up to weights and screwed right through your skin into your skull. It hurts like crazy and it doesn't allow you to move—not a fraction of an inch.

As I awoke, there were two doctors standing in front of me. My wife was on my left stroking my hand. I couldn't feel it at all. My mother and father were on my right as I was told bluntly that I was a quadriplegic.

Can you imagine waking up and trying to look down to see where your body went? It is eerie, spooky, and horribly unsettling to say the least.

I struggled against it, but how do you struggle with a body that won't struggle or respond in any way? There was no movement at that time—none.

The doctors did give me some good news. They said, "Hey, Chad, good news. We think you're going to get one wrist back and a shoulder and you might have some use of one arm but definitely not all of it. Other than that, you won't have any feeling in your body from the breast line down."

Good news? I wondered what "bad news" might sound like. Oh yeah, it would sound like this: "Hi, I'm St. Peter . . ."

Day sixty-three was pivotal for me. I had been sixty-two days in the hospital going numbly—literally—through rehabilitation. I went through the motions, unable to see what my future held; but being warehoused with nothing but steel and plastic keeping me alive sure as heck wasn't going to be it. Day sixty-three was also the day I met Art Berg. Or, rather, he met me.

Wright

Art Berg the speaker, I assume.

Hymas

Yes, also Art Berg the author, Art Berg the business owner, and Art Berg the wheelchair athlete. Art was also a quadriplegic. He's very, very well known in the speaking world. Of course I had no idea who he was. I was a farmer. I was an elk breeder. To me, Art was just another guy in a wheelchair whose hands didn't work so well—like mine.

He wheels his chair into my hospital room. Without a word, he throws himself onto my bed and takes off his clothes. That was quite a shock, but I was in no shape to run away. Then he puts them back on faster with the use of hardly anything more than most people do with the use of everything.

He then flings himself off the bed and back onto his wheelchair, looks up at me and grins. Finally he tells me his name, pulls a book out, signs it, and puts it on my bed. He had no better grip than I did, but he obviously had gotten a better grip on life than I had. I noticed the title, *Some Miracles Take Time.* The subtitle was, *The difficult takes time; the impossible just takes a little longer.*

He told me to call him sometime, then wheeled out the door just as he had wheeled in—leaving me speechless. My wife says that was the last time I was ever speechless.

So I called him. I didn't call him because I wanted to become a speaker, I called him because I wanted to get back to landscaping and ranching. I needed to ask him how to get through all this. How do you use the bathroom? How do I court my wife? How do I stay married? How do I get back to my life? He said, "You don't go back, Chad. You go forward."

I didn't pay attention. I didn't need cute philosophy, I needed answers. How do I show my kids how to jump off the left foot and shoot with the right hand in basketball? How do I mow my lawn? How do I make love to my wife? That was important to me and I know it is important to a lot of folks out there who are paralyzed like me—and who are paralyzed in a lot of other ways.

Art was a busy man—a professional speaker—one of the greats in the National Speakers Association. And here he was teaching me really personal stuff.

I asked him how he drove. He took me out and showed me. He showed me how to catheterize myself so I could go to the bathroom without assistance. He showed me how to ride a bike, shoot a gun, and discipline my kids from a wheelchair. He didn't just tell me, he took the time and showed me.

Art was married to a very, very beautiful woman, Dallas. I thought, "I am married to a beautiful woman and have two great kids. Art is married to a beautiful woman and has two great kids. My friend Mike Schlappi, also a wheelchair-bound national speaker, is married to a beautiful woman and they have a great family too—hey, maybe there are compensations in life."

I also learned that Art spoke professionally—and was paid very well for it. I thought this was pretty crazy. I didn't know that one could make a living just talking.

Wright

Well, you are making a good living at it.

Hymas

Yes, but that wasn't my plan. I just wanted to live a normal life.

One of the things I missed most was competition. I learned that Art set a world record back in 1993 going 325 miles—from Salt Lake

City to St. George—in his wheelchair. Could I do something like that? Just to prove to myself I could?

Art invited Shondell and me to go to Honolulu, Hawaii, with him to listen to him speak, so we did. Shondell and I decided to make it a second honeymoon, so we left our children at home and we went to a luxury hotel right on the beach, the Honolulu Marriott.

No, Shondell did not carry me over the threshold (give me a break). She sat on my lap and I wheeled her over in style!

We watched Art speak that night, and I was amazed that he spoke simply and powerfully from what most would call a weak position— that of a wheelchair-bound quadriplegic.

Afterward, he told me I could speak too. "Chad, be your own artist. Color your own picture and share it with the world." I think he was telling me not to steal his stuff! Those were the last words he ever spoke to me.

Wright
Why? What happened?

Hymas
We returned home on February 19, 2002. Five days later Art Berg died. He passed away in his sleep. Nobody was affected by that more than I was. I say that selfishly. I'm sure his family suffered more— but I was devastated.

I forced my way past my wife—I am always so sensitive—and pushed my chair down the asphalt country road for miles wondering what it was all about. Why didn't I just take the time to put one lousy quart of hydraulic fluid in that darn hoist? Hindsight sure is 20/20, isn't it?

As I pushed down the road, I did not realize I had just begun the training that would eventually lead to breaking Art's wheelchair record. How was I going to make it without Art? Who could fill his shoes (or rather, his chair)? He wasn't just a mentor to me to be a speaker, but to be a contributing "normal" human being, husband, father—man. I had lost my guide who was just starting to help me through this overwhelming maze of adjustment. However, maybe he had already given me what I needed.

As I headed for home, after having gone much farther than I should have, I grew weary. But I noticed how much easier it was if I looked up—if I focused on where I was headed. It sure didn't matter what was behind me. What is that scripture in Luke? "No man, hav-

ing put his hand to the plow and looking back is fit for the king-
dom . . ." (Luke 9:62).

What is behind is only as important as what can be learned from
it. Use that 20/20 hindsight to see the truth clearly. Then let the past
go and use what you learn to move ahead. Focus on your vision and
let its power move you ahead. I focused on the lights of my home and
found it much easier to get there, though I was weary to the bone.

Art hadn't left me stranded after all. He had given me exactly
what I needed—he taught me the power of clear vision, the power of
20/20 foresight. I could see something now ahead of me.

Wright

What did you see?

Hymas

A simple, clear goal. I was out there one day thinking about what
to do next, pushing my wheelchair along with the heels of my paralyzed hands, and I felt impressed to see if I could beat my mentor's
world record.

I trained for eighteen months. I pushed from Salt Lake City to Las
Vegas. I did set a new world record. Now, the details involved heat
and sweat and pain, but the essence was that I had a vision, kept my
eyes on the goal, I didn't look back (except when I wanted to quit and
my wife wouldn't let me), and I (we) won the prize—the trophy. My
wife claims the trophy—she says that if it wasn't for her I would have
given up. She is right, so now I call her my trophy wife.

Why did I go after a world record? Because—well—because I
wanted to. I didn't realize it would lead to something, I just wanted to
do it and so I did. And, after that, things started to happen.

Wright

What happened?

Hymas

Following the news coverage of my trek to Las Vegas, I was asked
to speak at a big convention. I hesitated. What did I have to say to a
bunch of able-bodied, successful corporate men and women? Then I
remembered how powerful Art was when he simply told his story—
just being real and having fun.

I gave my speech. I tried to be real. I had fun and I fell in love with
it. I made some national talk shows and I've been speaking profes-

sionally ever since. That first year I had seven speaking engagements. This last year we had 193. That's the short of the long story. It sounds easy but it wasn't. There is no way to move down the road quickly or easily—even with smooth asphalt and rubber tires.

Today, I am still learning how to get along. I travel by myself. I found that the more I depend on other people the more independent I become. Most people don't ever learn that. Some CEOs never learn that. I am independent, but I depend on others for help getting over a non-accommodating curb or transferring from my wheelchair. I have learned to ask—simply and specifically—for help.

Because I am willing to ask for help, I get to travel all over the world. This is possible because I ask simply and specifically and give positive feedback when others help me. Just like any CEO, if my people don't do it right I will get dropped on my head and that hurts!

I have learned that there are caring strangers all around who never saw me before and will probably never see me again but who are happy to help if I just ask. Some are strangers who don't even speak my language; instead, they speak the common language of caring humanity.

I have learned that it is the gift of clear vision and 20/20 foresight that gets the job done. I know exactly what I want and, because I can see it clearly, my instructions and requests are clear and precise. Even strangers who struggle with English get my intent clearly and I get to where I want to go safely and efficiently.

People are very giving if you are willing to depend on them. I found that the more I am willing to admit my dependence on others the more independent and powerful I become.

Wright

How does becoming dependent on others empower us?

Hymas

Not becoming dependent—admitting that we already are. What would happen if we would admit to our spouses and our kids that we depend on them? What if CEOs were willing to admit their dependence on their staff? What if they shared their vision and then simply and humbly asked their people to help them achieve it?

Wright

Maybe their people would pull together better?

Hymas

Right. And maybe the CEO wouldn't have to be there every single day and would have time to go on a vacation or spend time with the family or play golf or take sixty-three days off after dropping a two-ton bale of hay on his head. Better yet, maybe he or she would have time to do the simple but important things like adding a can of hydraulic fluid when it is needed and prevent the disaster in the first place.

Wright

Chad, you seem to know a lot of things about management that aren't in the textbooks. What characteristics have you observed in people who are most successful at getting their team to help them get what they want?

Hymas

They are men and women of vision—not just grandiose vision, though that larger vision is important. In his book, *Good to Great,* Jim Collins calls it a "Big Hairy Audacious Goal." They also see what needs to be done right now, today, and tomorrow. They let the energy of that vision move them through any problem, even if the solution isn't readily apparent.

Wright

Well, that makes sense. If the solution is obvious, who needs vision—or leaders for that matter?

Hymas

Right. Leaders have vision. They have 20/20 foresight. They see the future as clearly as others see the past. They learn from the past, but their focus is on the future—where they are headed, not where they've been.

Twenty-twenty foresight is a common trait among successful people. They see very clearly what hasn't happened yet but intend it to—and it does. They stay focused on the destination. They put their hand to the plow, they don't look back, and they reap the harvest.

Wright

Chad, you went through a lot of tedious, repetitive work just to relearn how to do the simplest things. Isn't that boring? What do you do when it gets boring and tedious?

Hymas

The road to success is paved with small and sometimes tedious and boring steps. Do you know how many yellow stripes there are between Mesquite and Los Vegas, Nevada? There are 6,752. I counted 'em on my record-breaking journey. That is tedium, but if what you do makes the vision of what you desire real, then you do what you have to do to succeed. Remember the Code of the West? "A man's gotta do what a man's gotta do." But we don't always do it. Why? 'Cause it's no fun. So, tedious or not, I say it like this, "I do what I gotta do, so I get what I wanna get."

Wright

Attaching tough work today to a great reward later, that's what you get to do, even if it is tedious?

Hymas

Exactly. Every successful leader I know of was clear about what he or she wanted and why, and was willing to do a lot of difficult, even tedious work to get there. These leaders approached even tedium with a certain degree of enthusiasm because they saw the direct connection to getting what they desired. Successful people are constantly focused on the prize with 20/20 foresight, and they let the thrill of that vision give them the energy to do what is necessary to get there.

After meeting Art Berg, I realized that I wasn't going to walk in a few weeks or maybe even a few years. But that did not mean that I couldn't achieve everything I wanted. I just had to see it differently. Successful leaders are willing to accept changing circumstances, yet keep their foresight 20/20.

The world of today is constantly changing. Technology is a great example. You have to be willing to relearn—even start all over again—just to keep from becoming a dinosaur.

Microsoft came out with a new version. My editor has it and so I'd better get it because the old version isn't good enough for what I want to accomplish. Twenty-twenty foresight helps you accept new circumstances and conditions without changing your vision.

On April 2nd I was just fine. On April 3rd a two-ton bale of hay altered my circumstances and I had to accept new facts and conditions. I had to relearn practically everything, starting with the simple things. I desire to live in normal society and eat at great restaurants with my wife or with clients; so what do I need to do to eat so I don't get food all over the people sitting next to me? What technology exists to help me? What do I have to learn or maybe invent so I can use utensils without assistance and without making a mess and splattering food all over? Am I willing to do that?

How can I drive without using my feet or hands? Can I use my wrists? Am I willing to learn to do that? How can I run my business? How can I be a husband? Not just a provider, but a real husband? This is very, very personal and I don't mind sharing it with you. The toughest thing that I've ever done in my life by far is to relearn how to be romantic with my wife. Face it. Considering a twenty-seven-year-old kid's ego, romantic intimacy is pretty important in his marriage.

So how did I deal with it? How did I save my marriage? I didn't. I was too thick-headed and wrapped up in my ego. It was my wife who saved my marriage. Well, I did do one thing right—I shut up and listened to her when she came to me and said, "Chad, you think you can't meet my needs—but you are wrong." I am a man. I am used to being wrong, so I kept listening. "You think my needs are the same as yours. They aren't. Men's needs are different than women's. Men really are from Mars and we women really do live on another planet—especially when it comes to love and romance."

My incredible, loving wife cut right through my thick-headed ego and changed the way I believe. My Shondell stuck it out when I was really tough to deal with. Because of her, more than because of me, we'll celebrate our twelfth anniversary this March.

For more than half of those years I've been in a wheelchair and during that half we have lived and loved better than the first half; all because of what my wife helped me learn about our relationship. She saved our marriage. I will forever love and respect her immensely for that. I take credit only for being smart enough to listen to her.

In my vision for the future, Shondell and I have a little girl. I am a quad. How do we produce a little girl? Well, I don't know, exactly, but I know we will if we focus on the vision of a bright beautiful little girl playing in a ray of sunlight on our carpet in our home, looking up and calling me "Daddy," then let the thrill of that vision pull us to it.

We did just that and solutions continued to come to us. We looked ahead with 20/20 foresight and let that vision work in us. It drove our creative engine and "voila!" we have a miracle. Through the miracle of modern science or adoption—or of a loving God—my Shondell and I saw with perfect foresight our little girl in our future. And now here she is in our present—our little girl from Guatemala—our little Gracee.

Dreams are coming true in my life—our life—because I am willing to focus on a vision of my own creation and have faith that the details will work themselves out.

Successful people, other CEOs, and other business and community leaders deal effectively with change by looking ahead with 20/20 foresight and seeing what they desire—clearly and in detail—they let their vision pull them forward. In my case and in Mike Schlappi's and Art Berg's situation, we let the power of that vision, *roll* us forward. This is the key ingredient in the formula for success.

Wright

I guess you have answered this already, but let me ask it anyway. Would these things that you have learned also apply to people who are not in wheelchairs?

Hymas

Definitely. Everyone has some sort of challenge. Mine is visible. Others' challenges may be invisible, but just as crippling. Someone has lost a loved one or someone's teenager makes a bad decision or someone is going through divorce or dealing with a dying parent. Someone is dealing with changes in the workplace. It can leave you feeling helpless—not knowing what to do next and, therefore, not doing anything. That is just as paralyzing as breaking your neck.

Paralysis is overcome more by vision and faith than by any other single thing. Look ahead with foresight and see with 20/20 foresight. Then exercise the faith to let that vision pull you forward.

My friend and fellow speaker, Kate Adamson, put it beautifully: "We focus on what we want, not on what we don't; on what we have not on what we don't; and what we can do, not on what we can't." It is that vision that pulls us into a wonderful future of our own creation.

By the way, Kate was more paralyzed than a quadriplegic. What can be more paralyzed than a quad? She was 100 percent paralyzed. Except for a stubborn heart that kept beating, Kate could do nothing. She could not move a finger or a toe. She communicated by blinking her eyes in a special code. Now she is a professional speaker and author just like me but she is better looking!

Kate could never have made it back—I mean forward—without focusing with 20/20 foresight—on her vision—not on her past injury and the unfairness of it. She is alive and inspiring others today because of it.

I might be paralyzed physically; others are paralyzed financially, technologically, emotionally, or mentally. Mike Schlappi was paralyzed by a bullet. My friend, Greg, was paralyzed by clinical depression, my editor is visually impaired by his DNA; but they all keep moving forward speaking and writing and accomplishing wonderful things by keeping their focus on their vision with 20/20 foresight.

Paralysis comes in many, many forms. How to deal with non-physical paralysis is no different from dealing with physical paralysis. I have lost 90 percent of my feeling and muscle control in my body.

Others have lost other things just as important—jobs, loved ones, financial security. How do they get through it? They visualize what they desire and focus on what they have, not what they have lost. They keep that vision in front of them and let that pull them through—like lassoing a shooting star.

During hurricane Katrina, 173 people stood on the rooftops of their homes that were covered in water. They refused to get on the rescue helicopters. According to some reports they actually shot at the helicopters! Now there were several hundred others who left their homes and were rescued. But 173 people stood there with guns in their hands refusing to leave their soggy possessions. What was our government's choice? They couldn't be forced—not when they were armed and dangerous—so they had to be left behind.

Those 173 people died. That's a fact. I don't want to offend anybody so I don't always share this with audiences, but that's the truth. Is that a fair price to pay for hanging on to what is already gone? Is it worth your life to not get what you can from your 20/20 hindsight and then get on with life with 20/20 foresight?

In a way, I had that same choice. Is it worth my life and my marriage and my kids for me to not change and maybe even die because I didn't want to change? No. "I gotta do what I gotta do so I will get to "have what I wanna have!"

Wright

Do you agree with most behavioral scientists that dealing with change by letting go of the past and moving forward with 20/20 vision is the most difficult thing human beings ever do?

Hymas

I don't know if it's the most difficult, but it is the most important. It can be difficult. It was for me. Many times I wanted to give up.

Then I would visualize my goal and that gave me the energy for the next step and the next, etc.

I still have bad days. Sometimes I look outside and see my kids playing ball and yearn to play with them. I admit I feel sad about what I have lost. Heck, I played college basketball. I love hoops and of course I want to play.

So I do. I roll out there in my chair and do what I can do. What can I do? Help my kids learn to keep their focus on the goal. I tell them to see what they want, not what they don't want. I teach them to focus on the basket and see the ball go where they want it to go. That is a perfect example of 20/20 foresight. The better their focus on the goal, the more consistently they score. Anyone who has played ball knows this. Does it work in business as well? In family life? It does.

Wright

So you not only get to play ball with your kids, you actually can coach them?

Hymas

That's right. I coach from the bench, so to speak. I don't have to show them, I just tell them and they believe me—because I am their dad. Of course that will wear off as soon as they hit their teens, but I can bask in the glory of coaching from the bench for a little while longer.

I could bemoan the fact that I can't play. But I don't focus on what I've lost. I focus on what I have and am grateful to my Creator for it.

Look, here I am in an incredible office, with a seventy-five-gallon exotic fish aquarium. It even has fish in it—and my little fishie friends are really glad that I saw Art Berg grip things with his wrists, and could see myself doing the same; because I can now grip a can of fish food and my little wiggly friends get dinner.

Because I was inspired by a great man to focus on my vision of the future, I have a beautiful home and a wonderful office with auto-graphed pictures and posters all over my wall from motivational speakers and world leaders I have met and who have changed my life.

Would I have all this had I not been hurt? Probably not. One thing for sure is that I wouldn't have my precious little girl—and she is worth it all.

Wright

If you could go back and change it would you?

Chad

No. No, I wouldn't change it. That doesn't mean that I don't want to walk again, I do want to. Because of the unique characteristics of my injury I still have significant muscle tone in my legs and I believe that somehow, through the miracle of science or the miracle of a blessing, I will re-establish those nerve connections. I would love to walk again. I would love to have feeling in my body. That's my "Big Goal." And so I will keep focusing on what I desire and let that clear 20/20 vision draw me ever forward.

But what if it doesn't happen? I'm not going to sit around and wait for it. There is too much for me to do today. I've got a daughter who depends on me to read to her. I've got two boys who love basketball and by golly, I can coach them from the bench. Maybe that will be the title of my next book, *Coaching from the Bench.*

I have an awesome life as a direct result of what I have learned and traits I have gained from the accident. I've got a beautiful wife who makes my life joyful and whom I love to make happy. I get to speak to thousands of people, some of whom depend on me as I depended on Art Berg. This week I'll visit three different states. My life is wonderful.

Wright

Most of the time when people have success like you do, they have a mentor who made the difference. I know that Art Berg had an impact on you because it was such an immediate thing and he had been through such a similar experience; but were there others who made a difference?

Hymas

Family. I have a great family. I grew up in a Christian home and faith was very important. When I got hurt, Dad quit his job of twenty-two years and took over my dream of being a rancher. That dream is still alive today. My dad kept my dream alive so that I could see it live and my boys could one day inherit it.

My income comes from speaking and writing. The ranch income is my dad's—and he sure earns it. He didn't have to give up his career for me. But he did.

My mother also quit her job to help me through rehab. She is an angel. I can never repay them for giving me my start in life—twice. Can you imagine teaching your son to feed himself—twice? I can never repay them; all I can do is make them proud of me again by moving forward with enthusiasm and vision.

Wright

What about your landscaping business?

Hymas

Remember what I said earlier about being willing to share the vision and hand over control to others? Well I did that, but not on purpose. It was thrust on me.

For seven years my dream was to plant trees, plant flowers, and grass, put in sprinkler systems, and mow lawns. That's what I did for a living. My brothers helped me build that business. We did it for seven years and I loved it. For a hobby, I raised elk. That's what we did for fun and we made a little profit on the side.

I had thirty-five employees before I broke my neck. When I was in the hospital I had to let every one of those guys go because I thought there was nobody else to run the business. It was my vision, right? Not theirs, right? So I gave each of them a few months' pay and told them that I was grateful for their service and was sorry I had to let them go.

But the rascals didn't go. They had taken over my vision. I had accidentally done something right in the way I had hired and managed my team.

When I arrived at home on day sixty-three all thirty-five of them were standing in my driveway with their families. Then, on cue, they stepped aside revealing a new cement ramp to my front door. Not some piece-of-junk ramp made out of plywood because of some government regulation; this was done right—a ramp built with love and respect.

I wheeled into my house and through tears of gratitude saw that they had built a deck all around my house so I could go out in the fresh air and see my elk any time I wanted to. There is nothing quite like watching baby elk play in the spring or adolescent elk trying out their head-butting skills in the fall to impress the ladies. I know building that deck wasn't cheap—but no matter what it cost it is priceless.

Then they took me back into the house and showed me where they had cut a hole in the floor and installed an elevator so I could get down to my office—and I guess so the kids could play on it because they think that's what it's for.

Finally, they showed me the master bathroom. They had torn out the extra sink and made a roll-in shower for me. I don't know why we needed two sinks anyway. They were both for Shondell—and she only has one face (a pretty one too).

You talk about leadership and successful people—I thought I had to shut the business down and let my employees go. Not only did they refuse to go, but most of them are still here. My landscaping business survived. It is not just my dream, it is theirs. Vision—20/20 foresight. Once mine, now theirs—ours.

Wright

Have you gained any specific expertise from this experience?

Hymas

Yes. Performance management—managing others by including them in your vision, whether long-range or short-range, thereby enlisting their willing and enthusiastic assistance. When you have to suck up your pride (something quadriplegics have to do all the time) and ask people to do simple things for you, you learn to get people to do simple yet noble things. The results are amazing.

Wright

If I had been speaking to you on April 2, 2001, at that stage in your life, what would you have told me your dreams and aspirations for the future would have been?

Hymas

I wanted a big family. I wanted to move forward in my coaching and see if I couldn't pursue maybe some collegiate refereeing opportunities. I had big dreams for my landscaping business. I wanted great things for my family.

Wright

And then the tragedy . . .

Hymas

Well, many people including my own mother said it was a tragedy; and indeed it was, or it seemed to be. But as I look back it wasn't so tragic after all. Change brings opportunity and this accident brought a lot of opportunity with it. Of course I didn't feel that way about it for awhile—and it certainly wasn't apparent.

Wright

Well, yes. The opportunity couldn't have been apparent immediately.

Hymas

I had shattered three out of seven of the vertebrae in my neck: C-4 C-5, and C-6. That caused me to lose the complete use of my feet, my legs, all my stomach muscles, two out of my three major chest muscles, most of the strength and use of my arms, and I lost the complete use and feeling in my fingers and hands. It sure didn't feel like an "opportunity." Could I still be a husband? Could I still be a father? Could I work?

Wright

How did you cope in those early days with that fear? Did you share your fear with others or were you in lonely isolation?

Hymas

I was isolated but not really lonely. I was in the hospital for sixty-three days. I was comfortable there because I was around people who were like me and I still had the belief that this wasn't really happening.

I was in all kinds of denial. The doctors told me that a high percentage of people like me lost their spouse within the first couple of months. I wasn't listening.

They didn't tell me I would lose Shondell because she wouldn't love me anymore. My Doctor said, "Chad, you are going to push her away."

I didn't understand what he was saying until I got home and then I found out what they meant.

My life was gone. I could not see tomorrow. I couldn't even see today. I couldn't see myself doing anything good or right or fun. When I dreamed at night, my dreams were always about my happy past— doing normal things as I had done before in a normally functioning body—working, playing ball, playing with my kids, standing hand-in-hand with my wife, Shondell, feeling her touch, watching the baby elk play. Then I would wake up to a body that didn't even exist. I wasn't feeling sorry for myself. I wasn't feeling much of anything. I was numb, emotionally and physically.

I found myself doing what the doctors told me I would be doing. I started pushing my sweetheart away. See, I didn't marry Shondell to watch her mow the lawn, put gas in my car, get me dressed, help me use the restroom. I didn't like watching her do that for me. And I saw myself begin to push her away.

One day Shondell was transferring me from the shower chair to this very wheelchair—and she accidentally dropped me. I looked up at her face from the ground and I saw a bead of sweat slide down her cheek. And that was it. I lost it. I'd had enough. I didn't marry her to watch her labor over me. I let myself believe that I was too much of a man for this and I let myself believe it was humiliating. I verbally kicked her out of the room.

She went out and stood on the other side of the door, quietly crying; but she would not go farther than a few feet away from me. I was too much into my own selfish pain to think about what that had done to her.

The phone rang. It was my mother-in law (of all people). I have a great relationship with Char, my mother-in-law. She asked to talk to me. She could have ripped me apart but she knew I was struggling. She let me explain to her for the next ninety minutes the very things I just told you in thirty seconds—over and over again.

"I didn't marry your daughter to watch her do this," I raved.

Finally she said, "Are you through yet?"

Sarcastically I replied, "Yes."

The second thing she said was, "This is the most selfish person I have ever seen you be, Chad. When you say it wasn't why you married my daughter, apparently you weren't listening to yourself when you made the promises you made on your wedding day."

And the last thing she said hit me like a brick to the face, "Chad, you want to know the greatest thing you can give my daughter?"

"What?" I replied flatly.

"You can give her your most gracious acceptance."

Ouch. I had to be a real man. I had to swallow my stupid pride and recognize her ability to give to me. Recognize what she really wants to do. Recognize her attributes, her skills, her counsel—everything a marriage should entail. Not only recognize it, but thank her for it. So I've tried to do that every day of my life from then on.

Wright

Is it hard?

Hymas

Yes it is difficult. Why? Not pride—lack of vision. Not looking with 20/20 foresight at how our life would look if I would let my wife be who she really is—my partner, my equal. But when I do and she does, wow! They say hindsight is 20/20. I say foresight—vision—is 20/20 because we create exactly what we see.

Wright

So that's the turning point? You caught the vision of what a real partnership would be?

Hymas

That's right; thanks to my mother-in-law.

Wright

Chad, is there anyone in your life who somehow prepared you for this, or taught you something that now you're able to use?

Hymas

I am where I am today mostly because of my family; but I often find myself thinking about a very special individual who helped prepare me for this day with the help of my dad. Her name is Melanie.

I was a "jock" in high school. I was cool. I don't think I was mean, but as high school athletes often do, I thought I was "all that." At lunch I sat in the cafeteria with my basketball buddies. At the middle table sat the Special Ed' kids—many in wheelchairs.

One of them was a girl named Melanie. When she ate, her food ended up on her shirt, on her lap, on the floor. She used a computer to talk. She often drooled.

I am ashamed to admit it, but for whatever reason my friends and I thought that was kinda funny. One day after basketball practice we were all at my house—downstairs in my room—laughing and joking about Melanie. There comes a knock at my bedroom door.

It was my dad—he had been standing on the other side of the door and had heard everything we had said.

He came in and sat down on the bed. He sat quietly for a moment and then quietly but firmly set us straight.

"Do you want Melanie to have a life filled with loneliness or filled with good friends?" He asked.

We mumbled whatever we could mumble with our feet in our mouths. Then Dad left the room. But he wasn't done with us yet.

The next day at school he cinched it. I was sitting with my buddies. Melanie was sitting at the Special Ed' table. My dad walked into the cafeteria and right over to our table. Quietly, he asked, "Chad, where is Melanie sitting?"

"Over there," I replied. "She's the one with the computer on her chair."

"You and your buddies, follow me."

We followed Dad over to her table. He tapped Melanie on her shoulder and said, "Melanie, my name is Kelly Hymas. This is my son, Chad. These are his friends," and he introduced each by name.

Then he asked her, "How would you like to go to McDonald's with us and grab a milkshake?"

She typed on her computer, "I'm sorry, sir; but my mother won't let me go out with strangers."

I thought that was a classic response.

Wright

(laughing) Very good.

Hymas

So Dad took Melanie to the principal's office. The principal called her mother and received permission from her. My dad then picked Melanie up out of the chair and deposited her on the front passenger seat. We piled into the van.

We went to McDonald's together—ten "jocks" and a girl in a wheelchair in a van that only seats six. And I was able to find out more about her. I also found out more about me.

Melanie became part of the gang. Did we change her life? I hope so, because she sure changed ours. Because she hung out with us, people realized what a wonderful, witty, fun person she really was. Melanie was elected Head Cheerleader.

I think about her every day because today I get to go through just a little bit of what she went through every single day of her life.

Wright

Chad, since your accident, has faith played an important role in the decisions you have made?

Hymas

I have tried to have more humility and more faith in the last three or four years (I say "in the last three or four years" because it took me a few years to figure it out. Is that okay to say?) But now faith is huge for me.

A vision isn't much good without faith. Or, I don't know, maybe a vision creates faith. Certainly a vision creates desire and desire is the driving force that pulls you ahead. All I know is that vision and faith go hand-in-hand. You can see clearly what you desire—that's vision—then you believe in it because you can see it in detail and that belief or faith moves you closer to the vision and that vision gets clearer and clearer until one day you realize why it is so clear. It is real. She is playing on the carpet in front of you, looking up, and calling you "Daddy."

Art Berg said, "What you see drives your beliefs and that drives your actions and consequently your results." I respectfully add, what you see drives your beliefs and that drives your actions and consequently your results. What do I believe about speaking for a living? What do I have to say? How will I say it? Do I see myself listening to my audience as well? How will that impact and influence them?

Art Berg built me a high platform and told me to move higher from there. And that's why I have the world record trophies I have. I'm not talking about the wheelchair run from Salt Lake to Vegas, which, by the way, I did in Art Berg's chair to honor him. I'm talking about all the other wonderful things I have because I didn't give in to my paralysis. I stayed focused on my vision and let it pull me forward.

Where is my focus, and what do I believe? Since my accident, 20/20 foresight and focus—seeing myself as the father of a little girl—and the blessings of Heaven—gave me my precious little daughter. Seeing myself connect with individuals in an audience of thousands has created my professional speaking business. I can now get dressed in forty-seven minutes; Art could do it twice as fast but I am proud of my accomplishment. I never thought I would do as well as I do.

It took me sixteen months to learn how to drive a car again and the first time out I drove less than one mile, but that is a world record for me—maybe it's a pretty small world, but a trophy win nonetheless. The fact that I was on the front page of the *Wall Street Journal*, that's a world record—for me. Those are trophies—Shondell even calls herself my trophy wife. I agree—you will too when you meet her.

These wonderful things that are happening in my life are things that I never dreamed of. Those are my trophies and they are way beyond anything I would have ever thought I would achieve until Art Berg taught me to look ahead with 20/20 foresight and let that vision drive my faith and my faith drive my actions—even the repetitive tedious practice of learning to shave, brush my teeth, and put on my own socks. And now I get to take my vision to the world.

Wright

When you speak, what vision do you want your audience to see?

Hymas

I want my audiences to catch the vision of the wonderful life they will live when they stay focused on their vision with 20/20 foresight and faith. They don't have to be religious to see a vision, they just have to be a little imaginative. And when they are, miracles happen.

Wright

You are one of those rare individuals who understand your right and obligation to make a difference where you are with what you've got.

As we sit here in this studio, on this particular day, it's only been a few years since the accident and yet you have accomplished so much. You own your own business. You travel around the country speaking to literally thousands of people. You are still actively involved in competitive sports. You are the world record-holder for quadriplegics in cross-country wheelchair. It has taken you a relatively few years to get to the point where you are today.

What have you discovered about yourself that you really don't believe you would have ever discovered had it not been for the accident?

Hymas

I learned I had the latent ability to see tomorrow and to act on that vision. I don't say that to say I am all that special. It is just something I was blessed with, I guess. Vision is the catalyst that creates extraordinary results. And I have the power to see what I want to see. I didn't realize I had that power before my accident. I was able to create a vision and let that vision draw me into it.

Today, when I wake up in the morning, I have the power to decide what I want to see. I can choose my vision—my 20/20 foresight. I get to decide what it looks like. I can choose to see it. I let that vision work in my mind, play in it, dream about it, and let that vision pull me into my day.

Wright

So, with the answer you just now offered, I hear you saying that this isn't really a special skill or trait—there is no one who couldn't do what you're suggesting.

Hymas

That's right. And it is not complicated. I was just average before and I'm still just average today. But all of us "average" folks have great power. We have the power to choose our vision—to choose what we see and how clearly we see it. Some are more naturally inclined, maybe even more easily imaginative, but it is a skill—a mental habit that can be learned by anyone who wants extraordinary results.

We can all see with 20/20 foresight. We can create our own vision and thereby create our own results. We've all been given that ability to choose what we want to see and therefore do with every twenty-four-hour day we are blessed to live. We can choose our future and create our own destiny. Vision is the single most important factor in a successful and joyful life.

Visualization is throwing out a mental grappling hook and pulling yourself toward it. Vision somehow becomes an active force as you hook into it; it also draws you toward itself. Anyone can do this.

Try it right now. Think of something you want to have or do—think of who you want to be. How does it look? Are there colors? How does it taste? Does it have a texture? A sound to it? How does it feel? Is it warm? How does it feel emotionally? Does it involve a happy marriage? A healthy bank account?

See how the more clearly you focus on the vision, enlisting as many senses as possible, creates energy, drive, and desire? Well, that energy and desire also creates solutions, methods, and techniques.

From deep in your subconscious—even from the very soul of you—depending on how important this goal is that you are visualizing, comes power and purpose and desire and drive—and technique and skill—sufficient to get you there.

Wright

You said before, when we first started this conversation, that people around you, even your mother saw this accident as a tragedy.

Hymas

She wouldn't call it that today.

Wright

That's my question.

Hymas

Yeah, she wouldn't. She would tell you this has been one of the most significant blessings of my life—one of the most significant blessings of her life.

I am better with my kids. I discipline them differently. My kids are my friends. Do they need discipline? Yes. But Christian is taller than his dad today. Try disciplining your kid from your knees. It is an incredible experience. You can teach 'em better from your knees. Everything's different and, honestly, many things are much better—even things you wouldn't think were.

Wright

Wonderful story. How about the future? How you see your life thirty years from today?

Hymas

Thirty years from today I see myself happy—still happy; whether I'm walking or not. I see myself happy. I see myself with my boys and my girl. I see myself involved with their families. And, most important, I see myself still married and deeply, romantically in love with my Shondell—the girl of my dreams.

I'll still be telling my stories and hearing others. And telling my story never gets old because it's different every time. Everyone is different and whenever I share it with others I relate to them in different ways.

Wright

Will you walk again?

Hymas

I have a dream. In my dream I am walking again. I see myself holding Shondell's hand as we walk down the street. I see myself playing ball with my kids. I see myself dancing with my wife again to "our song," "Save the Best for Last," by Vanessa Williams:

> *"Sometimes the snow comes down in June.*
> *Sometimes the sun goes around the moon;*
> *Just when you thought you were falling fast,*
> *You go and save the best for last."*

I'd say that was prophetic. But I'm not going to wait for that to happen. I'm not. There's too much for me to do today. I'm still a husband. I'm still a dad. I've got a job. One day, you might interview me and I'll be standing; wouldn't that be a story!

Wright

That'd be great. Thank you so much, Chad, for being a part of the program with us today. Thanks for offering us practical insight about hitching to the star of our own vision and using its power of vision to pull us forward.

Consider the horror of a life-threatening injury that ends up claiming your ability to walk. But, as we've seen today, that even confined to a wheelchair, Chad Hymas has, and is, accomplishing more than most people I know. How does he do it? According to him, the same way any of us can do it. It isn't complicated. Just decide that life is worth living and with that vision and focus—20/20 foresight—we have the ability to achieve any important goal and make a real difference regardless of obstacles that life throws our way.

Chad, thank you so much for being with us today on *Speaking of Success.*

Hymas

Thank you. It's been fun.

About the Author

On April 3, 2001, Chad was involved in a serious accident leaving him a quadriplegic; however, Chad's dreams were not paralyzed that day. Since then Chad has done the following:

- Established Chad Hymas Communications, Inc., a professional speaking company designed to motivate businesses and corporations to look ahead with 20/20 foresight, allowing the power of their vision to pull them forward.
- The *Wall Street Journal* calls Chad Hymas one of the ten most inspirational people in the world!
- Last year Chad spoke at 160 different events, traveling just over 180,000 miles.
- Chad has shared his personal message and entertained many audiences from organizations such as Wells Fargo, Blue Cross Blue Shield, VastFX, IHC, Coca Cola, and the Utah Jazz.
- He is a member of the National Speakers Association and is a CSP (Certified Speaking Professional). A designation achieved by fewer than 8 percent in the speaking industry.
- Past president of the National Speakers Association, Utah chapter.
- Maintaining his hobby and dream of managing a 5,100 acre elk preserve with his father, Kelly.
- He has raced in marathons, and in the summer of 2003, Chad set a world record by wheeling his chair from Salt Lake City to Las Vegas (513 miles).
- Participating in wheelchair athletic competition including basketball, rugby, wheelchair racing, and officiating basketball (a dream come true).
- Spending many hours with other injured individuals in therapy, encouraging them to overcome their challenges, focus on dreams and make them a reality, and to love life for all that it has to offer.

Chad says his greatest accomplishment is that he remains a devoted husband to his loving wife, Shondell, and proud father to their three children Christian, Kyler, and new little Gracee!

Chad Hymas

Chad Hymas Communications, Inc.

Phone: 435.843.5707 (office)

877.BOOK.CHAD (toll free)

Fax: 435.843.5010

E-mail: info@chadhymas.com

www.chadhymas.com

www.meetchadhymas.com (bureau friendly)

Chapter 8

PATRICIA CLASON

THE INTERVIEW

David Wright (Wright)

Today we're talking with Patricia Clason. Patricia Clason is a professional speaker, trainer, coach, consultant, and writer. As owner and director of the Center for Creative Learning, the focus of her work is on alternative methods of teaching and learning that produce high quality results. Her search for the best in the technology of human resource development has taken her as a student on many adventures through traditional and not-so-traditional training programs.

An important aspect of Patricia's presentations is that she addresses the psychological perspectives and principles behind the practical tools that she teaches. Patricia shares personal and real stories so people know that her practical wisdom comes from experience, not just books and good ideas.

Patricia, you often quote the wise philosopher, Anonymous, as saying, "You won't know when you get there if you don't know where you are going." How did you know when you got there? How do you define success?

Patricia Clason (Clason)

Success is the mastery of life—designing and creating a life with health, wealth, love, and creative self-expression in a flowing balance that works for me. As a result of my years of practice of Tai Chi Chuan, a Chinese martial art, I focus on principles and practicing those principles in order to master life.

In Tai Chi, we learn about the flow of the yin and yang—the empty and full—a flow that is constantly changing and adjusting. Mastering the flow means moving beyond resisting what life brings us and making it work *for* us.

When my daughter was young, my focus was more on raising her than building my business; that was a fulfilling and rewarding focus, a choice I will always be grateful I made. As she grew older and needed me to be there less, I shifted more of my focus to my business, building a client base and traveling more.

There are two key principles that permeate everything I teach: personal responsibility and full, free, and safe expression of emotion. These principles are also a consistent base under all of the teachings about success that I have read and experienced in my life.

One of the first things to be responsible for is the way we define success. Instead of taking on a definition of success from our parents, peers, or the media, each of us must choose how we will define success and experience satisfaction. There will always be someone who has more or less than you have, so comparing yourself to anyone else in order to gauge your success is a mistake. We all have talents that we express in a unique way. Not everyone can be a billionaire, powerful businessperson, politician, media star, or professional athlete. The roles needed to make our world work are many. If we each mastered doing what we do well with love, respect, excellence, and creativity, we would all have satisfaction and a lifestyle that fits us—in other words: Success.

Being in the moment—focusing *Now*—and doing our resourceful best is another important aspect of success. To call the result we achieve when making our best effort anything other than success requires moving out of the present moment into the past or future, comparing what is to what was or what could have been. Success isn't an end, a destination, or somewhere we are going. Success is being present to life in the moment and experiencing it to the fullest; we are always there and always arriving at the same time.

Wright

What does it mean to practice personal responsibility?

Clason

Success is directly related to one's willingness to be 100 percent personally responsible for one's life. When we blame anyone or anything else for *our* experience, *our* emotions, or *our* results, we give away *our* power to make changes and sculpt life to get the results we want.

At some level, we all know that we can't control other people or their actions. What we *can* do is take 100 percent of the responsibility for our choices, our actions and reactions, and our beliefs and emotions. These are some of the attitudes or behaviors of taking responsibility:

- Accepting what is—no blame, it just is,
- Instead of bragging or being prideful, simply owning our actions and results,
- Skipping the excuses, reasons, and justifications, and empowering ourselves by being accountable for our results—what we did or did not do,
- Repairing mistakes when necessary, and as soon as possible,
- Owning our beliefs, attitudes, and perceptions as just that—our beliefs, attitudes, and perceptions—not the absolute truth,
- Respecting others' beliefs, attitudes, and perceptions, and
- Changing our beliefs, thoughts, and actions in order to create different results.

Rather than waiting for someone else to do it for you, give it to you, or do it to you, or letting the world outside you determine your life, taking 100 percent responsibility gives you the opportunity to shape life into what you want it to be.

Wright

You talk about making core choices—fundamental choices—that affect the rest of our choices and actions. What are those core choices?

Clason

In order to have the life we went, there are certain choices we must make.

The first core choice is to *choose*.

We must choose what *we want* to make of our lives and then act on that choice. To not do so invites the world outside of us to determine our future, and just as surely to determine our dissatisfaction and struggle.

The second core choice is to define our purpose or vision for life.

Vision is our reason for being (*raison d'être* from the French). This vision or purpose is one without end—it lasts as long as we do. Once we have a vision, we then define our mission—how we will bring that vision into reality. Within that mission are the goals—the specific results we want to achieve along the way.

We also have to choose what kind of person each of us wants to be, and what qualities we want to develop in ourselves. These qualities are the values we hold that guide us spiritually in our choices and actions.

My personal values include:
- persistence and perseverance,
- patience,
- passion,
- flexibility,
- authenticity,
- compassion,
- curiosity,
- continuous learning,
- family/team consciousness,
- healthy boundaries,
- self-care,
- emotional intelligence,
- living life intentionally,
- respect,
- willingness to ask for and receive assistance,
- integrity and accountability,
- introspection (constantly examining strengths and weaknesses), and
- ethics.

My top three values are peace, love, and truth. I strive to make choices that are loving (even if it is sometimes tough love), truthful (in integrity), and that create peace.

The third core choice is to plan for success, using the tools proven to be effective over time in getting results.

Whether we are talking about building a business or a family, it is important to *have* a plan, *work* the plan, *review* the plan, *revise* the plan, and then begin the cycle again. As life brings us changes and challenges, the plan requires revision. That doesn't mean it was a bad plan or that we shouldn't have a plan. It is the nature of all plans that they change and grow over time.

As you work the cycle of planning, it is critical to continually re-orient yourself to your vision, mission, and values. Future pace: ask yourself, "What will my life be like five years, ten years, twenty years from now if I take this action, follow this path? Is that what I want? Can I live with myself and feel good about those results? Will my family and friends be proud of me?"

The fourth core choice is to act.

Taking regular, consistent action on the plans that we create is necessary to get results. While we may occasionally be pleasantly surprised by a goal that just seems happen all by itself, we need to work our plan. Also, continual development of habits of thought and action that support our vision and mission make it easier to handle the down times (challenges) and help us create the up times (celebrations) that are a part of the roller coaster ride we call life.

The fifth core choice is whether to play small or play large.

Playing small is about avoiding risk and holding back in fear. It's about withholding our talents and our potential to contribute. The result of playing small is that we live at the level of survival. We can be in "survival mode" even when we have a lot of money or other traditional measures of success yet we live in fear of loss, not truly enjoying or sharing life with others.

Playing large, on the other hand, is about taking a risk to make a difference—to contribute our talents and compassion to the world. It's about making a difference that helps create a better, safer world for others. In *Taking It Lightly,* the weekend emotional intelligence intensive I created, we say, "There is only one heart, and it matters to this one." This phrase is a combination of the concept of our being inter-dependent here on this planet (one heart) with the reality that making a difference for one affects all.

I love the story from Lauren Eiseley, *The Star Thrower,* which has been paraphrased into a very short story you have probably seen in many places. An observer sees a person on the beach early in the morning, throwing something into the sea. As the observer gets closer, it becomes apparent that the person is returning stranded starfish to the sea. The observer asks, "There are millions of starfish on this beach. You can help so few. Does it really make a difference? Does it matter?" The thrower responds, "Oh yes, it matters to this one."

There is a ripple effect each time a person reaches out in kindness or contributes to the world in a positive way, just like the ripples that flow when we throw a stone into the pond.

Playing large is not about how much money, acknowledgment, or media attention we receive. It is making your contribution regardless of the risk that it may not be popular or welcomed by some, or that it may not be seen or acknowledged by *anyone*. In fact, playing large is often focused on others—helping them to become co-creators in their lives. Instead of impressing others with your presence, it leaves them feeling good and strong and capable, impressed with themselves.

Wright

What do you mean by the principle of full, free, and safe expression of emotion?

Clason

Full, free, and safe emotional expression equals Emotional Intelligence. Neuroscience researchers and psychologists are now telling us that 80 percent of success in any job is determined by the level of emotional intelligence within the individual. I taught full, free, and safe emotional expression for twenty years before Daniel Goleman's book made "emotional intelligence" an everyday term.

The four key competencies of emotional intelligence as defined by Daniel Goleman include: knowing one's own emotions, being able to manage one's emotions, being able to relate to emotions in others, and being able to manage relationships.

Full expression of emotion does not mean explosive emotion. It means feeling emotions fully and expressing them safely. As we learn to experience our own emotions and the emotions of others safely, our relationships become easier and more satisfying. We develop ways to communicate even the deep emotions, which allows us to create intimacy, heal old wounds, or enrich our relationships. The flow of emotion—which is literally energy in motion—brings more aliveness.

Many people, and even some modern psychology texts, refer to anger, sadness, and fear as the "negative emotions," implying that they are bad and wrong. Yet every emotion has a time and a place; they are all natural responses to life's experiences. Even anger is useful and can be felt and expressed in healthy ways without becoming violence. When we are safe with all of our emotions and they can flow freely, they don't build to toxic levels, resulting in violence or depression. Instead, we experience the flow of life and joy and gratitude for all of our experiences.

My own process of developing my emotional intelligence escalated with a weekend intensive in 1983 called *Understanding Yourself and Others*. I became an instructor for that program, and then in 1986 wrote a new weekend program called *Taking It Lightly*. Since 1983, I have taught over 350 weekend intensives. Doing all of those weekends gave me an abundance of experience in feeling and expressing my own emotions, as well as developing and fine-tuning my emotional intelligence skills. Several thousand people have graduated from *Taking It Lightly*. It has been so gratifying to see their lives transform as they develop their emotional intelligence and live their lives with personal responsibility. This is, next to raising my daughter, my greatest success.

Wright

In your experience, what keeps people from success?

Clason

Being unwilling to practice—to do the work. One of the biggest obstacles to success is an unwillingness to do the work necessary to practice the principles. We often become sidetracked by techniques or offerings for quick success. We can be distracted or misled by the allure of immediate gratification; yet in the end this is not satisfying. It only causes us to want more and want it faster, like any other addiction.

We learn everything through repetition and practice, which develops the neural pathways that become our hard-wired patterns and beliefs about life. These neural pathways allow us to function easily because they allow us to do many things in life on autopilot. It took us time and practice to master walking, talking, eating, writing, reading, driving, and many other things we do in life. Can you imagine how difficult life would be if you had to *think about* tying your shoes, taking a step, or hitting return on a keyboard every time you did it?

Success is the same way. It takes time and practice, working the principles until you *become* the principles. My Tai Chi instructor always said, "Practice, practice, practice." Eventually the principles are integrated in you and you have mastery. Success then becomes as easy as taking a walk.

The other major obstacle for most people is the set of beliefs they hold about themselves, life, success, money, work, relationships, etc., that were formed as a result of their childhood experiences in these areas. These beliefs are usually fear-based and over time become automatic habits of thought and action—so automatic that many times people don't even recognize that these beliefs are running their lives. How often do you let a four-year-old make a decision that runs your life? Here's a secret: *people do it all the time!* Their lives are running on decisions that were made early in life and now are so subconscious that they are rarely, if ever, questioned. My Tai Chi instructor had another saying: "Pay attention, pay attention, pay attention!"

The most common self-defeating belief is, "I am not good enough," and it has many variations, usually with the same result—some form of self-sabotage. If we want success, we must become aware of our self-defeating decisions and replace them with ones that work *for* us!

Wright

Once you have success you're done, right?

Clason

No. Just like a martial art, if you don't continue to practice, you become rusty—not as flexible or strong.

Life will continue to offer challenges, obstacles, and changes for you to handle. In my experience, it's like a video game—we master one level, and then reach another where the obstacles are more challenging. So, in order to master the game, we continue to develop higher levels of skill and mastery. This comes from practice, practice, practice.

Wright

Do we have a responsibility to others in our success?

Clason

I believe we *do* have a responsibility to others—the responsibility of giving. There are actually three facets to this responsibility.

The first responsibility is to be a role model and mentor who teaches and empowers co-creators, who is accountable and holds others accountable, who lives in balance, and celebrates the successes of others. It is having gratitude for what we have been given and sharing the wealth (tangible or intangible) with others. I call this the responsibility to contribute or *to give back*.

One interesting aspect of success is that it attracts to itself scrutiny, jealousy, sabotage, and other negative energies of those unwilling to create their own success. We have a responsibility to continue acting in alignment with in our vision, mission, and values despite the often unconscious attempts of others to take us down because their misery loves company. This is the second responsibility of giving: *to not give up*.

In success, we can also be tempted with greed—the lust for the accomplishment and the resulting attention or benefits. Our responsibility is to pursue a practical and profitable plan for a worthy purpose, rather than doing "whatever" *just* to get the money or recognition. This is the third responsibility of giving: *to not give in*.

Wright

Who are the success role models who inspired you?

Clason

One of my role models is Earl Nightingale who said, *"Success is the progressive realization of worthy purpose."* Hearing this was a turning point for me as I began to recognize that success was not material things—the big house, fur coats, fancy cars, or lots of money. It rang true for me in my heart that a worthy purpose was the reason for living and true success was about living out that purpose, whether it included material wealth or not. There are many financially wealthy people who live simple lives and find their success and satisfaction in playing large and making the world a better place to live.

James Allen said, *"To put away aimlessness and weakness, and begin to think with purpose, is to enter the ranks of the strong ones who only recognize failure as one of the pathways to attainment; who make all conditions serve them, and who think strongly, attempt fearlessly, and accomplish masterfully."* This quote also had a deep impact on me. It reminds me that I will make mistakes, fall short, or fail, and that it is simply another step along the path. If I don't judge my failures as *bad*, or *myself* as bad for having them, then I can learn from my mistakes. If I am willing to learn, I won't fear failure. Learning also helps me be satisfied with my results and keeps me moving forward.

Fred Lehrman said, *"Why are you pretending you are not great?"* Fred was my original Tai Chi instructor; one of his gifts to me was this question. He taught me about owning my greatness—that I have a gift for the world, that my gift makes a difference, and that I can be proud of this gift.

We often compare ourselves with others who have done more, have more, do it better, etc. Or we think that we have to accomplish big things, be recognized by the world, or be famous. Making a difference one person at a time is as important to the planet as impacting thousands at a time. Our names don't have to be in the media or history books for us to have made a great contribution.

Mother Theresa said, *"Do it anyway."* Mother Theresa is cited as having a poem on her wall called *Anyway* that was about doing what was right regardless of the response of others. I learned from her that living my life following my vision matters to the one heart, one person at a time. She did what she believed was the right thing for her to do in alignment with her values and spirituality. She is also an example of success and satisfaction that is not materially based.

There are those who will succeed in the material world, some in great measure. There are those who will succeed in other aspects of life. Some will succeed at being good parents and raising good children, others succeed at finding a job that they love or a vocation that contributes to the world. Living a simple, satisfying life is also success. It is not ours to judge another person's path of success or to compare it to our own or to anyone else's path.

Wright

Is there anything that you suggest people do and/or not do in their search for success?

Clason

- Don't look for magic formulas as the easy way out. They don't work.
- Remember to nurture your relationships and your spirituality, or all that you achieve will still leave you feeling empty.
- Pay attention to your body—good health is critical to being able to enjoy the fruits of your success.

- Don't do anything just for the money. Selling your soul for material wealth will eventually destroy your creativity and passion, maybe even your physical health and relationships.
- Take action today—*now*. We do not know how many more seconds or days or years we have left to live. Make this moment and every moment the best it can be. Live it fully. Appreciate it fully.

My parting wisdom is: The world is abundant with opportunity, like a deep, deep well of fresh water. You have a choice—will you just sip because you think there's not enough, or will you drink fully and freely with gratitude?

About the Author

For over thirty years, Patricia Clason has traveled across the continent doing speeches, workshops, and media appearances as a professional speaker, trainer, consultant, writer, and coach, giving over 4,000 presentations for corporations, associations, government agencies, and non-profit organizations. Now the owner and Director of the Center for Creative Learning, which offers programs for personal and professional development at offices in Milwaukee, Madison, and Detroit, Patricia has written many articles, training programs, and personal growth seminars. She hosted radio and television interview shows for ten years and is also a sought-after guest.

As a consultant and business coach she works with large and small companies as well as with individuals in the areas of start-up, marketing, management skills, and career building.

Patricia was the first to receive the Registered Corporate Coach designation from the National Association of Business Coaches (now the Worldwide Association of Business Coaches). *Ask the Coach,* Patricia's question and answer column on career coaching, appeared regularly in *Employment Times* and is currently on *MilwaukeeJobs.com.* Her articles are also often printed in business and trade publications and in online newsletters.

To keep all this together, and still have time for her family and herself, Patricia must truly practice what she teaches in the areas of communication, time and stress management, and motivation, as well as business marketing, management, emotional intelligence, and ethics.

Patricia Clason
Patricia Clason, LLC
Center for Creative Learning, LLC
2437 N Booth Street
Milwaukee, WI 53212
Phone: 414.374.5433
E-mail: patricia@lightly.com
www.patriciaclason.com
www.lightly.com

Chapter 9

MARY WOLF

THE INTERVIEW

David Wright (Wright)

Today we're talking with Mary Wolf. She is a speaker and strategic consultant specializing in working with people and their companies to achieve unparalleled success. She is a highly motivational force in helping people go beyond their personal expectations, and she is a strategic thinker who has the ability to keenly assess situations and deliver fast results.

Mary is founder of Mary Wolf Enterprises, LLC, and she brings twenty-five years of experience in organization and leadership development with Fortune 500 companies. She provides strategic consulting, executive coaching, talent alignment, leadership and management development, team enhancement, and training, as well as speaking engagements. Her programs are customized for high impact. She works in all industries and work environments. She is listed in *Who's Who of American Women,* and in the *Cambridge Who's Who Registry.* She has been on local radio, quoted in the *Wall Street Journal,* and has been the focus of newspaper business articles. She served as an executive women's delegate to China and a guest lecturer for Rider University. She serves on several organizations' boards of directors, and is active in many professional organizations.

Mary Wolf, welcome to *Speaking of Success.*

Mary Wolf (Wolf)

Thank you David, thank you very much.

Wright

So what has been your journey to success?

Wolf

Well, David, I started out about twenty-five years ago. I had a small successful retail business and was also an adjunct professor at a community college when the Dean called me in one day and said he wanted to start a consulting piece to the college and he wanted me to head it up. This was a little foreign to me at the time for I had really no background in that field; but I'm not one to say no so I said I would be delighted to do it. I asked him to please send me to New York.

In New York I conducted some research, attended some seminars, and figured it all out. I then began my journey in consulting.

I found that I loved consulting because it combines the three areas I'm passionate about. One is business, two is people development, and three is learning. I found that this part of consulting and designing training programs and coaching people really turned me on so I applied for a job at RCA as a stand-up trainer; I was lucky enough to get that. I sold my retail business and started my journey to my career in organizational development.

I have found that my guiding path has always been the internal urges I feel—the areas of life that I feel very passionate about, the things I love to do, the kinds of things I'm willing to stay up all night for, to take risks. I'll put these into three major areas:

1. *Professional*—My barometers are these: am I doing the work I love? Am I making a difference? Am I respected and known for the work? Am I sought out by others?
2. *Personal*—Relationships with my family and friends are very, very important to me. I need those relationships to be wholesome, reciprocal, and very highly functioning. I work hard on that. I also value my good health, fitness, spirituality, and my emotional state. I want to be an emotionally healthy person.

3. *Financial*—I set my own targets and I create ways of getting there.

I set goals for myself every day and ask myself periodically, am I where I want to be? If not, what do I have to do to get there? And the peak of achieving success for me is to be the architect of my own life, to chart my own course, and to decide how I want to live my life, and then I make it happen.

Wright

Have you found that there is a secret ingredient successful people seem to have?

Wolf

Most definitely, and I've whittled them down to twelve key areas of success. One is that successful people have a bias toward action. They always ask themselves, how can I? They don't sit around and think about why this happened or why that happened. They're always questioning how they can do something and how they can conquer obstacles. They follow-up, they follow-through, they don't say what they're going to do without doing it. They take action and they're always anticipating everything that might be coming their way, they're always looking around the corner.

The second one is that successful people go inside to flourish outside. In other words, they set goals, they know their strengths, they know who and where their resources are, and they call on them. They adjust their sails in the direction of the strong winds that move them forward to achieving their goals. They're like mountain-climbers—they know they can rest and lean on their team when they're tired and not judge that as a weakness but as a strength in their climb to the top.

The third ingredient successful people have is they never stop learning and yearning for more. They know they will never reach the end—success is always a work in progress. Success is a journey and they enjoy the ride!

The fourth ingredient is woven through all successful people—their passion. They're always in touch with what they love to do, they surround themselves with people they love, and they create their plan around that.

Number five is successful people internally explore who they are as well as the world around them. They rely on their strengths and they have full confidence in themselves. They know where to turn when they need help; they know they cannot do everything themselves and they don't try. They capitalize on their talents and their strengths and they trust those around them to fill those gaps. The total picture is what counts with successful people.

Ingredient number six (another major ingredient) is that they have the courage to live out loud. It is a courageous act to put yourself out in the world and to stand up to criticism—there's going to be a lot of that—and there are a lot of unknowns. The secret here is that little ole belief in yourself and the knowledge that you are a winner no matter what—you can handle challenges that come your way. David, sometimes we just have to figure it out as it comes to us. Knowing how to do things and knowing how to take care of ourselves is also very important.

Number seven is that they put joy in their work. This comes from their passion and they work in that joy. Their work is not work, it's more like play. You'll find people who love what they do thrive on it, it shows, and it's contagious. People are attracted to them for this joy they provide and put out into the world.

Number eight is that successful people know what they stand for and what they don't stand for and they use their energy wisely.

Number nine is they always trust their gut. They check things out cognitively and intelligently but their decisions are usually swift. They use their intuition and they keenly apply their knowledge.

The tenth ingredient is that successful people are secure in their decisions even in the face of doubt. Again, they always trust their gut.

The eleventh ingredient is they use their energy to fight for what they believe in, not against what they don't believe in.

Number twelve—the final ingredient successful people have—is that they do not perceive a difference between what ifs and what is. Even though they certainly know that there is a "what if—" their passion and determination propel them forward. They love the uncharted course.

Those are my twelve keys to success, David.

Wright

So do you have a formula that has served you well?

Wolf

I do David. I surround myself with positive people from whom I can learn and people who can also learn from me. When I am with people who want to be around me it fortifies my strengths and it energizes me to challenge myself to rise to new heights.

Years ago I heard a statement that has resonated deeply with me to this day and it's this: "Successful people are willing to do what unsuccessful people are not." That's it in a nutshell. Successful people do what it takes to reach their goals and align values with their actions. They jump hurdles, they build bridges, they take risks, they hit brick walls, and they create innovative ways to get around them. They use detours as opportunities.

Successful people have clarity on what they say yes to and what they say no to and the consequences of both. Life comes at us quickly these days, everybody knows that, and successful people innately know what to grab onto and what to let go of; they do it quickly, never taking their eye off their goal.

So that sums up my little formula David.

Wright

I know there are a lot of skills that go into being successful, but would you share with our readers at least three skills that you think are critical in creating a path to success?

Wolf

Yes I will. One of the things that I've observed (and I certainly know within myself) is I just put one foot in front of the other and keep moving forward in the direction of my goals. I create clear actions every single day that move me forward. And here's another clue that I think is so critical in regard to successful people—they know when to rest and the benefits of play and I mean "play" in the true sense of the word. Play activates the right brain, which is your creative side. That can serve you well and help you be innovative and refreshed back on the job. These are some really critical skills that are not real tangible but that successful people really put into play.

The second one is that successful people have contingency plans and they're ready to activate them.

The third one is, as I said before, that they know who their resources are. They know who they can depend on and who has their best interests at heart. They know what skills and talents they need at any particular time and who has them; they then go after those who have those skills and talents.

Wright

So what has been your biggest challenge?

Wolf

Ah David, my biggest challenge is managing my emotions—my emotional intelligence. Change is inevitable but growth is optional and time and time again I have witnessed that managing emotions is the biggest downfall of people. Conversely, good management of emotions can contribute greatly to their success. Once again, it's a journey inward—checking into what's really going on inside, acknowledging it, accepting it, having insight about it, and making strong decisions not to display inappropriate behavior but rather to use your intellect to express your feelings in a thought-provoking way to move you forward.

Sometimes you just might be down for the count but know that you always have a choice. Although it might not be easy or obvious you will get another chance.

One of my mantras has been that old song, *The Gambler,* by Kenny Rogers. When you examine it, success is actually gambling or betting on yourself to win, so I like this song:

> "You got to know when to hold 'em,
> Know when to fold 'em,
> Know when to walk away and know when to run."

I say that in my head quite frequently and it serves me well. I remind myself daily that I only have so much energy to use that day and so I use it wisely. I make priority decisions around my daily goals that take me one step further to my big goals. I always know that there are going to be interruptions so I plan for them. That way I diminish my stress level, which as we all know consumes our energy. So I count on the unexpected every day because it's as sure as anything else to show up. I remind myself that when things seem insurmountable today they'll be a piece of cake tomorrow.

I also remind myself that the greatest success is paying it forward and doing that, there's always a bias toward action.

Wright

So how do you navigate the challenges that come your way and come out on top?

Wolf

Well, I really observe this keenly—some people let things happen but successful people *make* things happen. So I've learned how to ride the speed bumps in the road, when to slow down, and when and where to speed up. I reach out when I need to and I check out data, information, and knowledge. I then turn what I've learned into wisdom to shed light on the situation.

Sometimes you've just got to get away—sometimes that's the secret to success. Throw it in the proverbial pile, walk away, and do something totally and completely different. We get so entrenched in our own processes and thoughts. They can become a whirlpool that has its own power. We can lose perspective and getting away helps. Go to the movies when you're over the top. Go to the beach, take a hike, go for a bike ride, go shopping, go to a museum—do whatever it takes to give yourself the space you need when you need it. This is truly working with yourself and going inward so you can be effective outwardly.

Wright

How important do you think people skills are to success?

Wolf

Well, let me put it this way: is there anything—anything in the entire world—we do that doesn't ultimately involve people? I don't think so. Understanding differences and what your hot buttons are, what pushes your patience, how to interact with all types of people, and how to handle different behaviors so that you can create win-win situations are keys to all successes. Whatever we do we're working through people.

I live by the platinum rule. Most people know the golden rule, which is of course to "do unto others as you would have them do unto you." My platinum rule is "do unto others as they would have you do unto them," so I watch, I listen, I learn. Successful people are keen listeners.

Wright

So do you have any advice that you give to beginners?

Wolf

Yes I do, because it wasn't so long ago I felt like a beginner. My advice is to create your own definition of success. That's so important.

Everybody needs to have a personal definition of what success is for them.

Then make a list of the top 100 things you want to achieve in life, put them in priority order, create a timeline, identify steps that need to take place, identify possible obstacles and back-up plans, create your action plan with goals, dates, and just chip away at it every single day.

Another piece of advice I have is listen to those urges inside of you. Know what your passion is and know that passion is the fuel and your belief in yourself is the lubricant for your energy force.

Create your personal mission, vision, and value statement and keep it in front of you at all times no matter where you are. Put a copy on your desk, put a copy in your laptop, put a copy anywhere you go and keep it in front of you as a reminder.

Know what you stand for and what you stand against—that's so important.

Know that the biggest risk in life is really truly not taking a risk. Everyone is afraid but the successful do it anyway.

I love Stephen Covey's circle of control and circle of influence. We have to put our energy to work wisely and focus on our circle of control and know that a satisfying life of peace, joy, contentment, and happiness come ultimately from pushing ourselves to the limit. Create a life you love and when it's all said and done, look back and admire your canvas. You started with a blank one and created a masterpiece. It's uniquely yours.

Develop a quiet knowing that even in the face of adversity you can take control—the circle of control. Insulate yourself from negative forces, know that there is a safe haven and balance is the key so when you're tired, rest, play, and come back with gusto. Know that there's a high cost to doing nothing, much greater actually than taking risks. And live on purpose, know what your excellence is, observe, ask, and do, get feedback along the way.

Being productive is possible every minute. That may even mean reflection time, play time, down time; but you need to engage your creativity.

I like to form a coalition. I have an advisory board I use—people I turn to who will give me advice on the tough stuff.

Believe in yourself, in your natural intuitive capability and take quantum leaps.

Know what motivates you. Have a knowledge of what's important to you and develop the willingness to make the right trade-off. Discipline yourself to do what you don't really want to do at times.

Know that success is very personal as well as public. There will always be naysayers who usually sound like they really know that bad things are on the way and you know what, they just might be right; but put your energy into positive outcomes and go forward. Surround yourself with winners and people you can learn from. Challenge yourself, learn from the masters, internalize your success, build on it. In the end know you can do well by doing good.

Wright

So what would you consider your biggest motivator to be?

Wolf

I'd have to say it's my drive, my unwillingness not to give up, my ability to see the future, my ability to taste success before it materializes, and recreating over and over again something out of nothing.

Wright

So how do you know what you don't know?

Wolf

Ah, that's a good question. By paying keen attention to what's going on around me, by picking people's brains, by being curious, by admitting that I have a lot to learn. I have an 80/20 equation that looks something like this: I know 80 percent of what I need to know to be successful at what it is I want to achieve. The other 20 percent I either have resources for or I just simply don't know it, so I listen and I learn.

I have a little acronym that I'd like to share with you.

SUCCESS:
S—Start at the beginning.
U—Upward is always the path.
C—Clarity
C—Creativity
E—Enjoy the ride.
S—Strategize.
S—Stop to reflect.

Wright

What's next for Mary Wolf?

Wolf

Ah, what's next for Mary Wolf? I just want to keep on growing my company, Mary Wolf Enterprises. I'm very excited about this book. I intend to market it and do some public speaking.

I've also moved toward a new area of my life—real estate investment—so I intend to get really sharp on that end and make that another business of mine.

I'm also opening a new business called Street Smart Sales Academy®. This is specifically geared toward salespeople who work strictly on commission, which is a tough row to hoe.

I'm excited about that journey as well. Thanks for asking me David.

Wright

Well, what a great conversation. I really appreciate your taking all this time with me today to answer these questions.

Wolf

It was my pleasure.

Wright

Today we've been talking with Mary Wolf. She is a speaker and strategic consultant. She specializes in helping people and their companies achieve unparalleled successes. She is a highly motivational force in helping people go beyond their personal expectations. Mary is a strategic thinker who has the ability to keenly assess situations and deliver fast results. And I don't know about you, but I think she knows what she's talking about.

Wolf

Thank you David.

Wright

Thank you so much for being with us today, Mary, on *Speaking of Success.*

Wolf

It was my pleasure.

About the Author

MARY WOLF, founder of Mary Wolf Enterprises, LLC, brings twenty-five years of experience in organization and leadership development with Fortune 500 companies. She provides strategic consulting, executive coaching, talent alignment, leadership and management development, team enhancement, and training, as well as speaking engagements. Her programs are customized for high impact. Mary works in all industries and work environments. She is listed in *Who's Who of American Women*, and in the *Cambridge Who's Who Registry.* She has been on local radio, quoted in the *Wall Street Journal,* and been the focus of newspaper business articles. She served as an executive women's delegate to China and a guest lecturer for Rider University. She serves on Boards of Directors, and is active in many professional organizations.

Mary Wolf
Mary Wolf Enterprises, LLC
7415 Fairlinks Court
Sarasota, FL 34243
Phone: 941.780.2578
Fax: 941.360.3196
E-mail: marywolf77@aol.com
www.mwolfenterprises.com

Chapter 10

DETRI MCGHEE

THE INTERVIEW

David Wright (Wright)

Today we're talking with Detri L. McGhee. She is president of DLM and Associates. She has spent over twenty-five years in the financial services world as an insurance agent, a securities registered representative, a market development vice president, and then as training coordinator for one of the largest independent insurance firms in America. Detri led the on-site training of Wells Fargo Bank's first Insurance Representatives. Upon leaving that field, Detri owned a quilting shop for three years. Her Criticism Management System and its principles were compiled from over thirty years' experience in business and personal life. She now dedicates full time to sharing that information. Detri's CD and workbook are titled, *Criticism Management: Using the Cunning C-A-T to Tame the Dragon of Criticism.*

Detri, welcome to *Speaking of Success.*

Detri L. McGhee (McGhee)

Thank you David, it's great to be here with you.

Wright

How do your Criticism Management principles and techniques propel people more quickly and easily toward success?

McGhee

Successfully handling criticism is a universal problem. From birth to death we are in danger of—and receive—criticism.

Just when we get wrapped in warm blankets and cuddled in Mom's arms for a moment, criticism hits. We are shuffled off in the arms of strangers only to be unwrapped and tugged upon. We experience one problem after another. At one point they stick us with a needle. Do we object? Most assuredly we do! So we are criticizing them for hurting us. And, we feel justified. After all, they criticized us first. They told us that our body wasn't perfect as it was and they needed to change it in some way. Well, of all the nerve. That *hurt!*

A simple test of whether any criticism management techniques and principles can benefit us is to ask this: "Do I ever get frustrated, depressed, mad, hurt, sad, defiant, incapacitated, or feel rejected? Or have I ever lost my temper?" You can bet that criticism or one of its siblings—grumbling, complaining, griping, or ingratitude—is at the root of the problem. Upon close inspection we can see that criticism in one form or another is included in any negative, painful situation of life. From birth to death it continues. At every turn we're faced with people telling us what to do and how to do it, where to go, how to get there, and even *when* to be there. We are told who we are and who we should become, what to learn, and how to learn it.

As we travel through our world, seldom do we feel that we are doing things right. In today's world many people don't even *know* how to define "right." Even the most self-confident, powerful, charismatic people in the world know how criticism stings.

The natural, undeveloped temperament of my youth included a much-too-deep desire to please everyone. I had a feeling that no matter what went wrong with anyone in my life—a loved one, classmate, coworker, or friend—it was somehow my fault. I felt that I should have been able to avoid the problem or at least fix it quickly and to everyone's complete satisfaction. That's a no-win situation. It took me quite a few years of heartache to realize that fact. Even today I sometimes feel twinges of inferiority or guilt when the people around me aren't happy.

Accompanying those feelings was the problem that criticism tended to incapacitate me—to make me want to hibernate and to run from trying. It was years before I found out that I was not alone. There was also this nagging *fear of success* that was as strong in me as any fear of failure. Actually, it was even stronger. I really didn't have much fear of failure. I had been told that I should just get up and try again, learn what I could and apologize sincerely if appropriate. Like the old song lyrics, "Pick yourself up, dust yourself off, and start all over again." My parents and teachers *expected* me to succeed and allowed me a reasonable number of mistakes along the way.

But when it came to adult life, I observed a different set of rules. I saw that failure was common, even pitied. People often reach out to you. Mediocrity is acceptable; it goes unnoticed so to speak. But with real success there is a heavy backlash to endure. Often, the one at the top is a target for everyone else. Just look at sports. People root for the underdog and then if they become too successful you will hear many people say, "I hope they get creamed. I'm sick of them winning." Then there's the sad truth that sometimes success does change people so they really *do* deserve some criticism. Deserved or not, people who excel will receive criticism—and lots of it.

For those dealing with failure right now, criticism management techniques can help to pinpoint the cause and uncover a strategy for turning that failure into success. For those in the midst of success, sometimes this wisdom is needed even more. In the search for and discovery of these criticism management principles I also learned that as we mature we *should be* evolving into a balanced personality that develops our natural strengths and works through our natural weaknesses. I deeply wanted that balance in my life and through seeking that, the concept of Criticism Management was born.

Wright

"Criticism Management"—I don't believe I've heard that exact term before. Did you coin that phrase?

McGhee

Well David, I guess perhaps I did. I don't remember hearing the term before I began using it. Because of my career, I've studied a lot about communication and sales skills. I grew up professionally on Earl Nightingale's tapes and self-help books. I've seen some work on how to give criticism but I have never seen any in-depth discussion on how to take criticism—*any* and *all criticism,* constructive or not—and make it work *for* me instead of trying to ignore it or letting it harm me.

In trying to learn from all the success gurus, another problem invariably cropped up for me. Without fail they all gave strong advice to always, always, *always* avoid negative people. Even my favorite early mentor, Dr. Norman Vincent Peale, consistently advised avoiding negative people. He said negative people bring us down, try to crush our dreams, and offer only discouragement.

Of course, he was right. However, what if that negative person is someone you love, right in your own family, with whom you don't *want* to sever your relationship? Are we doomed then to depression and failure because we spend so many hours with someone like that? Isn't there some wisdom in all of creation that can help us to succeed and have happy, fulfilling lives while dealing with (rather than deleting) that relationship? That is an important function of criticism management techniques. *That* is what makes it worth the work to discover the system, the techniques, and the principles.

Wright

Was there a crisis time that actually started you writing these concepts down?

McGhee

Yes, David, there was. In my early thirties I received some substantial and undeserved criticism (at least, that's the way I viewed it). I reacted to it rather inappropriately. Because of my reaction not only did I have to deal with undeserved, incorrect criticism, but I had to acknowledge some deserved, correct criticism of my inappropriate reaction!

I'm not sure what hurts more, David—undeserved criticism that's *wrong* or deserved criticism that is *right!* That's a little like asking what hurts more—a broken leg or a broken arm. The answer, of course, is, "Whichever you have at the moment."

Through the years, I have found that the best way for me to really learn from something—to learn how I truly feel—is to put my concerns and questions on paper, then write and rewrite and *re*-rewrite my answers to those issues *until even I agreed with the answer.*

Who said it first? I don't know, but the first person I remember hearing say this was Mark Victor Hansen. He said, *"Don't just think it—ink it!"*

Wright

So this material was originally developed for your *personal* use. How did you find out that others would be so interested in learning to handle criticism more productively?

McGhee

Through the years, I've shared bits and pieces in various places—with a women's network group that I co-founded, the local Life Underwriters Association, church groups, a women's conference, and bank management teams. People always responded positively and added to my understanding that I had only *begun* to see the tip of the iceberg where this topic is concerned.

For instance, one year, as secretary of the local Life Underwriters Association, I worked with the group officers as we diligently sought to increase membership. Our programs were very important in that process. At one of those meetings a mild panic set in when it became clear to our vice president that the program presenter was a no-show. He was familiar with some of my Criticism Management principles and he turned to me just *beaming* with this great idea he had suddenly had. He said, "Detri, get up and share what you told me about Criticism Management. It's good stuff. Save my backside here, okay?" So I took my outline, which I had printed on the back of my business card, and winged it. About twenty minutes later we adjourned.

Immediately, one of the most successful and respected agents who was approaching retirement and who was also the kindest, most supportive mentor to all of us, approached me. I was taken aback, David. He literally had tears in his eyes. He said, "Detri, how I wish I had heard that fifty years ago! I see so many missed opportunities, especially with my family. Thank you for sharing that." As he continued to speak I began to realize that he had heard some things *that I hadn't said!* He had applied these principles to *his* life and while I was envisioning and speaking of a C-A-T that looked like a lion to me, he was seeing a Bengal tiger!

His reaction touched me and made me dig deeper. Once that happened I began to discover how many famous and powerful people struggle in this area, sometimes in professional relationships and sometimes in personal relationships.

Wright

"Famous people"? Will you give us a few examples?

McGhee

One of the first that comes to my mind is Jessica Savitch. Do you remember her?

Wright

As a matter of fact, yes, I do!

McGhee

She was so popular and beautiful. She was a newswoman on the rise in the world of journalism at a time when Barbara Walters was about the only truly successful woman in the broadcast industry. Jessica met an untimely death in a car accident. As I read a book about her life (I believe it was *Golden Girl* by Alanna Nash), Jessica seemed so perfect on television with the cameras rolling. Yet, when the camera went off she could fly into hateful tirades and venomous outbursts. She was apparently unstable and rather unsuccessful in personal relationships. One insight that jumped off the pages of the book at me was when she said that she could not get inner peace because she never came to terms with the criticism she received as a child from her father.

I thought, "Oh, if we could all *truly feel* what our words infuse into another soul, perhaps we would praise more, love more, listen more, speak less, and do what my mom always advised, *'If you can't say something nice, just keep your mouth shut!'* "

Mark Victor Hansen is another example. I heard him speak many years ago in Pine Bluff, Arkansas. He was great—energetic, upbeat, encouraging—yet he later said that during those early years he had a lot of problems promoting his own books and other materials. He said that *he feared being criticized*—that people might say he was just out for the money and pushing his own agenda. Can you imagine that—someone with his gifts and talents with that fear? It just blew my mind! I began to realize that I was not alone, I really wasn't.

And, another is Oprah. Do you remember when she experienced the controversy and the lawsuit about her comments concerning eating beef?

Wright

Yes, I do.

McGhee

Well, all that led to her professional friendship with Dr. Phil and we know what happened there. But wouldn't you think that someone as brilliant and "together" as Oprah would already have all the answers? Naïvely, I did.

Wright

I read in your materials that you have some strong opinions regarding annual job performance reviews. Well, just let me quote you if I may: "Inadequate Criticism Management skills virtually *guarantee* that annual job performance reviews, at their *best*, are useless exercises consuming valuable time, energy, and emotions, and, at their worst, they are monsters of destruction." Will you tell us how you came to feel so strongly about this?

McGhee

Well, you know what they say, "Been there, done that." I probably wrote that right after an annual job performance review. (Laughter.)

Actually, I have never had a bad job performance review. But, I do remember one year, even after I heard several nice things, some compliments and things looked fine, there was *one suggestion for improvement*. And, in my mind, that *one suggestion* canceled out all the praise I'd just heard. Of course it shouldn't have . . . but that wasn't the issue! The fact was: *it did!* If I had known *then* what I know *now,* I could have enjoyed the praise and then I could have *wisely used the suggestion* to propel me further, faster. If I had chosen wisely, I could have made that suggestion (criticism!) into a speedy growth process.

Anyone who has worked in an office environment can testify as to how tense and worried employees are when yearly review time grows near. Everyone is edgy. Some people come back from their sessions in tears or red-faced with anger. Others never hear a word their supervisor says unless they talked about a raise. Some overreact at the least suggestion for improvement (as I unwisely did) and others overlook valid criticism, determined to believe that if the boss says anything negative that he or she "has it in for them."

I don't know who had this idea first, but I really like it. Let's have "Reverse Job Performance Reviews"—the employee gets to tell the boss what the boss can do to make things better. It probably wouldn't work too well in most cases unless the boss applied Criticism Management techniques first in his or her daily life.

Are you familiar with Bill Schorr's comic strip *The Grizzwells*—poppa bear Gunther and his little porcupine friend Pierpoint?

Wright

Yes. I like that one.

McGhee

My very favorite is when Gunther's little friend, Pierpoint, asked, "How do *you* handle criticism, Gunther?" Big old papa bear Gunther said, "Hmm. Gosh little buddy, I don't *know*. No one has ever had *the nerve* to criticize me before. Why? You got a problem with that!?" And little Pierpoint quickly and wisely replied, "Nope. Uh-uh. Nada. Zip. No way."

Sadly, though, most managers and bosses come across to their employees just like big papa bear Gunther—"Do not *dare* criticize *me!*" As I watched the fear and dread in my own life and in the lives of friends and coworkers, I thought about how much wasted time, energy, and emotions were generated. I was strongly encouraged to keep digging and to find some ways to first of all help myself and then to help others cope with life's difficult situations. No, not just "cope"— I wanted to *find success* in the midst of life's difficulties. The Criticism Management principles have been of great help to me. I know they can be for others, too.

Wright

Tell our readers a little about this "C-A-T with the power to tame the dragon of criticism." What's that all about?

McGhee

David, I am a very simple person. I wanted a tool that I could use that would be easy to remember. You know, advancing age does that to us—we're lucky if we can remember our age! Anyway, I wanted a tool that was easy to remember, simple to apply, and yet powerful enough to effect change right away. I also wanted it to be so durable, flexible, and useable that it would grow with me, year by year.

The C-A-T stands for three steps in the evaluation technique that can be applied to any criticism to make it work for us. The "C" stands for Categorize, the "A" stands for Analyze, and the "T" stands for Take action. So many applicable analogies came to me when I thought of a cat. When you think of a cat, David, what does your mind's eye see?

Wright

Well, I have three cats.

McGhee

So you see a housecat?

Wright

Yes. This is not a philosophy that I thought up—it was on a t-shirt I saw one time that said, "Dogs have owners and cats have staff."

McGhee

That is so true! Some people do see a housecat or a little kitten. Someone might see Garfield or the big black cat of Halloween. Sometimes when I think of a cat (of course, now I'm always linking it mentally with criticism) I see a massive Bengal tiger or a feisty bobcat or even a fierce lion—the king of the jungle.

I got to thinking, as I thought about the cats, how would I like to be like a cat? It is said they have nine lives and that sounded pretty good on some days. Also, no matter how they fall, they always seem to land on their feet.

Then I observed that we are already like them in a lot of ways. Like people, cats come in infinite varieties—each kitten different from any other—and they're so sweet when they're cuddling. But even the youngest kitten can bite to the bone if they're threatened. Unfortunately, I know this from personal experience. I once tried to wash pesticide off a kitten that was just days old. It had been accidentally sprayed and I promise you, it is not a good idea to put a kitten in water, no matter how limp and lifeless it may appear.

Also, like our tongue, you can't totally tame a cat. Like our mind, a cat can't be completely kept from wandering. I also got to thinking, have you ever seen anyone herd cats? It is just not going to happen. Then I thought of the big cats—the lion (king of his domain) and the tiger who struts in fear of nothing. The analogies keep coming even now.

So, just how do we start to conquer a criticism? The first thing to do is to write down the criticism as we see it. And then, as the C-A-T is used for evaluation, we follow a simple outline where each of the three sections is further broken down into a set of two to four subquestions that trigger our thought process.

Basically, here's the entire formula:

1. **Categorize**—Break the criticism into bite-sized pieces. Take each part and ask, is it:
   a. Correct or Incorrect
   b. Deserved or Undeserved
   c. Solicited or Unsolicited
   d. From a Friend or Foe
2. **Analyze**—In this step we learn how to get to the root of the problem.
   a. Take your categories in step one and analyze each part. (The CD and workbook amplify the process and explain the importance of each category.)
   b. Re-assess the steps and *be honest until it hurts*. (It can help to pretend it is a criticism you *gave* rather than *received*.)
3. **Take Action**—Whether we want to or not, we are going to do something with every criticism we receive.
   a. Ignore It. We may *try* to ignore it, but that's like ignoring a donkey that comes into your living room, sits down in your lap, and won't get up—it is virtually impossible.
   b. Get Angry, Get Even, or Get Ulcers. Or, maybe give ulcers to someone else. This is the most common and most unwise option. It is usually followed with attempting Step 3.a.: Ignore It.
   c. Take Positive Action (this is our goal):
      i. Discard it with a clear mind or,
      ii. Use it for profit.

When you see the system in its entirety you begin to see why each step is important and then you personalize it to fit your temperament and current life needs.

At first glance, we might think step one, Categorizing, and step two, Analyzing, are basically the same thing. But in the categorizing element of handling criticism we'll learn to be very detached. We are merely breaking the criticism into bite-sized pieces necessary to "eat this elephant." Then in step two we will dissect each category personally, deeply, and honestly. Here is where we learn how to get to the root of the problem, to dispose of any chaff properly and completely, then salvage each grain of truth or wisdom for our own gain.

Let's quickly examine the deserved or undeserved section. Parts of the criticism might fit into each category. We need to consider that.

Just because the criticism was undeserved doesn't mean we're wise to ignore it. Within that situation might be the seeds of greatness. Wisdom may be there that is unavailable to us from anywhere else. Where each part fits will have a great impact on the final outcome of what we will *do* with that part of criticism. And remember—we *will do something* with every criticism we receive. The key is to do the right thing with each part so that we are benefited and not harmed.

My goal in seeking wise Criticism Management is two-fold: (1) Gain from everything of value that comes into my life, even if it comes from criticism and, (2) Recognize when something is useless and throw it away.

Here is a little trick I have to play on myself from time to time when I have a nagging thought or hurt feeling that I just can not seem to dispose of or release: I pretend it is an empty toothpaste tube, therefore, I can and should throw it away without guilt or remorse.

David, my mom and I are both really bad pack rats. Sometimes we've even been known to save empty paper towel and bathroom tissue tubes. (Did you know they make great stands for paper dolls and fabulous spy glasses?) But, even Mother and I don't save empty toothpaste tubes. They're totally useless. Trash! I don't remember how many I've tossed away because I don't care. I send them to destruction without a pause.

Sometimes turning loose of painful situations or comments or criticisms and so forth is not easy. Sometimes I have to help myself. After I have taken a criticism through the C-A-T process, and if I find it totally useless but nevertheless painful, I have been known to take the written criticism and envision it to be an empty toothpaste tube. I'll take it in my hand, I'll smile at it, I may even speak to it, saying something like, *"I have* total control *over you. You are worse than worthless to me. You are in my way staying here. You are g-o-n-e, gone for good—for my good!"* And then I toss it in the trash. If it has been a particularly painful criticism I might have a really long, nasty speech for it. I have been known to take the trash outside to the bin right that moment.

So, I work through each step, and once it is complete, I have a guaranteed positive result if I follow the principles, even if that result is being able to finally turn loose of the pain that the criticism caused.

Wright

I am wondering, Detri, this sounds like it *could* be a very time-consuming and lengthy learning process. How long does it take a person to *profitably use* this information?

McGhee

That's a very good question, David. The neat thing about this information is that we learn something from day number one. If we just pay attention to the concepts and principles presented we will keep learning and benefiting from that knowledge until the end of our days.

If I may, let me illustrate how it works with an analogy. Do you remember when you learned to drive a car?

Wright

Yes, I certainly do.

McGhee

I just soaked it up because I wanted to get all the benefits of that ability. I was young and I wanted to go! Of course it took time and effort. I made some silly mistakes along the way but it was exciting from the very first day. I hate to think how my life would have been all these years living in rural America if I had been unable to drive.

It is similar to learning to play golf, or swimming, or parenting, or the sales process. We learn as we go. What may start out tedious and even feel strange at first can be, as in the case of golf, a life-enhancing project, even *fun*.

When I get in the car now I don't even think about how to start it or which pedal is the brake. The myriad of little things I learned earlier automatically go to work for me and I simply begin to drive. Even relatively new golfers don't have to think, "Now, how do I put the ball on the tee?" The principle, once learned, becomes a habit.

In a similar manner, once you have become familiar with the Criticism Management Techniques and experienced the exciting, positive results of this knowledge, it becomes ingrained into your thinking process. From then on, when criticisms, suggestions, ideas, or complaints come your way, you will find yourself automatically responding to them in a more positive, helpful way.

Remember my goal? It was to create a tool that was easy to remember, simple to apply, and powerful enough to effect change right away, yet so durable, flexible, and useable that it would grow with me year by year.

Wright

I understand that your original subtitle was changed from "Using the Cunning C-A-T" to "*Slay* the Dragon of Criticism" to "Using the Cunning C-A-T to *Tame* the Dragon of Criticism." What made you decide that it was better to "tame" these dragons than to "slay" them?

McGhee

That was one of those "ah-ha!" moments. I was years into this process when it dawned on me that I still wanted to "kill" all the criticism and negativity and complaining that came into my life. In my mind it was a nasty, mean old dragon and it deserved to die! Then one day I thought: "If I found a dragon—*a real, live dragon*—would it be worth more to me if I killed it or if I tamed it?" I thought, "How *blind* I have been!" Criticism isn't bad; it is my reaction to it that determines its value and effect on me. It's a fact of life. I'm making a bumper sticker that says, "Criticism happens."

Criticism is often disguised as a comment.

I remember when I was new in sales—insurance sales, at that. I heard every insurance joke imaginable, over and *over!* People would tell me, "I could *never* be a salesperson." I felt I needed to defend my career choice at first. Now? I would probably smile and sweetly say, "Well, you know, you're probably right. It *does* take a *really special person* to do this job."

Criticism may come as a suggestion: "Perhaps you should not wear pink."

Sometimes it is disguised as a rule: "To work here, you will have to cut that hair, young man."

Or, it might come as a question, "Are you really going to wear *that?*"

Well, anyhow, David, I want this journey-making to continue and grow. I also hope and pray that other people will be blessed by this insight and share their wisdom with me, too. So, I decided to give away my C-A-T outline. I placed it on my Web site along with some of my favorite training pieces, all as a gift from me to anyone who would take the time to consider the Criticism Management system.

Wright

You're *giving away* your C-A-T outline?

McGhee

Yes. I want this information available to anyone who wants to help themselves or others. I know that having just the outline and illustrations given on the Web site will help some people. I also know that there is a plethora of valuable information that is provided in the training programs, on the CD, and in the workbook that isn't available anywhere else.

Wright

The more we talk, the more ways I see how just about everyone can benefit from understanding these Criticism Management techniques.

McGhee

I couldn't agree with you more.

Wright

Who do *you* think will benefit most from your work?

McGhee

Oh, probably human beings from age five to ninety-five! Seriously, the speeches, training workshops, CD, and workbook are geared toward adults and older teens. Whether applied to work or personal life, the principles are the same. Each on-site workshop is tailor-made for the profession, industry, or group involved. Because of my career background I have somewhat of an insider's understanding of the insurance, securities, banking, and medical professions, from the CEO and Board to the janitors. As a marketing VP, I had to make presentations to the CEOs and Boards. I also trained the salespeople on sales skills and products. In addition, every employee and Board member had to be trained on referral techniques and compliance issues. It was extremely challenging and interesting to develop training concepts that would reach people at *their learning level.*

I have a true appreciation for and understanding of salespersons, managers, Board members, quilt-lovers, owners of small businesses, parents, Christians, and women. And, oh yes, waitresses! That was my first job at age fourteen in our town's only hamburger joint.

Wright

What would you like to see in the future for this information?

McGhee

We do have a special edition coming out soon for women and one for Christians. My deep desire, David, is to see this information translated into a useable format for school children of all ages. The peer pressure and bullying that they are experiencing right now, as well as the lack of being able to properly respond to the various teaching methods, are greatly related to a lack of Criticism Management skills. We just have to get this information on their level and make it fun.

Come to think of it, the C-A-T is a really good beginning. What child isn't fascinated by kittens, and lions, and tigers! *Oh my!*

Wright

What an interesting conversation. I've learned quite a bit here today and I can't wait for this book to get in the hands of our readers. I think you can help them immensely.

McGhee

Thank you. It's been a lot of fun working on this project and visiting with you.

Wright

I really appreciate all this time you've spent with me. It was nice of you to take the time to answer all these questions.

Today we've been talking with Detri McGhee. She has spent over twenty-five years in the financial services world as an insurance agent, securities registered rep, and in the corporate market. She is now dedicating full time to sharing the information she has accumulated over her past thirty years of experience. Her CD and workbook that she has alluded to are titled, *Criticism Management: Using the Cunning C-A-T to Tame the Dragon of Criticism,* which is very interesting—at least I think it is. I look forward to learning even more!

About the Author

DETRI L. MCGHEE, CLU, CHFC, conducts workshops and training sessions and enjoys speaking to a wide variety of groups using tailor-made applications in Criticism Management. Her CD book and workbook are titled, *CRITICISM MANAGEMENT: Using the Cunning C-A-T to Tame the Dragon,* and are available by phone, mail, or through her Web site. Special discounts apply if you mention this book.

Detri L. McGhee, CLU, ChFC
President
DLM & Associates
20161 US Hwy. 425 South
Star City, AR 71667
Phone: 870.370.0160 / 870.628.1464
E-mail: detri@criticismmanagement.com
www.criticismmanagement.com

Chapter 11

JACK CANFIELD

THE INTERVIEW

David E. Wright (Wright)

Today we are talking with Jack Canfield. You probably know him as the founder and co-creator of the *New York Times* number one best-selling *Chicken Soup for the Soul* book series. As of 2006 there are sixty-five titles and eighty million copies in print in over thirty-seven languages.

Jack's background includes a BA from Harvard, a master's from the University of Massachusetts, and an Honorary Doctorate from the University of Santa Monica. He has been a high school and university teacher, a workshop facilitator, a psychotherapist, and a leading authority in the area of self-esteem and personal development.

Jack Canfield, welcome to *Speaking of Success.*

Jack Canfield (Canfield)

Thank you, David. It's great to be with you.

Wright

I talked with Mark Victor Hansen a few days ago. He gave you full credit for coming up with the idea of the *Chicken Soup* series. Obviously it's made you an internationally known personality. Other than recognition, has the series changed you personally and if so, how?

Canfield

I would say that it has and I think in a couple of ways. Number one, I read stories all day long of people who've overcome what would feel like insurmountable obstacles. For example, we just did a book *Chicken Soup for the Unsinkable Soul.* There's a story in there about a single mother with three daughters. She contracted a disease and she had to have both of her hands and both of her feet amputated. She got prosthetic devices and was able to learn how to use them. She could cook, drive the car, brush her daughters' hair, get a job, etc. I read that and I thought, "God, what would I ever have to complain and whine and moan about?"

At one level it's just given me a great sense of gratitude and appreciation for everything I have and it has made me less irritable about the little things.

I think the other thing that's happened for me personally is my sphere of influence has changed. By that I mean I was asked, for example, a couple of years ago to be the keynote speaker to the Women's Congressional Caucus. The Caucus is a group that includes all women in America who are members of Congress and who are state senators, governors, and lieutenant governors. I asked what they wanted me to talk about—what topic.

"Whatever you think we need to know to be better legislators," was the reply.

I thought, "Wow, they want me to tell them about what laws they should be making and what would make a better culture." Well, that wouldn't have happened if our books hadn't come out and I hadn't become famous. I think I get to play with people at a higher level and have more influence in the world. That's important to me because my life purpose is inspiring and empowering people to live their highest vision so the world works for everybody. I get to do that on a much bigger level than when I was just a high school teacher back in Chicago.

Wright

I think one of the powerful components of that book series is that you can read a positive story in just a few minutes and come back and revisit it. I know my daughter has three of the books and she just reads them interchangeably. Sometimes I go in her bedroom and she'll be crying and reading one of them. Other times she'll be laughing, so they really are "chicken soup for the soul," aren't they?

Canfield

They really are. In fact we have four books in the *Teenage Soul* series now and a new one coming out at the end of this year. I have a son who's eleven and he has a twelve-year-old friend who's a girl. We have a new book called *Chicken Soup for the Teenage Soul and the Tough Stuff.* It's all about dealing with parents' divorces, teachers who don't understand you, boyfriends who drink and drive, and other issues pertinent to that age group. I asked my son's friend, "Why do you like this book?" (It's our most popular book among teens right now.) She said, "You know, whenever I'm feeling down I read it and it makes me cry and I feel better. Some of the stories make me laugh and some of the stories make me feel more responsible for my life. But basically I just feel like I'm not alone."

One of the people I work with recently said that the books are like a support group between the covers of a book—you can read about other peoples' experiences and realize you're not the only one going through something.

Wright

Jack, with our *Speaking of Success* series we're trying to encourage people in our audience to be better, to live better, and be more fulfilled by reading about the experiences of our writers. Is there anyone or anything in your life that has made a difference for you and helped you to become a better person?

Canfield

Yes and we could do ten books just on that. I'm influenced by people all the time. If I were to go way back I'd have to say one of the key influences in my life was Jesse Jackson when he was still a minister in Chicago. I was teaching in an all black high school there and I went to Jesse Jackson's church with a friend one time. What happened for me was that I saw somebody with a vision. (This was before Martin Luther King was killed and Jesse was of the lieutenants in his organization.) I just saw people trying to make the world work better for a certain segment of the population. I was inspired by that kind of visionary belief that it's possible to make change.

Later on, John F. Kennedy was a hero of mine. I was very much inspired by him.

Another is a therapist by the name of Robert Resnick. He was my therapist for two years. He taught me a little formula called E + R = O that stands for Events + Response = Outcome. He said, "If you don't like your outcomes quit blaming the events and start changing your responses." One of his favorite phrases was, "If the grass on the other side of the fence looks greener, start watering your own lawn more."

I think he helped me get off any kind of self-pity I might have had because I had parents who were alcoholics. It would have been very easy to blame them for problems I might have had. They weren't very successful or rich; I was surrounded by people who were and I felt like, "God, what if I'd had parents like they had? I could have been a lot better." He just got me off that whole notion and made me realize the hand you were dealt is the hand you've got to play and take responsibility for who you are and quit complaining and blaming others and get on with your life. That was a turning point for me.

I'd say the last person who really affected me big time was a guy named W. Clement Stone who was a self-made multi-millionaire in Chicago. He taught me that success is not a four-letter word—it's nothing to be ashamed of—and you ought to go for it. He said, "The best thing you can do for the poor is not be one of them." Be a model for what it is to live a successful life. So I learned from him the principles of success and that's what I've been teaching now for more than thirty years.

Wright

He was an entrepreneur in the insurance industry, wasn't he?

Canfield

He was. He had combined insurance. When I worked for him he was worth 600 million dollars and that was before the dot.com millionaires came along in Silicon Valley. He just knew more about success. He was a good friend of Napoleon Hill (author of *Think and Grow Rich)* and he was a fabulous mentor. I really learned a lot from him.

Wright

I miss some of the men I listened to when I was a young salesman coming up and he was one of them. Napoleon Hill was another one as was Dr. Peale. All of their writings made me who I am today. I'm glad I had that opportunity.

Canfield

One speaker whose name you probably will remember, Charlie "Tremendous" Jones, says, "Who we are is a result of the books we read and the people we hang out with." I think that's so true and that's why I tell people, "If you want to have high self-esteem, hang out with people who have high self-esteem. If you want to be more spiritual, hang out with spiritual people." We're always telling our children, "Don't hang out with those kids." The reason we don't want them to is because we know how influential people are with each other. I think we need to give ourselves the same advice. Who are we hanging out with? We can hang out with them in books, cassette tapes, CDs, radio shows, and in person.

Wright

One of my favorites was a fellow named Bill Gove from Florida. I talked with him about three or four years ago. He's retired now. His mind is still as quick as it ever was. I thought he was one of the greatest speakers I had ever heard.

What do you think makes up a great mentor? In other words, are there characteristics that mentors seem to have in common?

Canfield

I think there are two obvious ones. I think mentors have to have the time to do it and the willingness to do it. I also think they need to be people who are doing something you want to do. W. Clement Stone used to tell me, "If you want to be rich, hang out with rich people. Watch what they do, eat what they eat, dress the way they dress. Try it on." He wasn't suggesting that you give up your authentic self, but he was pointing out that rich people probably have habits that you don't have and you should study them.

I always ask salespeople in an organization, "Who are the top two or three in your organization?" I tell them to start taking them out to lunch and dinner and for a drink and finding out what they do. Ask them, "What's your secret?" Nine times out of ten they'll be willing to tell you.

This goes back to what we said earlier about asking. I'll go into corporations and I'll say, "Who are the top ten people?" They'll all tell me and I'll say, "Did you ever ask them what they do different than you?"

"No," they'll reply.

"Why not?"

"Well, they might not want to tell me."

"How do you know? Did you ever ask them? All they can do is say no. You'll be no worse off than you are now."

So I think with mentors you just look at people who seem to be living the life you want to live and achieving the results you want to achieve.

What we say in our book is when that you approach a mentor they're probably busy and successful and so they haven't got a lot of time. Just ask, "Can I talk to you for ten minutes every month?" If I know it's only going to be ten minutes I'll probably say yes. The neat thing is if I like you I'll always give you more than ten minutes, but that ten minutes gets you in the door.

Wright

In the future are there any more Jack Canfield books authored singularly?

Canfield

One of my books includes the formula I mentioned earlier: E + R = O. I just felt I wanted to get that out there because every time I give a speech and I talk about that the whole room gets so quiet that you could hear a pin drop—I can tell people are really getting value. Then I'm going to do a series of books on the principles of success. I've got about 150 of them that I've identified over the years. I have a book down the road I want to do that's called *No More Put-Downs,* which is a book probably aimed mostly at parents, teacher and managers. There's a culture we have now of put-down humor. Whether it's *Married With Children* or *All in the Family,* there's that characteristic of macho put-down humor. There's research now showing how bad it is for kids' self-esteem when the coaches do it so I want to get that message out there as well.

Wright

It's really not that funny, is it?

Canfield

No, we'll laugh it off because we don't want to look like we're a wimp but underneath we're hurt. The research now shows that you're better off breaking a child's bones than you are breaking their spirit. A bone will heal much more quickly than their emotional spirit will.

Wright

I remember recently reading a survey where people listed the top five people who had influenced them. I've tried it on a couple of groups at church and in other places. In my case, and in the survey, approximately three out of the top five are always teachers. I wonder if that's going to be the same in the next decade.

Canfield

I think that's probably because as children we're at our most formative years. We actually spend more time with our teachers than we do with our parents. Research shows that the average parent only interacts verbally with each of their children only about eight and a half minutes a day. Yet at school they're interacting with their teachers for anywhere from six to eight hours depending on how long the school day is, including coaches, chorus directors, etc.

I think that in almost everybody's life there's been that one teacher who loved him or her as a human being—an individual—not just one of the many students the teacher was supposed to fill full of History and English. That teacher believed in you and inspired you.

Les Brown is one of the great motivational speakers in the world. If it hadn't been for one teacher who said, "I think you can do more than be in a special ed. class. I think you're the one," he'd probably still be cutting grass in the median strip of the highways in Florida instead of being a $35,000-a-talk speaker.

Wright

I had a conversation one time with Les. He told me about this wonderful teacher who discovered Les was dyslexic. Everybody else called him dumb and this one lady just took him under her wing and had him tested. His entire life changed because of her interest in him.

Canfield

I'm on the board of advisors of the Dyslexic Awareness Resource Center here in Santa Barbara. The reason is because I taught high school with a lot of kids who were called at-risk—kids who would end up in gangs and so forth. What we found over and over was that about 78 percent of all the kids in the juvenile detention centers in Chicago were kids who had learning disabilities—primarily dyslexia—but there were others as well. They were never diagnosed and they weren't doing well in school so they'd drop out. As soon as a student drops out of school he or she becomes subject to the influence of gangs and other kinds of criminal and drug linked activities. If these kids had been diagnosed earlier we'd get rid of a large amount of the juvenile crime in America because there are a lot of really good programs that can teach dyslexics to read and excel in school.

Wright

My wife is a teacher and she brings home stories that are heartbreaking about parents not being as concerned with their children as they used to be, or at least not as helpful as they used to be. Did you find that to be a problem when you were teaching?

Canfield

It depends on what kind of district you're in. If it's a poor district the parents could be on drugs, alcoholics, and basically just not available. If you're in a really high rent district the parents not available because they're both working, coming home tired, they're jet-setters, or they're working late at the office because they're workaholics. Sometimes it just legitimately takes two paychecks to pay the rent anymore.

I find that the majority of parents care but often they don't know what to do. They don't know how to discipline their children. They don't know how to help them with their homework. They can't pass on skills that they never acquired themselves. Unfortunately, the trend tends to be like a chain letter. The people with the least amount of skills tend to have the most number of children. The other thing is that you get crack babies (infants born addicted to crack cocaine because of the mother's addiction). In Los Angeles one out of every ten babies born is a crack baby.

Wright

That's unbelievable.

Canfield

Yes and another statistic is that by the time 50 percent of the kids are twelve years old they have started experimenting with alcohol. I see a lot of that in the Bible belt. The problem is not the big city, urban designer drugs but alcoholism. Another thing you get, unfortunately, is a lot of let's call it familial violence—kids getting beat up, parents who drink and then explode—child abuse and sexual abuse. You see a lot of that.

Wright

Most people are fascinated by these television shows about being a survivor. What has been the greatest comeback that you have made from adversity in your career or in your life?

Canfield

You know it's funny, I don't think I've had a lot of major failures and setbacks where I had to start over. My life's been on an intentional curve. But I do have a lot of challenges. Mark and I are always setting goals that challenge us. We always say, "The purpose of setting a really big goal is not so that you can achieve it so much, but it's who you become in the process of achieving it." A friend of mine, Jim Rohn, says, "You want to set goals big enough so that in the process of achieving them you become someone worth being."

I think that to be a millionaire is nice but so what? People make the money and then they lose it. People get the big houses and then they burn down, or Silicon Valley goes belly up and all of a sudden they don't have a big house anymore. But who you became in the process of learning how to do that can never be taken away from you. So what we do is constantly put big challenges in front of us.

We have a book called *Chicken Soup for the Teacher's Soul.* (You'll have to make sure to get a copy for your wife.) I was a teacher and a teacher trainer for years. But because of the success of the *Chicken Soup* books I haven't been in the education world that much. I've got to go out and relearn how do I market to that world? I met with a Superintendent of Schools. I met with a guy named Jason Dorsey who's one of the number one consultants in the world in that area. I found out who has the best selling book in that area. I sat down with his wife for a day and talked about her marketing approaches.

I believe that if you face any kind of adversity, whether losing your job, your spouse dies, you get divorced, you're in an accident like Christopher Reeves and become paralyzed, or whatever, you simply do what you have to do. You find out who's already handled the problem and how did they've handled it. Then you get the support you need to get through it by their example. Whether it's a counselor in your church or you go on a retreat or you read the Bible, you do something that gives you the support you need to get to the other end.

You also have to know what the end is that you want to have. Do you want to be remarried? Do you just want to have a job and be a single mom? What is it? If you reach out and ask for support I think you'll get help. People really like to help other people. They're not always available because sometimes they're going through problems also; but there's always someone with a helping hand.

Often I think we let our pride get in the way. We let our stubbornness get in the way. We let our belief in how the world should be interfere and get in our way instead of dealing with how the world is. When we get that out of that way then we can start doing that which we need to do to get where we need to go.

Wright

If you could have a platform and tell our audience something you feel that would help or encourage them, what would you say?

Canfield

I'd say number one is to believe in yourself, believe in your dreams, and trust your feelings. I think too many people are trained wrong when they're little kids. For example, when kids are mad at their daddy they're told, "You're not mad at your Daddy."

They say, "Gee, I thought I was."

Or the kid says, "That's going to hurt," and the doctor says, "No it's not." Then they give you the shot and it hurts. They say, "See that didn't hurt, did it?" When that happened to you as a kid, you started to not trust yourself.

You may have asked your mom, "Are you upset?" and she says, "No," but she really was. So you stop learning to trust your perception.

I tell this story over and over. There are hundreds of people I've met who've come from upper class families where they make big incomes and the dad's a doctor. The kid wants to be a mechanic and work in an auto shop because that's what he loves. The family says, "That's beneath us. You can't do that." So the kid ends up being an anesthesiologist killing three people because he's not paying attention. What he really wants to do is tinker with cars. I tell people you've got to trust your own feelings, your own motivations, what turns you on, what you want to do, what makes you feel good, and quit worrying about what other people say, think, and want for you.

Decide what you want for yourself and then do what you need to do to go about getting it. It takes work.

I read a book a week minimum and at the end of the year I've read fifty-two books. We're talking about professional books—books on self-help, finances, psychology, parenting, and so forth. At the end of ten years I've read 520 books. That puts me in the top 1 percent of people knowing important information in this country. But most people are spending their time watching television.

When I went to work for W. Clement Stone, he told me, "I want you to cut out one hour a day of television."

"Okay," I said, "what do I do with it?"

"Read," he said.

He told me what kind of books to read. He said, "At the end of a year you'll have spent 365 hours reading. Divide that by a forty-hour work week and that's nine and a half weeks of education every year."

I thought, "Wow, that's two months." It was like going back to summer school.

As a result of his advice I have close to 8,000 books in my library. The reason I'm involved in this book project instead of someone else is that people like me, Jim Rohn, Les Brown, and you read a lot. We listen to tapes and we go to seminars. That's why we're the people with the information.

I always say that your raise becomes effective when you do. You'll become more effective as you gain more skills, more insight, and more knowledge.

Wright

Jack, I have watched your career for over a decade and your accomplishments are just outstanding. But your humanitarian efforts are really what impress me. I think that you're doing great things not only in California, but all over the country.

Canfield

It's true. In addition to all of the work we do, we pick one to three charities and we've given away over six million dollars in the last eight years, along with our publisher who matches every penny we give away. We've planted over a million trees in Yosemite National Park. We've bought hundreds of thousands of cataract operations in third world countries. We've contributed to the Red Cross, the Humane Society, and on it goes. It feels like a real blessing to be able to make that kind of a contribution to the world.

Wright

Today we have been talking with Jack Canfield, founder and co-creator of the *Chicken Soup for the Soul* book series. As of 2006, there are sixty-five titles and eighty million copies in print in over thirty-seven <u>languages</u>.

Canfield

The most recent book is *The Success Principles*. In it I share sixty-four principles that other people and I have utilized to achieve great levels of success.

In 2002 we published *Chicken Soup for the Soul of America.* It includes stories that grew out of 9/11 and is a real healing book for our nation. I would encourage readers to get a copy and share it with their families.

Wright

I will stand in line to get one of those. Thank you so much being with us on *Speaking of Success.*

About The Author

JACK CANFIELD is one of America's leading experts on developing self-esteem and peak performance. A dynamic and entertaining speaker, as well as a highly sought-after trainer, he has a wonderful ability to inform and inspire audiences toward developing their own human potential and personal effectiveness.

Jack Canfield is most well-known for the *Chicken Soup for the Soul* series, which he co-authored with Mark Victor Hansen, and for his audio programs about building high self-esteem. Jack is the founder of Self-Esteem Seminars, located in Santa Barbara, California, which trains entrepreneurs, educators, corporate leaders, and employees how to accelerate the achievement of their personal and professional goals. Jack is also the founder of The Foundation for Self Esteem, located in Culver City, California, which provides self-esteem resources and training to social workers, welfare recipients, and human resource professionals.

Jack graduated from Harvard in 1966, received his ME degree at the university of Massachusetts in 1973, and earned an Honorary Doctorate from the University of Santa Monica. He has been a high school and university teacher, a workshop facilitator, a psychotherapist, and a leading authority in the area of self-esteem and personal development.

As a result of his work with prisoners, welfare recipients, and inner-city youth, Jack was appointed by the state legislature to the California Task Force to Promote Self-Esteem and Personal and Social Responsibility. He also served on the board of trustees of the National Council for Self-Esteem.

Jack Canfield
Worldwide Headquarters
The Jack Canfield Companies
P.O. Box 30880
Santa Barbara, CA 93130
Phone: 805.563.2935
Fax: 805.563.2945
www.jackcanfield.com

Chapter 12

STEPHEN G. LIPSCOMB

THE INTERVIEW

David Wright (Wright)

Today we're talking with Stephen Lipscomb. He is a business consultant, avid golfer, and a professional member of the National Speakers Association. His expertise has driven him to focus on leadership development, selling strategies, and entrepreneurial development. Stephen has become addicted to the lessons that golf shows us about our lives. You might say he's golf-centric! He sees things from the greens that others obliviously walk and drive by.

Stephen works with progressive thinking and acting companies and individuals globally. He consults with Senior Teams, delivers powerful keynotes, and implements employee progression solutions.

He teaches men and women the power of doing business on the golf course. As he likes to say, "Human progress is like making your way around the golf course—it takes practice and patience and persistence!"

Stephen, welcome to *Speaking of Success.*

Stephen Lipscomb (Lipscomb)
Thank you, David!

Wright
I know you've heard many definitions of success, how do you define success?

Lipscomb
I think that a lot of times people look at success from the standpoint of what they have, how large their house is, what country club they belong to, what college they've attended, what style of Rolex are they are wearing—that sort of thing.

For me success has always been about what you have to offer and who have you become as an individual. Often people lose that perspective in their quest to be successful. Success is often related to someone being taken advantage of for another's personal gain. I think truly successful people put others' interests first and then look at how they can become better people. That is success because no matter where you go you are going to contribute something.

It's often mentioned that people have millionaire status because they are privileged. I believe that if you have millionaire mentality you will be a millionaire no matter where you go. If you're broke today, you can become a millionaire tomorrow. It's not just privilege; it's a mindset and a conditioning that we have to adhere to.

Wright
What would you say would be the biggest contribution to your professional success?

Lipscomb
I think it really goes back to childhood. I'm from Philadelphia, and being a Philly kid, things didn't come easy. We are all products of our environments; I just didn't believe that I had to be a victim of mine. I came from a divided household, so money was not in surplus by any means. When my mother would go shopping for me (I was about eleven) she would buy me the clothes that wouldn't wear out—clothes from Sears and Roebuck. They weren't the most fashionable clothes, so I'd get picked on and laughed at—I remember saying to my mom, "Hey, I would love to wear the types of clothes that the other kids in the neighborhood are wearing."

"Here's how much I'm spending," she would reply. "If you want to get those clothes or those sneakers, then you have to come up with the rest."

So I started very early learning how to make money in the neighborhood raking leaves, washing cars, shoveling snow—whatever I could do to make some money. And of course she got half of my earnings, so I would learn responsibility by a making a contribution to the household. So I would say that the biggest contribution was learning a solid work ethic that was instilled in me as a boy.

Wright

Aside from personal role models, who are the people who have served as your role models for success?

Lipscomb

David, there have been people I've met, and people I've never met and only have read about or listened to their audio programs or viewed their videos.

I think that some of the biggest role models are people in one's immediate life, like mothers, grandmothers, or other family members. Perhaps it could be a daughter or a wife. Then there are people like myself who become what could be considered as "people watchers." We watch the progress in others' lives. Perhaps our role models are spiritual leaders and how they apply Bible principals. My secular examples are: Jim Rohn, Zig Ziglar, Les Brown and Tony Robbins. The list goes on by—watching peoples' lives, their struggle and progress or their vicissitudes. I enjoy watching the athletes because I think that they are living a life very similar to being on stage as professional speakers; they have to perform for an audience.

It's a very lonely existence oftentimes being in our line of work, because we show up and then we go back to a lonely hotel or spend much time traveling from place to place.

So I think my role models include a lot of the greats out there, from reading the books they've written, listening to the seminars, and watching them in action.

Wright

What do you think are the biggest obstacles people face in trying to become successful?

Lipscomb

I think the biggest obstacle that people face is their own mindset, which oftentimes is contributed to by other people's opinions. Once a person sets out to do something, the pitfall that exists is it will be shared with everybody. Those with whom they share cannot help them to achieve their goals or success, so therefore others' opinions become their reality. For example, they might hear comments like, "We tried this before," or, "We did this before and it didn't work." "Who do you think you are? You're from this part of town," or, "Your skin color is this," or, "You don't have enough education to do such-and-such." I believe people become bogged down with the nay-sayers in their lives and those who have never really tried to do anything other than exist off the corporate dole or remain at the generation plant where a whole generation of family has worked. I believe that is the problem.

People need supportive environments to be successful, surrounding themselves with enough positive thinking and progressive people. Then they can share their goals with the people who can help them achieve them. If negativity sets in, the "stinking thinking" sets in, and as a result they are back doing what everyone else is doing, saying what everyone else is saying. They then have settled for being non-progressive in their lives.

Wright

How do you know what you need to be successful?

Lipscomb

You need to measure your success based upon your own abilities. If you're a carpenter today how realistic would it be to think that tomorrow you could be a cardiologist or something similarly outrageous? You have to be realistic. People say, "Use the power of positive thinking," and have a "positive mental attitude." That's true, but you need a level of realism as well. What are your skill sets? Look at what you have today—what do you offer? What do you like? What do you do well? Start there. I think the biggest thing people don't recognize is that success takes a period of time, and you build it in small chunks.

I remember I had the opportunity to meet the former heavyweight boxing champ Evander Holyfield. One of the things he said was that when he was training as a boy his trainer kept saying, "One day you'll to be the champ. I know you're going to the champ"—and then Evander said, "I didn't think it would take twenty years!" Sometimes people fool themselves into thinking that it's going to be an overnight thing, but nothing like success happens "overnight"! Everything is built upon something else and then we look back over a course of life and work history. That's where success comes from—by aligning yourself with what your attributes are, your passions, your physical wherewithal, a strong educational background, or whatever it is— align yourself with your strengths.

Wright

Would you tell our readers a little bit about what drives you to be successful?

Lipscomb

I think thankfulness—being thankful that I've had the opportunity to rise above mediocrity, and that started with a mindset and it keeps me motivated.

By knowing I have something to offer people that can benefit their lives, that adds to my drive to be successful. If they just hear one message that can start the process of change in their lives, then I would want to be a contributor to that!

Everything starts with self-discovery, which is the beginning of self-development. I believe that if I can help young people or professionals transition to a better place in their lives, then that's great. That's what keeps me going.

Jehovah God has gifted me with my attributes and my passion and my persuasiveness, so that's what keeps me trying to be better and do better. I'm never satisfied with what I have today, but I strive to become a better person each and every day.

Wright

Is it important to balance your success in your life? If so, how do you balance your success with your life?

Lipscomb

Life can get away from you, David, there's no question about it. When you're on the road 80 percent of the year doing domestic and international work like in Singapore or Europe, it gets rough. Anyone who says that it's "the glamorous life" also knows there's a lot of hard work that has to be put into it. You go from bad meals to bad hotel beds to noisy rooms to no ventilation. It is really not as glamorous as it appears to be sometimes. So when you have down time you must look at your health and your relationships. You also need to look at your nutrition and exercise.

You really have to find a way to balance it all out because the world and what you do for a living can take the last bit of energy right out of you, and balance is necessary. If you have children, take time to be with them. If you have a wife, take time to be with her. If you have other people in your family, you must take time to be with them because that makes you a stronger person to the audience and a stronger person to the commitment you make in the corporate world. It makes you a better you, and more powerful as a professional.

Wright

In the past you've spoken about passion being our compass for life and how it's the main factor in attaining success. Do you think that passion alone is enough?

Lipscomb

No, passion alone is not enough. It's almost like saying, "I can dream." However, a dream and a goal are two different things. A dream is something of a fantasy and a goal is something that you work at. And you realize that you achieve your dreams by virtue of working through goals and segments and chunks of life. Passion is something that keeps you in there; it keeps you coming back when you get knocked down. Here's a phrase from the well-known speaker, Les Brown: "If you can look up, you can get up." That has stayed with me over the years, because passion is what keeps you going—you have to have enough reasons why! And you must have some skill behind that passion.

You can be passionate about something; however, no one may want it. We need to be marketable and we need to be sure that we are offering people something they can use—something they can really benefit from. It's not just about profiting from something we are passionate about. It's others benefiting from something we are passionate about that they can take into their lives and that has value to them.

Wright

Les certainly walks his talk, he's been a friend for many years, but boy, I tell you, at one point in time when he had cancer, a lot of folks didn't know if he was going to come out of that or not.

Lipscomb

Yes, I'm familiar with that. We shared the platform a number of years back when he was just starting that whole process and it was very difficult for him. I'm glad to see that he's made much progress and is still making great things happen.

Wright

Why are more people not in tune with their passion if it's something all people possess?

Lipscomb

Again, I think it's a matter of "other peoples' opinions," it's a matter of tradition, and it's a matter of how failure is viewed. A lot of times people try things and fail. You can probably finish this quote, "Behind every successful man there is a . . ." What would you say, David?

Wright

"Woman."

Lipscomb

Okay, you say woman, that's also true. I'm going to say that behind every successful man is "a lot of failure"! The reason there is a lot of failure is because failure is something that takes place in order to find the "passion of success." Again, we go back to the reasons why a person does something that is closely related to the passion. And what happens with the failure is that people look at failure and they take it personally. They look at rejection, and take it personally. We have to understand that failure is an event, failure is not the person. When we recognize that, a person can then tune into his or her passions.

We also talk about "stinking thinking" and "rag mentality" and "brag mentality." Some people prefer to sit around and complain as opposed to actively doing something. "Rag mentality" is to blame the government, blame the administration, blame where you live, blame the water—they want to blame everyone and everything instead of looking in the mirror. And then the "brag mentality" sets in—"Oh, I'll buy this car," or "I'll join this country club, now I'm successful," but really often they're just in debt. That is what keeps people from tuning into their passion, it's called honesty. We need to be authentic.

When people become authentic they are then in a position to find their real selves within their passion.

Wright

We all know what the dictionary definition of passion is, but how do you define it?

Lipscomb

As I said earlier, the definition of success is defined by the phrase, "behind every successful man there is a lot of failure." I recall failing in my first marriage. After a very bitter ten-year relationship I was working in a commission-only job. I remember going forty-five days without receiving compensation. So I wasn't in the best place of my life financially at this point. When forty-five days went by someone said, "Why don't you just go and get a real job?"

I was a training consultant for a well-known organization—the Dale Carnegie organization—and I was doing some really great work with them. I knew that this was going to be the thing that was going to jump-start my career. To define "passion" is to do something that you would love to do without being paid for it, and I wasn't getting paid—I knew I would eventually get paid for it—so I hung in there. I soon broke a record for the largest six-figure sale the company had known at that time. That took care of my financial situation and I was back on the success track. I tell you, passion is defined for me as the answer to the question, "What would you do if you woke up tomorrow and money wasn't an issue?" And that, for me, is passion.

People who go to work for money first soon lose their passion. If you do what you like (passion) the money will come. People get that backwards. They go to work for the money instead of going to work for what they believe in and what makes them have a sense of purpose, progress, excitement, and fulfillment, which is motivation.

Wright

How did you conclude that speaking was your passion?

Lipscomb

David, people would tell me that I had presence and persuasion. I got into speaking from the sales and marketing side of things. I was making presentations and conducting sales and public speaking seminars. I would also make regular presentations at The Theocratic

Ministry School as a student. Then one thing led to another—Toastmasters and then the National Speakers Association.

Wright

You talked about people who influenced your life like Les Brown and Zig Ziglar. How can people help others succeed?

Lipscomb

We must become aware that people are constantly observing us. I go back to my old neighborhood; people often say that we are a product of our environment. I always say that we don't have to be victims of it. We can profit by our environments by virtue of understanding that people are listening to what we say; they are watching every move we make, and whether we accept it or not we *are all* an example and a role model. What will we chose to show them?

I'll give you one small example. The barber shop is the hub for most neighborhoods. As a rule men get together there and they talk as they get their haircuts, because it takes a while. I remember recently there were some young boys in the shop and the barber commented that their generation was lazy and hopeless. I asked him, "Why would you say something like that? Why would you condition their mindset; that their lives were hopeless? Subconsciously they will live up to that reputation, so why not give them a fine reputation to live up to? That negative projection will guide them until either they change environments or expand their thinking by other resources and experiences." (Unfortunately, that may never happen.)

We have to be careful about what we say because once we say it, it can never be taken back. That's one thing I would say—to be careful about what we put out there. Put positive messages out there! You can't measure success by saying that everyone's going to be at the same place. We are not all going to be at the same place. It doesn't mean that a carpenter who has a carpentry business is not successful. It doesn't mean that a landscaper who has a landscaping business is not successful. If you're not working in a lucrative position in a corporate ivory tower, that doesn't mean you're not successful.

We have to recognize that success is based upon giving the best of ourselves that we can give and making sure that our speech and our conduct is such that people say, "Wow! That person is really trying. That person is really setting a good example." That's what we can do to help other people.

Wright

Would you say that when people follow their passion, and excel at it, the passion brings success, or does success bring more passion?

Lipscomb

I think that when they follow their passion, passion is going to bring success, but we can't distort it. We have to recognize that we will have to start with small chunks and recognize what it is.

Some people actually speak for a living who have started out giving free speeches. Some of those same people are now getting paid hundreds of thousands of dollars to make presentations around the world. So yes, that will make you more passionate.

I think people need to be honest with themselves and understand that it's not an overnight thing. Many people have talked about overnight success and "getting rich quick." I believe that your passion does bring you more success if you recognize and remain thankful for everything you have, and not become greedy. As a result of that, yes, passion does bring more success and success more passion. But at first it's going to be a lot of hard work, with some disappointment along the way.

I remember back in 1995 saying that speaking was what I wanted to do for a living, and it's taken a good part of ten years to get where I am. I'm still not where I really want to be. I'm well along my way in doing what I love to do. If it takes twenty years, that's fine. If it takes thirty years, well, as a result of the experience from the journey, I would hope to have become better as a person from it.

Wright

What makes your perspective unique?

Lipscomb

I don't know that it's so unique, but for me it just appears to be a conditioning—a mental contract—there's "no growth in comfort" and "life is a choice." Find the solution, experience the highs and lows of life, "let it go," and keep it moving.

Some people may have careers with little disturbance. Most professionals in my field have come from corporate or educational positions to consulting and speaking. I didn't take the traditional track. I had to change my environment from a tough Philly kid to the military first, and then formal education. From there I transitioned to the corporate world. I started a few businesses along the way and I've had successes in my businesses and disappointments. I've had successes in corporate and disappointments. Each challenge and change has led to a new area of growth and opportunity.

I think that if anyone says he or she has had a challenge-free career, I'd wonder if that person is really being authentic. Honesty with self is what allows people to "grow through" things and helps them recognize their value. So I think being authentic is what makes a difference—that you've been there and have the battle scars and you're still willing to get up every day and say, "Let's do it again!"

Wright

Tell me, what is the difference between a coach and a directional consultant? I understand that you are a directional consultant, is that right?

Lipscomb

That's correct. The difference is that a coach is someone who is going to be in there with you by virtue of what you're currently doing. So we coach and we are helping people along the path they have already aligned themselves with. When you're looking at a directional consultant you're mapping out a place for them to go.

As an example, I was working with an executive from a Fortune 500 company. I saw that his leadership was not being respected. He had the title, but he didn't have the respect. When you don't have respect, things get done behind your back and over your head. I recommended that he think about and create an exit strategy.

If you don't have an exit strategy, someone may have one for you, and it may not be in your best interest. Then you're stuck at that point.

The suggestion I made was for him to use his educational background and his corporate experience in banking and financial services to start his own consulting practice and provide a service. He had a great educational "pedigree."

I suggested that he be a consultant because he was not very effective as a department leader. He was rather spineless and people walked all over him. I told him, "If you can't function in this environment, you might want to try functioning in a different environment where you make the rules. If you want to win at the game, sometimes you have to make your own rules!"

I continued to working with him for a solid four years. He had still not followed my recommendations. He just went from job to job. Often he's out of work. If he had followed my original recommendation he probably would be well on his way to making a very successful practice. He had something to offer, but he was not very effective in the role he had, so coaching him was doing very little for him. Sometimes you have to get a different direction, a different mindset, and a whole new environment for you to function and thrive in.

The challenging mindset is that people believe we all have strengths and weaknesses, that's the common thought. In my opinion we all have strengths and limitations. However, our limitations don't have to limit us. So if you have a limitation, you can either delegate the responsibility, take additional training, or just get rid of it altogether and take on something that is more in alignment with your strengths. That is the challenge, and that is where directional consultation comes into play.

Wright

What is the message you want people to hear so they can learn from your success?

Lipscomb

The message is that people really need to ask themselves, "What is it that I want to become?" more than "What can I get?" People think being a millionaire is all about the money. If you set a goal to become a millionaire, it's not so much the money you have, it's what you become as a result of going through that challenge of getting it. It's the ups and downs, the highs and lows, the fake-outs, and all the stuff that comes with business and success. And learning to read people and understand their intentions. I think it's really what you become. If people can just put that in perspective—to *become* more as opposed to *having* more—it's important because if you become more you'll get more!

You asked me earlier if passion follows success, and does success add to your passion. Yes, passion does feed on itself if you have your priorities aligned correctly.

Give more of yourself, help other people, become a mentor to someone, collaborate with someone who's just getting started in the business. Help people out as best you can. The more you give, the more you get. That's scriptural.

Wright

What an interesting conversation, Stephen. I really appreciate your taking all this time with me to answer all these questions. It's been enlightening and I've learned a lot.

Lipscomb

Thank you, I appreciate it, and I thank you for arranging this interview.

Wright

Today we've been talking with Stephen G. Lipscomb. He works with progressive thinking and acting companies and individuals globally. He consults with senior teams; delivers keynotes and implements employee progression solutions. Stephen is into training and playing golf—he teaches men and women the power of doing business on the golf course. As he says, "Human progress is like making your way around a golf course—it takes practice, patience, and persistence," and he's certainly convinced me of that today.

Stephen, thank you so much for being with on *Speaking of Success.*

Lipscomb

Thank you, David.

About the Author

STEPHEN G. LIPSCOMB is a professional speaker and consultant with expertise in leadership, entrepreneurship, and selling strategies. Stephen has parlayed seventeen years of corporate sales and human relation experience into the creation of a premier training and development company. Since 1995, A.I.PLINC has focused on the development of leaders and managers in progressive organizations.

Formerly a training consultant and speaker for Dale Carnegie Training, Inc., Stephen validated his expertise by becoming certified to facilitate thirty professional development seminar programs. His proficiency in sales, marketing, and management has earned him several awards and accolades, an International Achievement Award, in addition to other regional awards. Stephen's expertise is internationally recognized in the areas of employee performance and organizational cultural change.

Progressively involved in personal, professional, and organizational development for the past thirteen years, Stephen's experience has served Technology, Pharmaceutical, Commercial Banking, Telecommunications, and Specialty Sales industries.

Stephen's voracious appetite for reading and learning spans numerous diverse subjects, including business, finance, biographies, psychology, health, and fitness. His desire for education and wisdom easily translates to generating fresh ideas that have become the signature for his consulting success.

Stephen believes it is important to give back to the community and serves on committees that benefit the neighborhood, youth, and those less fortunate. He frequently speaks to progressive college students and leads discussions on career development and employment marketability.

Stephen's personal philosophy, borrowed from his mentor Sam Iorio, is that "the short-cut to success is the long way." He believes that when a person stands up to speak, he or she should speak not to impress but to be understood.

Stephen G. Lipscomb
A.I.PLINC
SE Pennsylvania
Phone: 302.275.4624
E-mail: plinc@plincorg.com
www.plincorg.com
sgl@sprint.blackberry.net

Chapter 13

LAUREN BROWN-PERRY

THE INTERVIEW

David Wright (Wright)

Today we're talking with Lauren Brown-Perry, JD. She teaches undergraduate courses in the Career Core and Criminal Justice Departments at Bryant & Stratton Business College in Milwaukee, Wisconsin. She previously taught at Herzing Career Technical College in Madison, Wisconsin, as well as the University of Wisconsin Madison Law School. Lauren is a consummate teacher and trainer, having trained business owners, corrections officials, and law enforcement executives on a variety of legal and management issues. Lauren has developed curriculum and training materials for a broad range of topics such as business law, trial advocacy, and community advocacy. She has trained many volunteers and community members on social justice and legal issues.

Lauren has advocated on behalf of low income, marginalized populations, and formerly incarcerated men and women while serving as a community coordinator for an interfaith social justice agency.

Lauren practiced law in Illinois and Wisconsin for over twenty years as a former deputy and assistant prosecutor, defense attorney, guardian *ad litem*, UW law professor, and attorney in private practice. She handled business, criminal, juvenile, and family matters, trying over one hundred cases in her extensive legal career.

Lauren credits her success with her faith in God and support of her husband, Martel, and their daughter, Ayilé, who is a student at a historically black college in Tennessee. Lauren values the love and support of her four sisters, her brother, and many nieces and nephews. "These are the keys to my success!" she says.

Lauren, welcome to *Speaking of Success.*

Lauren Brown-Perry, JD (Brown-Perry)
Thank you.

Wright
What is your definition of success and how do you measure it?

Brown-Perry
To me success means accomplishing what you set out to do, doing it well, and being satisfied with your accomplishment. I measure success by how I feel about my accomplishments and mostly how my accomplishments help others.

Wright
Do you have a motto?

Brown-Perry
I have something I remind myself of all the time: try, try, and never give up!

Wright
When we talked before you said there were at least ten elements of your success. Will you list and explain them for our readers?

Brown-Perry
First and foremost is faith. I believe that faith is what carries us through as individuals. I have a strong faith in God and a strong faith in people as individual human beings. Faith is what has carried me throughout my life. There have been times when I felt that if I didn't have faith I don't know where I'd be.

Motivation is one of the elements of my success—being motivated to do what it is I set out to do.

Determination is very important because you can get easily distracted or become disinterested in something that you're doing, no matter how much you want to do it.

Perseverance is very a much a part of being successful. Along with motivation and determination, perseverance gives you that ability to strive forward and keep going.

Dedication is also necessary to succeed. You have to be dedicated to what you want to do, again, because you can be easily distracted or taken off task.

You have to be a risk-taker to be successful, in my view, because success does involve stepping outside your comfort zone and outside of the box, so to speak, in pursuing excellence.

This leads me to excellence—excellence in what you're doing. You have to strive for and constantly achieve excellence. You keep raising the bar to excel in your excellence.

I believe one has to be selfless in what one is doing. By this I mean that whatever you do, first of all do no harm. This comes from the Hippocratic Oath that doctors take. At the same time you're there to help others. By helping others and feeling that satisfaction in helping them you are actually showing and feeling success yourself.

You have to have a desire to be successful. Something within you must help you strive to go forward—to encourage you to pick yourself up after you have setbacks.

Last but not least, I also think you have to have humility. Humbleness is something I work on every day. I think humility is very, very important to me in being successful.

Wright

Of all of these, which one or two do you think are the most important elements?

Brown-Perry

The most important one for me is faith. The other one I would say is humility.

Wright

Why would you say that?

Brown-Perry

For faith, it's the head of my life and what keeps me going. I think humility is important because you can get too full of yourself. I said earlier that one of my measures of success is being able to be selfless about it and to help others. Because of that you have to focus not so much on yourself but on how you can assist others.

Humility is hard for most of us, particularly people who are accomplished and who are very successful. I think humility is one of those characteristics that is a challenge. I know it is for me from time to time.

Wright

It's been said that if you're walking down the road and you see a turtle sitting on a fencepost you can bet he didn't get up there by himself. So who are two of the most influential people in your life as far as your success is concerned? Who helped you "get on top of the fencepost"?

Brown-Perry

I would say my parents—primarily my mother, who passed away some years ago. I'm the oldest of six children. She raised us for the most part by herself. She started college and then decided to get married and have a family. She attended college at a time when not many African American women were going to college. Even though she didn't finish, she instilled in us the desire to go to college. She was uncompromising in terms of education and so I thank her a lot for that.

The other person is a man who owned his own real estate business and who I worked for one summer. His name is Mr. Shelton. Mr. Shelton grew up in Chicago and came from modest means. He was a friend of our family and was always in business. He always treated people with respect. He was an excellent businessperson. I learned a lot about dealing with people, clients, and customers from him. He maintained humility throughout his business career.

I would say my mother and Mr. Shelton were the most influential people in my life as far as my success is concerned.

Wright

In regard to your mother's uncompromising position on education, was she still alive when you received your doctorate of jurisprudence?

Brown-Perry

Yes, she was. As a matter of fact, I had been practicing about nine years when she died. She was there when I received my license. I actually graduated early—I didn't graduate with my class, I received my JD in the mail before my class graduated and so I didn't go through the graduation ceremony. When I was admitted to the State of Illinois Bar, she attended the ceremony. She had a chance to see me grow and be successful in my legal career.

After my first year of law school, I found out that my mom's high school classmates had voted her most likely to be successful. Everyone thought she would be a lawyer. Even though she was very supportive of my choices and my career, she never told me about that until I was in law school, which I thought was interesting.

Wright

Tell us about the parts of your background that contributed the most to your success.

Brown-Perry

One is my humble beginning. I grew up in public housing in Chicago in the sixties. The turbulent sixties and seventies had a great influence on my ultimate success. Even though I had humble beginnings I spent time with businesspeople like Mr. Shelton. I was around people who were positively desirous of success not only for themselves but for us as kids growing up in our community. Both of my parents instilled success in us. My mother worked in some of the schools we attended. My dad had a middle school education. He highly valued education and was a stickler with us about that. Education was our ticket out of public housing and humble beginnings.

I'd say the Civil Rights Movement had an influence on me. I say that not because of the discontent and racial problems that were going on in the country, but because it was a time when a lot of folks were thriving and showing an entrepreneurial spirit. They were at their best in some ways during that time in our country.

I also appreciated being viewed as a competent individual, not just a female, not just an attorney, not just an African American person, but as a competent person in my field. I'm considered an expert in several areas of the law as a result of that. I was allowed to grow, develop, and make mistakes, ask questions, be supported, and valued all throughout my life by my family, educators, and those who had the most influence in my life. The support of my family and friends has been a valuable asset to me. I actually have seven close childhood friends. We are still friends who are accomplished, successful people in our own fields.

I was told "no" a lot. I heard, "You can't do this. You shouldn't try that." That was just an incentive for me to try harder. When people tell me no, part of me says, "Okay, this is a challenge; you're going to be ready for the challenge and you're going to show people they are wrong." Being told no actually contributed to my success. When I hear the word "no" now I consider it to be just another word; to me it means just try again and that's what I'll do.

Wright

Would you share one or two of your personal success stories?

Brown-Perry

One of the things that I am just so very proud of is having a supportive husband. All couples have their issues but my husband has been very supportive. I met him after I graduated from law school. He's seen me as a professional person, a career woman, an attorney, teacher, and trainer. I have known him all of my professional life. We have a daughter who is in college. She is majoring in hospital administration and she's going to pursue her MBA. I always tell her she's going to take care of her parents one day! That's also a personal success story—having a wonderful child who is a motivator in my life. My students can tell you that I talk about my daughter a lot. I check in regularly with her to be sure I'm using a generation-appropriate teaching approach with them.

Another success story concerns an outline for a book for a group of formerly incarcerated men and women. They call their group "Voices Beyond Bars." I wrote the outline about five years ago. Earlier this year, twenty men and women shared their stories about what their life was like during the first twenty-nine days after release from prison. That book is now published. I am so proud of that and I tell them, "This is just one of many because you can have the first sixty days, the first six months, the first couple of years, and so on." There are so many subsequent books they have the opportunity of doing. I am really thankful they were able to get that done. They are the only ones who can really tell their story. They've done it and the book is doing well.

Wright

Why did you pick those two stories to share with our readers?

Brown-Perry

Because one is personal to me—I've produced a daughter who is doing well and is the light and love of my life. Family is very important to me and I believe that one measure of success is how much you give back.

Certainly you're going to give back to your family but how much do you give back to others you don't have a responsibility for or obligation to? That's also the reason why I picked the second story because there is a disproportionate number of African American men and women who are in the criminal justice and prison systems. I've learned a lot about myself and about our society by working closely with these men and women, most of whom are parents and married and who have families they do their best to support.

Wright

Will you share a couple of business strategies that contributed to your success thus far?

Brown-Perry

I think first and foremost you must be thoroughly prepared. You should know about the success journey you are on. If it's being an entrepreneur, you need to utilize all the tools available to you.

I have tried many cases over my legal career. I had to be thoroughly prepared for those cases. (By the way, I won most of the cases I tried both as a prosecutor and as a defense attorney.)

The second business strategy that I think has contributed to my success is that of perseverance and risk-taking. I use those terms together because I think they are that important. Risk-taking involves cutting-edge thinking, trailblazing, and being unconventional.

Another aspect is perseverance. Markets go up and down, clients and customers are not there all the time so you do have to persevere.

Wright

Why do you say that you are still on this success journey?

Brown-Perry

First of all, I would say that I don't think God is through with me yet. There's more He has in store for me to accomplish and to realize in life.

Looking at my journey so far, I know I have a lot of accomplishments but I feel that the greatest one is yet to come. I believe I'm still on this journey because I'm a life-long learner. I think there are always ways to improve. Even if you're at the top of your game, there is room for improvement. Being published as a college student is quite an accomplishment. I am looking forward to publishing more books and articles.

I have more to give back. I said earlier that one measure of success is how much you help others and how much you give back. I'm not through with that yet. I've been very blessed in my life and I want to share that blessing. By sharing your blessing you are blessed even more. So that's why I say I'm still on this journey.

Wright

As you have made your decisions down through your career, has faith played an important role in that?

Brown-Perry

It definitely has. I go to the Master first and ask for direction and pray on it. I know that if I do my best and He is at the helm, everything is right with the world. I have faith that all will turn out. Things turn out one way or another but things turn out the best when you take the proper approach. I believe that if you have faith you can do anything. I am a living testimony.

In college, I read a report about the public housing project I grew up in. At that time, Robert Taylor Homes was the largest housing project in the world. It doesn't exist anymore. The report was dismal and it contained so many negative statistics about where I grew up. That wasn't my experience. Frankly, if I had believed that report, I probably wouldn't be where I am today!

Faith is really important. I know that my faith can overcome my circumstances. That was a real challenge because it was like telling me "no" and I was not going to amount to anything in life. I grew up with a number of people for whom that is true; but I knew it wasn't true for me. My parents told us that we may be living in the projects but it was not our end destiny.

I believe every generation needs to do better than the previous one, that's why I'm expecting so much from my daughter and her generation to accomplish so many more things than my generation was able to do.

Wright

As you consider the young people of today, what advice or suggestions would you give to aid in reaching their success?

Brown-Perry

I think they need to stay true to themselves. They are subject to a lot of peer influence. Depending on who your peer group is or who you more readily identify with, it can stunt your dreams and your fantasies and the goals you set. So stay true to yourself.

I say this to the students in my college classes who are in the age range of seventeen to twenty-five—do not give up. I tell them that they can accomplish anything they want to accomplish. First of all you have to dream and I even say fantasize about it—you have to visualize it for yourself. Then you have to make a decision about what it is you want to do and develop a plan of action. You are setting goals and implementing that plan—you're preparing yourself.

It's one thing to say you want to be a doctor when you grow up. It is another thing to determine that because you want to be a doctor, you're going to get used to reading, developing good study habits, and looking into the field of medicine. There are so many different specialties from which to choose. You have to associate with people in that field and ask questions and learn all you need to know about it. Then you have to believe you can do it. You have to see yourself at the end of that journey actually becoming a doctor. Then you have to excel so you will receive that satisfaction and then you have to give back— help others. As opportunities were made available to you, you have to help create them for others.

I also tell them to smile because it takes more muscles to frown than it does to smile. When they get my age they'll be glad that they smiled a lot. I also tell them to have fun. What's life without fun?

Wright

I appreciate all the time you've taken with me today to answer all these questions. I've certainly learned a lot. I wish you well. It seems that you're doing some great work and you have done some great work throughout your life.

Today we've been talking with Lauren Brown-Perry. She teaches undergraduate courses in the Career Core and Criminal Justice Departments at Bryant & Stratton Business College in Milwaukee. She has advocated on behalf of low income, marginalized populations, and formerly incarcerated men and women while serving as a community coordinator for an interfaith social justice agency. She actually walks her talk—she does what she says and she says we ought to help others. I don't know about you, but I believe her.

Thank you so much for being with us today, Lauren, on *Speaking of Success.*

About the Author

LAUREN BROWN-PERRY, JD, teaches undergraduate courses in the Career Core, and Criminal Justice Departments at Bryant & Stratton Business College in Milwaukee, Wisconsin. She previously taught at Herzing Career Technical College in Madison, Wisconsin, as well as the University of Wisconsin Madison Law School. Lauren is a consummate teacher and trainer, having trained business owners, corrections officials, and law enforcement executives on a variety of legal and management issues. Lauren has developed curriculum and training materials for a broad range of topics such as business law, trial advocacy, and community advocacy. She has trained many volunteers and community members on social justice and legal issues.

Lauren has advocated on behalf of low income, marginalized populations, and formerly incarcerated men and women, while serving as a community coordinator for an interfaith social justice agency.

Lauren practiced law in Illinois and Wisconsin for over twenty years, as a former deputy and assistant prosecutor, defense attorney, guardian *ad litem,* UW law professor, and attorney in private practice. She handled business, criminal, juvenile, and family matters, trying over 100 cases in her extensive legal career.

Lauren credits her success to her faith in God and the support of her husband Martel and their daughter, Ayilé, who is student at a historically black college in Tennessee. Lauren values the love and support of her four sisters, her brother, and many nieces and nephews. She says, "These are the keys to my success!"

Lauren Brown-Perry, JD
1028 E. Juneau Avenue #724
Milwaukee, WI 53202
Phone: 414.469.9281
E-mail: lauren_brownperry@yahoo.com

Chapter 14

ALEX ZOLTAN SZINEGH

David Wright (Wright)

Today we're talking with Alex Zoltan Szinegh. He is Senior Regional VP for North America, Exit Realty Corporation International. Alex is a true "rags to riches" story. Armed with only a tenth grade education, this immigrant from Hungary has surmounted all odds to become an internationally recognized speaker, trainer, and performance coach. Alex has personally sold over 2,300 properties; he has run successful businesses, trained thousands of people in the art of "street smarts" and "how to succeed in spite of your circumstances and past." Alex is refreshing, funny, educational, and positively "in your face" with a candid style. He tells it like it is. Alex is a family man with four children, ages thirty-six, thirty-two, twenty-nine, and a four-year old. He also has five grandchildren. Alex's main drive to succeed in life has been his family, and his biggest supporter and inspiration is his wife, Cindy.

Alex, welcome to *Speaking of Success.*

So, what is your definition of "success"?

Alex Zoltan Szinegh (Szinegh)

You know, it is so interesting—over the years people have asked me what my interpretation of "success" is. Going back to my early days and getting out into the workforce, I would have thought that "success" meant I make a certain amount of money, or I achieve a certain level, or I get a certain title, or I acquire material possessions. As the saying goes, "The guy with the most toys wins." I always thought that success was measured by things and status. As I journeyed through different jobs I gained a lot of education. I held many really great jobs and "success" became something different every time. Success started to become more of a vision, more of a lifestyle, more of an attitude than material possessions.

In my training and my coaching with people I talk about the wheel of life. I talk about all the different parts of life—spiritual, family, physical, mental, financial, fun, and business. I think true success, in my opinion, is the ability to balance the different parts of your life in such a way that you're comfortable with yourself, your surroundings, and the people around you. That's what success is—the ability to balance, to be able to achieve whatever you set your mind to, and make the decision that this is where you want to be, that you've arrived at that position.

When I say "arrived" at that position, I don't think we ever arrive at success, it's more of a flow, it's something that's always fluid, it is a journey more than a destination.

My first job out of school (I quit school in the eleventh grade) was in a factory; I was making $47.50 a week. I remember my boss coming to me and said, "Alex, we're going to give you a raise," and the company gave me a $2.50 a week raise. I always thought that once I made $50 a week I would be "successful" and I could go and buy a car. My first car cost $45. I know I'm dating myself but it was amazing and the car actually ran, so I thought that at fifty bucks per week, "I'm a great success."

Over the years I kept thinking that way. I thought, "If I make ten grand a year I'm a success. If I make a hundred grand a year—" Then I thought, "Well, once you make your first million you're a success—I always wanted to be a millionaire." But when you lose it all, then you think, "Maybe this isn't success." The biggest drive for me is family. I believe that having a good family life, being healthy, and just enjoying what you're doing is important. I think you can really truly call yourself a success if you happen to find the thing that you are really passionate about, love it, and be able to do it; that is when everything falls into place.

Wright

So if I understand you correctly, you're saying that success to you is a journey rather than a destination?

Szinegh

Absolutely. I didn't want to use that cliché, but I've watched a lot of great speakers—Jim Rohn, Tony Robbins, Robert Kiyosaki—I've read many, many books, listened to tapes, and I've attend many seminars. It seems that all of these people who are really successful talk a lot about the whole aspect of the journey. Unfortunately, we discover that too late in life. If we discovered it a little bit earlier I think we'd all be a lot better off. I think teaching goal-setting and more life skills on how to become successful would help a lot if it was taught in the earlier years of schooling.

Wright

How do you know when you are successful?

Szinegh

I can only think of one word, it's called "peace" with yourself—you have peace inside yourself. There was a survey done and it was discovered that people would rather die than be a public speaker, for example. You are successful when you are not afraid of anything in life and you're content with your position in life. You have the goals and desires to grow and get better, but you have arrived at a position where you have achieved a happy balance in every part of life—physically, mentally, emotionally, financially, spiritually, family, and in business. You have this feeling of euphoria that life is great and every day is great, and every moment is great. I think, for me, that's what it feels like.

Wright

What do you think it takes to become successful?

Szinegh

There are many different opinions about that. I think a lot of people believe they can take a course or a seminar and once they follow some step-by-step process they will become successful. I feel the process really starts when you find your passion.

Success is the journey, it's the process, it's that feeling versus the actual belief that one has arrived in a particular position. I think it's a never-ending, changing, shifting, drifting, moving target. I heard this at a seminar, "Set your goals as high as you want, as far as you can see, and when you get there you're going to notice that you can see farther." I've seen people doing demonstrations where they say, "Stretch your arm as far as you can," and you stretch and stretch and they'll ask if you're at the limit that you can stretch it and the audience says, "Yes!" Then they say, "Give me another quarter inch," and then the people stretch even farther. And there you are—you can go another quarter inch, you can stretch *farther*—you can definitely go farther.

I think one of the biggest killers of success today in our society is complacency. It's "settling" for only so much in your life all around you in all the different categories; it's "giving up." I heard a speaker say that the opposite of success is not fear, it's complacency. People get complacent, they "settle," they give up, they put their dream aside. I talk to people who are overweight and they make statements like, "I'm big-boned, it's in my genes, my family was always this way." If they don't have any money, they say, "Well, we were never rich, so we understood that it's okay for us not to be successful." I think one of the biggest misconceptions is when people quote the Scriptures and they say, "You know, it says right in the Bible that money is evil." Not true. What it says is that *the love of money* is evil (1 Timothy 6:10). It says right in the Bible that you are supposed to be rich (3 John 1:2), you have a responsibility to become rich—that is the only way you can help others.

In my training sessions I talk about this and sometimes people say, "You know what, I think what we need to do is we need to serve society, we need to help people, and we need to help the poor." My opinion is if you want to help the poor, step number one is *don't join them!* You can't do a lot of good if you haven't taken care of yourself.

I fly almost every week. Before the plane leaves the ground the flight attendant will say, "In the event of the loss of oxygen an oxygen mask will drop from the ceiling. If you're traveling with a child, you put yours on *first.*" In other words, if you can't take care of you, you can't take care of anybody!

I think that's where we are in our society—we settle for too little, and we settle for less than we can be. And when we do that, we not only hurt ourselves, but we hurt all those people around us who trust us and count on us—those we are responsible for and whom we could give to.

I see it in my own family. I have three brothers. My older brother is brilliant. He has a college education and he's smart. Over the years I've watched him and he could have been a lot more successful if he had put a little more effort in certain areas, but he never chose to do that. He "settled." I see people in my training programs who "settle." They say, "Well, I just want this much. I don't want to go too far because if I get too rich or I get too successful I'll lose all my friends." We hold each other back sometimes.

The bottom line is this: find something you really love to do (something you can get passionate about), start doing it, continue to learn about it. Get extra training (you could even get a coach), dedicate your life to it, and success in all parts of your life will be virtually guaranteed.

Wright

Do you feel not having a formal education has slowed you down?

Szinegh

I don't think so. I really truly don't. It's not that I'm against education, I'm not against education, but I'm for a specific type of education. I think there are missing elements in schooling and teaching. I wish there had been somebody smart enough among my teachers and my professors and people who were teaching me along the way who knew about, for example, personalities and DISC behavior profiles tests. I also think I would have been a lot better off if, when I was in grade five and grade six and even grade one, somebody had taught me the value of money. But educators are not trained to do that. I wish that somebody had placed more of an emphasis on health and had said, "This is what you need to do to become healthy."

I believe that what we need to do is take the wheel of life to children. We need to show them the wheel of life and we need to show them that if they want to be successful in life, if they want to excel, it's not when they get straight A's or straight B's or whatever—it's got nothing to do with academic knowledge.

I believe that some of the things we desperately need training in early in life include: goal-setting, planning, specific skill development, and better time management.

As I was sitting in school when I was in grade seven and eight, I used to think to myself, "Why on earth do I need to know algebra? What benefit will I get out of knowing what the capital of Turkey is?" Why do I need to know this stuff? When I really thought about it, I realized that there was so much stuff put into my brain that was irrelevant to my life. I discovered more and more, as I started to read books, attend seminars, and listened to great speakers, that all of that stuff was just "stuff"! Unfortunately, our school system and our educational system are not designed to teach us all of the practical things of life.

You know, David, you've been in the Real Estate business and you know as well as I do that when somebody gets a real estate license, they may be called a real estate agent because they passed the test, but they sure as heck don't know how to sell real estate or how to deal with people, do they? The "real" training starts after they get a real estate license.

Wright

Right.

Szinegh

They only learn enough to pass the test, and I think that's a shame in our society. And here's another thing I think is a big problem about education: we are punished and we are kept being told what we "don't know" and what we do *wrong* as opposed to saying, "Oh, you've got all these things right! It seems to me, Alex, that you are leaning toward these kinds of things in your life. Why don't we enhance that and why don't we spend more time at what you're good at, versus beating you up with what you're not good at?"

When I was at an event this weekend, most of the speakers talked about how one can make it on one's own. In my life I would never have gotten as far as I did unless there had been other people who supported me or helped me. We call that "team effort" or "team work"—working together and building a relationship. In school you're never taught that. What are you taught? Early in life we are trained to *compete*. "Why can't you be like your big brother Johnny? Why do you do that? Why can't you do better in school? Your brother got better marks," so you're always competing in a win/lose situation—we're not trained to work as a team.

I presented this speech to a very large audience a couple of weeks ago on teamwork. It was interesting—my boss, Steve Morris, said to me, "I want you to speak about teamwork."

I started to think about my life, and I thought I was never a great team player because I thought about sports immediately. I always did individual sports—gymnastics, running, wrestling, one person against another, or me against myself. We were trained and conditioned to the win/lose mindset. I thought about teamwork and that a person is a team member in his or her family. I realized I had to look into this and start thinking about it. I even thought about school—if you want to practice teamwork how could you do that in a test? The concept of "teamwork" would involve your looking to your neighbor and saying, "I'm not sure about this answer. Would you help me with it?" That wouldn't be teamwork, it's cheating—you would get punished!

So in school you're not trained to work as a team, you're not trained to work in cohesion with other people. I think our education system needs improvement. All my kids finished schooling through grade twelve, so they all received more education than I did.

The best example is my oldest daughter, Michelle, who went to college. She lived at home and for years she watched me fail and succeed, fail and succeed, and go broke and lose money and make money, and succeed in business and fail again. During those years I'd be encouraging her and the rest of my children to read books like *Think and Grow Rich* by Napoleon Hill. I was trying to educate my children about success and about life.

Michelle went to college because she said she wanted to learn to become better. She enrolled and chose as her major business administration. She was in college for a couple of months when she came home and said, "Dad, my professor is telling me all the same things that you've been telling me."

"Why don't you ask your teacher how many businesses he has owned and operated?" I asked.

So she asked him, and she discovered that he had never run a business! He was somebody teaching my daughter how to become a success in business and he had *never* run a business!

I just got a pilot's license not too long ago. I was flying with this gentleman who was seventy-five years old. He had specific knowledge as a flight instructor. He would have scared the pants off me if I'd had to fly with him if he had only had book knowledge versus actual flight experience. But because he had actual experience, I trusted him—I felt safe. He did maneuvers with the little plane that were incredible, that scared me; but at the same time I felt very secure and safe that he could do it. And I think actual experience is what we don't learn in school. Sometimes we are taught by people who have a lot of "book learned" experience versus real life experience.

Wright

If you had to do it all over again what would you change?

Szinegh

Well, first of all, if I could do it all over again, looking back over the decisions I've made and the things that I've done, I think what I would do is definitely listen to my gut—my instincts—a lot more because over the years I missed a lot of opportunities. My gut feelings said I should do it, and I didn't go for it, and other times my gut says don't do it and my head or my heart said do it or greed said do it and I lost money and I got hurt and things happened. So I think the first thing I would do is listen to my gut instinct more.

The other thing I would do is I would definitely have gotten more education in specific areas. I would focus and make a decision about what I wanted to do with my life. I should have set my goals earlier, I should have read more books, and I should have followed more successful people. I should have taken coaching earlier in my life. I should have listened to people—not people with a bunch of degrees and a bunch of initials after their names—I would have listened to people who were in positions where I wanted to be. I wish I had awakened earlier in my life. I wish I had gotten smarter earlier.

I had parents who were average, middle-class folks. My father was just a regular working man working from paycheck to paycheck. My mother had a certain philosophy of money. I programmed myself according to their standards and their thinking. It took me twenty to thirty years to undo some of the programming I had acquired during my life at home.

I love everything about my life—I love the failures *and* the successes, because that's what got me here. When a great man was asked, "What do you think about the obstacles in your life? You had so many problems in your life," I heard him reply, "I used those obstacles as stepping stones to get me where I want to be." I think that's what happened with me. But if I could do it all over again, I would pay more attention. I would open up my eyes more, but unfortunately I did not have the role models back then.

I would definitely go for more specific training and knowledge, and it would be nice if more specific training was available in our school system today such as teaching people about the various personalities and how to get along with others.

I got married very early. I got married when I was nineteen years old and I became a father at twenty. It took me probably twenty years to figure out how to be a father. You go to a department store and you buy a toaster and it comes with instructions. But when you become a father, there's no instruction manual that comes with the kids. When you bring the baby home from the hospital you have to learn how give infant care by doing it. That's the educational process of understanding about how to grow and how to develop.

I used to think I was a terrible father. I wasn't a terrible father—I was just a certain type of personality. I have four children, and all four children are different personalities—very specifically different. I look at them now and I think, "I know why they did that." But back then I didn't know. So, being a certain personality type, and as a father, I thought that everybody should be like *me*, and I treated my children that way.

I think that's the reason I failed in business so often. The golden rule says, "Do unto others as you want it done to you." I kept doing that to others and it doesn't work—everybody is different.

I wish I had taken more people skill training and learned more about understanding others because it's through others that we grow. So if I could do it all over again, if I had the brain power back then that I've got today, who knows where I would be now! But you know what? I'm very happy where I am. I am very satisfied with where I am, and I know where I'm going and I'm excited about my life.

"I've gone through one marriage that didn't work because I didn't understand my spouse. I didn't understand her personality. People say to me, "It sounds as if it was tough and you must wish you had never married her." No, I don't wish I hadn't married her—she's a terrific woman; with her I have three wonderful children and now I have five grandchildren. I am actually thankful to her for the experiences and the lessons she taught me. Every experience was added to the next one—every experience is built on the one before it.

Wright

For a guy your age you seem to have a lot of energy, so would you tell our readers what makes you go?

Szinegh

I think the biggest thing that makes me go is being excited about life. A lot of people ask me, "Don't you ever get down?" When I look back at my life, twenty or thirty years ago I used to really get unhappy. I would be depressed for months sometimes. I'd go out drinking and partying as a diversion.

I'd also smoke. Then as I saw people around me—my father died of cancer, my wife's father died of cancer—I'd see people get sick around me, so I decided to quit smoking.

I knew that my mindset had to do with attitude. So I began to read books. What really got me excited was the very first motivational book I ever read. It was *Think and Grow Rich* by Napoleon Hill. I saw that there was hope for everybody! What excited me, and what really built this energy into me, was the opportunity and the understanding I gained that I have total control over my life. I *do* have control.

I know there are people who are going to say, "Wait a minute. God controls our life, we were put here." But I don't think that God put idiots on the earth. I think we are given a brain so that we can think for ourselves, and we can direct and control our life. That's exciting! It's exciting to me to get up in the morning and have a focus and know that I'm going someplace and doing something that I really love and have a passion about.

I think passion drives people, and the problem today is that people don't have the energy and don't have the passion. Most people hate their jobs, they're just in a job—they only do enough work so they don't get fired. They only get enough pay so that they don't quit. People are just not passionate about life. They are not passionate about their marriage, they are not passionate with the way they live, and they feel trapped. They feel that they don't have the option or an opportunity to move ahead or have total control over their life.

I saw a perfect example of that this morning, and I'm going to use this in my training today. I was having breakfast in the hotel. I had finished working out and there was a lady with two little children who were about four or five. As they walked in, they got their breakfast from the buffet and the lady put the plate and the orange juice and everything down on one of the tables. One little girl sat where this lady told her to sit and the other little girl sat at another table. The lady said to her, "No, honey, I want you to sit over here."

The little girl said, "No, I like this table and this is where I want to sit."

"No, no, honey, this is where we are going to sit."

I was watching this tug-of-war between the woman and the child. Within two minutes the lady, the plates, and everything went over to the other table, and this four- or five-year-old child was in full of control of the situation. She had said, "This is where I'm going to sit and this is where I am going to be," and she moved this adult person over! I was *amazed* just watching it.

There are so many people who think they have no control in life because they don't *ask* for it. That's where I think I get my energy from—it is the knowledge that I do have control. I can make a difference. I *can* make a change. I love what I do.

The other thing that I do (and I talk with people about this all the time) is that I exercise on a regular basis. Energy creates energy! This morning I was running on the treadmill. I didn't take long— probably twenty to twenty-five minutes. Exercise like that pumps your blood and gets you going. I don't understand all the physiological details but I do know that exercise creates endorphins in the body and chemical reactions that make you feel good. It's all about life!

Last night before I went to bed I spoke to my little girl over the telephone. It made me feel good to talk with her. All these things around me opened my eyes. Over the years I have become in awe of the little things. It's almost like I have more energy now.

I'm fifty-seven and every day I want to do as many push-ups as the number of years I've lived. This morning I thought, "I can do better." So this morning, in forty-five seconds I knocked off seventy push-ups! I thought, "That's not bad for an old guy!" It's the "excitement" that I felt that I could stretch and do *more*! Challenges like that keep me going and give me the energy.

I joined Exit when there were two offices and about fifty agents. Now we have a thousand offices and over 30,000 agents! I helped build that, and that gives me excitement.

I don't know who said it, but in one of the trainings I attended someone said, "If you give it away, you get more of it." I think that is one of the things that gets me energized and charged up—when I give it away. When I do a training or when I do a seminar—when I give something to somebody else—it just charges me right up. I'm like the Energizer bunny that just keeps going and going. I think that's where it comes from—it comes from different parts of my life.

Wright

Your company Exit is growing at a rapid pace. What makes your company so unique?

Szinegh

This is absolutely incredible—I met the founder of Exit by accident. I've been in the real estate business for twenty-three years. There's no security in most jobs today, is there? Jobs are getting downsized, companies are closing, pension programs are going down the drain, and executives are stealing other people's money. Look at Enron—there's no future and no security.

Steve Morris, the founder of Exit, has been in the Real Estate business for many years. He said, "We have these huge problems in Real Estate and one of them is that it takes so long to get paid. Another problem is you can't stop; you cannot stop in this business. Once you get on it, it's like running on a treadmill. If you stop on a treadmill you fall flat on your face. Real Estate feels like that—you've got to keep going and keep selling and waiting for the next commission check. There's no wisdom passed down—nobody's going to help you because it's a competitive business. Everybody's competing against everybody else."

What Steve Morris did is look at the problems in real estate that have plagued the industry for fifty years.

He always said that agents are a very important asset to the business. Most corporation owners make a huge mistake of thinking it's their idea, it's their equipment, it's their product, it's their office building, it's all the money they have in the bank. They think all those things are their assets. I feel a lot of corporations think that as long as they have a good idea and something that looks good, that that's what makes the corporation. Steve believes passionately, and transposes this to all of his people, his executives, his brokers, and every salesperson, that *they* are the assets of the corporation! He said, "Why don't we pay tribute to the assets that we *have?*" So he built a system of rewarding people for helping him grow the corporation. Give them a piece of the action.

I've worked for many different corporations—huge Real Estate corporations—and their attitude was, "Give me your money every month, pay your bills, and don't bother me." But Steve believes that if you help the corporation to grow, he rewards you.

His program is called a "Single Level Residuals." That means if I bring someone into the corporation, the company rewards me for bringing that person from another company. That's how it works at Exit.

When I first joined the company I thought, "Oh yeah. Okay, if this thing ever works I'd be surprised." But it was amazing how quickly it started to catch on and Exit started to grow.

Can you imagine if you have an office of five agents and each of them brings one, and then next month each of them brings in one again? The growth and the compounding of numbers is phenomenal! So the company believes in rewarding its people.

The other thing is education. The biggest problem in the real estate business is lack of education. As I said before, the business is so competitive that most realtors do not want to mentor people who are new in the business.

In Exit we have systems in place that will build and rebuild and educate and push forward all of the agents in the company.

One of the most significant components that has driven this corporation is Steve's philosophy of passion about the company, about its people, and his ability to pass on this excitement. Steve practices affirmations. He does eight to ten pages of affirmations every morning and he's been doing it for maybe twenty-five or thirty years. Here's his method in his own words, "Write down what you want to happen that day. Write down your future and talk about what you want to take place." He projects this and he passes it on to his people.

He demonstrates just incredible leadership. I think that's what grows the corporation. That's also what grows a family—"leadership." A leader is somebody who has followers. If nobody's following you you're just taking a walk!

To this point, the company's success has been basically the passion, the incredible focus, and excitement. I think that's what drives it. You look around today—what corporations have passion? I think we lose that human factor and the company's employees become just numbers—they become statistics—they're not as important as they should be.

I think what makes our company so unique is that those who work here feel *important*—every single one of us. There's another system Steve put in place. Every agent pays a very small franchise fee, which is much smaller than most of the other real estate franchises. From that fee we take a little bit of money—only $5—and we put it toward Habitat for Humanity, the organization that builds houses for people who can't afford to have them. And what's amazing is, those tiny little $5 contributions have so far amounted to over $865,000 in donations to Habitat for Humanity!

Even the secretaries benefit. We take $5 out of every transaction and we put it into a secretarial fund. At the end of the year, based upon the seniority of the person and who worked there, and based on their hours and other factors, the secretaries in every office get a bonus. Now tell me, how many companies take part of their earnings and give it back to the secretaries? So every part of the organization is *giving*, which creates cohesion. I think that's what drives the company and that's what makes it so successful! What we say at Exit is, "It's real estate re-invented."

Wright

What is your advice to someone who is struggling to succeed?

Szinegh

The first thing is, recognize that you're struggling.

Jim Rohn has been my mentor over the years and he doesn't even know it. I've listened to him, I've watched him, I've personally met him several times, I've read his books, and I listen to his tapes. He says there's a day that turns your life around. He talks about many days, but he says that there's a particular day—he calls it the day of disgust—when you actually become disgusted about where you are. You've actually discovered you're struggling and you've actually understood you're in a hole. So stop digging!

When you undergo the revelation that you're struggling, step number one is to make that decision that you *are* struggling.

Step number two is to make the decision and understand that you *can* make a difference—you can *change*. If you change, your results will change.

Then what you need to do is to seek out people who are in positions you want!

There are two ways to learn in life: one is to make your own mistakes, and the other is to learn from the mistakes of others. Some of us couldn't live long enough to make all the mistakes, so we need to find role models—it's all about modeling. A lot of people don't understand that. We never learned about that in school.

I mentioned earlier I got my pilot's license to fly these little ultralight airplanes. My teacher has flown since he was fifteen years old. He was seventy-five years old when I was his student. He had been flying for sixty years. He has trained over 6,000 pilots without a single accident. So I knew he had the expertise and qualifications to teach me.

That's what people need to do. People need to seek out individuals who have the skills and knowledge to teach others about their field of expertise. People also have to be teachable and coachable. I think most of our society wants "instant this" and "instant that." We go to the drive-throughs and we want instant coffee.

I was reading in a magazine a few days ago that there's a place where quickie divorces can be done. There are other places where they hold five-minute dating. Relationships change very quickly; people are not putting any emphasis on relationships.

What people have to do is realize they're struggling and then seek out somebody who is doing better, somebody who can help them.

I went to a gym one time and the guy behind the counter was probably fifty pounds overweight! I thought, *"Hello!* Look at the equipment! Look around you!" You've probably heard this saying "Never go to a bald barber."

There's lots of help available out there. People who are reading this book really need to understand that there's an incredible amount of support out there. Find someone who has practical knowledge—knowledge gained from experience. I've known people in real estate who have all these initials after their names and the only thing they don't have is *m.o.n.e.y.* All they have are degrees. They're into "learning," but as Tony Robbins told me, "Alex, don't let your learning lead to knowledge. Let your learning lead to *action.* What's really interesting is this: if you are stupid and broke that's okay; but if you are smart and broke it's a sin!"

The solution is to seek out people who are knowledgeable and take that knowledge and apply it, practice it, role-play it, work with it, and get better at it! And that's what I teach in my trainings.

Wright

What a great thought and a great conversation. Today we've been talking with Alex Szinegh. He is the Senior Regional VP for North America, Exit Realty Corporation International. And as we have found out today, he tells it like it is from his experience, which is real knowledge.

Thank you so much, Alex, for being with us today on *Speaking of Success.*

Szinegh

Thank you, David. I'm hoping that when people pick up this book they understand that they can accomplish anything in life if they set their mind to it! They can if they evolve and surround themselves with enough people who can support them and who know what to do.

I'm hoping that people will take this part of the book and dissect it and call me or send me an e-mail. Whether they have a problem or if they are just on the way up (or on the way down)—whatever direction—I want them to let me know what they're thinking.

I made a DVD series, and on the front of that DVD there's a sign that says "No Bull." We say it like it is—I will tell you the truth. Unfortunately, most people don't want to know the truth, but I'll tell you the truth. Please get in touch with us and give us your comments.

About the Author

ALEX ZOLTAN SZINEGH is Senior Regional VP for North America, Exit Realty Corp International. Alex is a true "rags to riches" story. Armed with only a grade ten education, this immigrant from Hungary has surmounted all odds to become an internationally recognized Speaker, Trainer, and Coach. Alex has personally *sold* over 2,300 properties, he has run successful businesses, and trained thousands of people in the art of "street smarts" and "how to succeed in spite your circumstances and past." Alex is refreshing, funny, educational, and positively "in your face" with has candid style. He tells it like it is. Alex is a family man with four children ages thirty-six, thirty-two, twenty-nine, and a four-year-old. He also has five grandchildren. Alex's main drive to succeed in life has been his family. His biggest supporter and inspiration is wife Cindy.

Alex Zoltan Szinegh
P.O Box 750516
Las Vegas, NV 89136-0516
Phone: 702.334.5570
E-mail: alexszinegh@exitrealty.com
www.alexszinegh.com
www.ExitOnlineUniversity.com